Please also visit the **250 Laws of Love** website

for further insights and bonuses:

www.250lawsoflove.com

"A relationship is like a tandem bike.

It is not possible for one person to pedal while

the other one is braking."

CONTENTS

250

LAWS OF LOVE

Petr Casanova

Published by © First Class Publishing a.s.,

Washingtonova 1624/5, Praha 1, the publisher of FC magazine and FirstClass.cz portal in Prague in 2015 as its first book publication

First edition

www.firstclass.cz

www.250lawsoflove.com

INTRODUCTION | VALUES

THE FIRST TEN COMMANDMENTS

TIME IS MOST PRECIOUS OF ALL

had a classmate in secondary school. He got ill. At that time, the type of cancer he suffered from was incurable.

He was 18 years old and knew that he could die at any time.

Like today.

He lost the motivation to study, he stopped going to school.

He stayed at home, in the care of his mother. He felt the four walls of his room pressing down on him and so he decided to go outdoors. Haphazardly. He wandered soullessly through the streets, until he found himself standing in front of a book shop.

He looked through the shop window and spotted a girl of a similar age as himself inside. She must have attracted him, because suddenly he found himself in the shop, walking as if in a dream state towards her, until being interrupted by her question: *"May I help you?"* He shyly blushed, because she had the most beautiful smile he had ever seen in his life. All he wanted to do was to kiss her. Instead, his lips began to hesitate and stutter: *"Well, I just wanted to buy a book. This one."* – he pointed in a random direction.

"And do you want it wrapped?" the girl asked, smiling even more. Yes, he did.

She went away, returning with the wrapped book a moment later. He was uneasy and left the store hurriedly. On the way home, he walked through the same streets which suddenly seemed different. More colourful. Livelier. More beautiful.

He put the book at the bottom of his wardrobe.

On the second day, he ventured to the shop again. He plucked up courage, deciding definitely to confess his feelings to the girl this time. But because of the disease which was quickly taking its toll, he had lost his willpower as well as his reason. For this reason, the scenario was repeated. Every time, he asked her to wrap up any book. He always silently paid and left.

This situation was repeated for more than a week. Finally, he dared to leave his phone number next to the cash register as she was wrapping up the book. He fled. And never returned.

A phone rang in my classmate's home on the Wednesday. His mother picked it up: *"Who's speaking?"* It was the girl from the shop. She wished to speak to the boy.

Floods of tears flowed from the mother's eyes. *"You don't know? He died yesterday..."* There was a deathly silence, interrupted only by the mother's weeping. She hung up and went into her son's room. She wanted to remember him, at least through the belongings that he had left behind.

She opened the wardrobe and breathed in the scent of his clothes. Suddenly she saw a pile of wrapped items at the bottom of the wardrobe. She unwrapped one of them − a book!

She opened it and a card slipped out of it.

"Hi, you looked handsome today. Lucy."

She unwrapped the next book.

"Where have you been? I thought of you all day long. L."

And quickly the next:

"Would you like to go to the movies on Sunday? L." and a telephone number below the message.

The mother picked up the last book, which was on the very top of the pile.

No card fell from this one, the message was inscribed right on the first page:

"I love you. Forever yours, L."

• • •

If you have the most loving feelings for someone who is unaware of them, there is no reason to hide them. Express your feelings – let the person know what he/she means to you. You might be surprised that your feelings are reciprocated. But act before it is too late.

DO NOT HESITATE TO
MAKE POSITIVE CHANGES

I was born on 30th August. I was the youngest and smallest in every class I attended. I used to listen to others. I did not consider whether what they urged me to do would be good for me. I automatically believed that older people, especially parents and teachers, were there to help me, to show me the way and to pass only the good on to me.

I became accustomed to the fact that whenever I had an idea to change something in my life that I desired, I was regarded as stupid by others. Whenever I wanted to be myself, I heard how naïve I was and that I should obey those who were more experienced and who knew better. Be good, do what others want you to do, study, get a job, a family, a car, a flat. And I, stupid young child, never asked: And then will I be happy?

Today, I regret all those years that I lived according to others. They prevented me from the change that I felt within to be necessary – to follow my dreams, for which I felt enthusiasm and motivation. I made the mistake to suppose that other people had a patent on reason and that their way was the only correct one.

If the youngest and smallest boy in the class was standing in front of me, and he wanted to be different, I would tell him loudly to follow his heart. I'd hesitate to claim that there was anything that he could not do, because I cannot know what somebody else can or cannot do; I only know what I myself am capable of. So if I did not have faith in any of his abilities, I'd be saying more about my own limitations, not his.

And, in particular, I would tell him not to trust people who confuse age with experience. Regardless of the intended change which motivates you, try to remember these 10 basic principles essential for a contented relationship:

12

HUMAN LIFE IS SHORT

We all know that life is short and death awaits us all. Yet we are always caught unawares when the Grim Reaper slashes his scythe near us. At such times, we seem to disconnect the fuel driving the running wheel in which we run like hamsters for our whole lives, without actually knowing why. Only then do we realise that we really only live once, only now.

Death is the only certainty in life and it is good that it reminds us of this fact. We should not ignore it or fear it. Rather than Death, let's fear an unlived life. Death is not the greatest failure we can encounter. A much greater failure is to die inside long before, while still alive.

Do not fear Death. Rather fear *"the time before death"*, so that you do not waste your present opportunities, and the most precious commodity in life. No, it is not health, because also those on the Titanic were healthy. The most precious thing you have now is time. None of us knows exactly how much time we have left. But with every passing second, we have one second less.

If you have a problem with time, don't worry, you will learn to cope with time.

ONLY THE LIFE WHICH YOU YOURSELF CREATE AWAITS YOU

W e like to renounce responsibility for own lives. We ask others what we should do. But no one else can know what is right for us. We have the answer within ourselves. We just have to find it.

Firstly, recognise that your life is really yours alone. Others can persuade you, manipulate you, try to change you, but they cannot decide for you. They can walk by your side, but never in your shoes. Try to let the way you walk be in line with your intuition and desire. If there are no previous tracks, don't be afraid to step into the fresh snow and make your own new footprints in it.

It is always better to stand on the first rung of your own ladder, which you desire to climb, than to be on top of someone else's ladder where you feel uncertain.

Life is this ladder. Where you reach is entirely your own choice. No, nobody will live life on your behalf. And you will never live any differently from what you have created.

A step taken by self-will and with passion is always worthwhile. It does not matter how miserable the place is where you find yourself at present. A journey of a thousand miles also starts with the first step. In life, it is not so much about the distance you walk, but about the direction taken.

The heart is the indication of direction. If you follow where it directs, you are in harmony with your desires. The reward for the courage to follow your heart is a feeling of self-fulfilment.

If you have a problem trusting in intuition, don't worry, you will learn to trust intuition.

OVERWORKED DOES NOT MEAN PRODUCTIVE

You know this from your job. You are stressed, can't keep up. In the evening, you flop down on the couch, thinking how useful and effective you have been. A diary full of scheduled appointments gives you a sense of importance and indispensability. But this is just an illusion.

Being overworked is not a virtue for which you should be respected and praised. Exhaustion rarely equals productivity and usefulness, but is rather an example of bad time management and choice of priorities. It is one of the most important virtues to be able to say "*no*" when appropriate. Beware of resembling a hamster in a running wheel. Unstoppable all day, but still in the same spot.

If you feel like that, spend more time on building something which provides real meaning. Because this is productivity. It is insufficient merely to tick off what is expected, even in a relationship. Often a single meaningful action is much better.

If you have a problem with productivity, don't worry, you will learn how to achieve productivity.

SUCCESS IS USUALLY PRECEDED BY FAILURE

From childhood, one is taught that a mistake is bad, shameful, reprehensible. Those who err should be ashamed. One should be spanked for a bad grade. However, most mistakes in life are inevitable. At birth, life is a clean sheet. A baby has no experience. Any progress can only occur if you are unafraid of treading where you have never before ventured.

All the mistakes ever committed in life are an invaluable source of learning. Each subsequent step is usually wiser. It is no disgrace to make a mistake. The only real disgrace is not to learn from the mistake.

If you are afraid of change or failure, you do not take the necessary steps for improvement. Error is not an enemy. It is an ally. An indicator of reserves and potential improvement. Every success is the result of a previous failure.

If you have a problem with acceptance of mistakes, don't worry, you will learn acceptance.

CHANGE NEVER OCCURS BY ITSELF

You can be on the lookout for change. You can think about it. But it does not occur. Because a change is the result of what you do, not what you think or talk about. Everything carried in the mind is a mere assumption. And it remains an assumption unless it is made real. This book will show you what is really important. Thereafter, you will learn how to muster the courage to build your entire remaining life around these answers. That is, how to act.

Any assumptions without action are useless. And if you wait for the perfect moment, you may waste an entire lifetime waiting.

Waiting with hatred and envy, feeling that others are luckier and have a better fate. No, they have nothing like that. They only take action for the sake of their happiness and a better life.

Actions are all that count in life.

If you have a problem making your wishes come true, don't worry, you will learn how to make your wishes come true.

YOU DO NOT HAVE TO WAIT FOR AN APOLOGY IN ORDER TO FORGIVE

One can argue for an entire lifetime about who is more correct. However, this will probably not lead anywhere. Because all of us have our own truth.

This book teaches that life becomes much lighter if you are even able to accept that some apologies never come from others. Regardless of how much hurt has been caused by someone else, the key to overcoming this disappointment and heartache is to be grateful for every experience, whether positive or negative. *"Being grateful"* means sending a single thought to the relevant person: Thank you for the lesson.

Stop squandering happiness, time and energy unnecessarily. Try to cancel the rental of the two chambers in the brain, the left and right hemispheres, where all bad memories and objections are supposed to be stored for life. Through forgiveness, you can disinfect this apartment within the brain.

Forgiveness is a service provided primarily to yourself. In so doing, you are committed to no longer using the past against the present. Forgiveness is in no way an amnesty for the person who has caused the hurt. The other person has nothing to do with it. Forgiveness is primarily a pardon for yourself. Because you do not need somebody else's apology to stop suffering.

If you have a problem with forgiveness, don't worry, you will learn forgiveness.

SOME PEOPLE ARE SIMPLY BAD

As kids, we had to get used to company. Teachers assigned us our classmates, neighbours our peers. We did not know them and had nothing in common with them. Yet we learned how to get along, get close, make friends with them. Often we had to. Our parents explained to us that we had to get along with everyone who crossed our path. That it would also be like this in life. They dictated to us who were appropriate friends for us, and who were not.

Those times ended long ago. Not everybody who once crossed our path belongs in our entire life. We have to learn to move away from those who cause bad feelings, and to surround ourselves with those who make us happy. We are not all cut from the same cloth. Sometimes it may initially appear tasty, but even a nice looking morsel is confirmed only after tasting. Or after it is eventually digested in the stomach.

We are not children anymore, to maintain at all costs, under threat of a beating, a relationship which does not benefit us. Let's learn to find the right people to revitalise, encourage and inspire us. Thanks to them, we will improve our own lives.

If you have a problem in choosing people, don't worry, you will learn how to choose people.

8ᵀᴴ LAW

NOBODY IS OBLIGED TO LOVE YOU

It was explained to us in childhood that if we acted to please others, they would like us. And so we learned to pander, fawn and expect bonus points. Somehow, in the effort to adapt to the wishes of others, we forgot what we wished for ourselves. We sold ourselves for fake friendships which were often false and conditional – by not being ourselves.

It is good to be kind to others. But it is paramount to be kind to oneself. That is why we should never return love as a merchandise, quid pro quo. Let's not allow ourselves to be judged through other people's eyes and to constantly feel inadequate. Let's choose a partner who can see the value of who we currently are. Who will love us as fallible as we sometimes feel, as unattractive as we sometimes feel, as incomplete as we really are.

Let's find people who will love us despite everything. And let's be grateful if they allow us to continue to be ourselves. Because such a relationship is invaluable.

A relationship in which one person is not obliged to love the other person.

And yet, or perhaps just because of it, there is love.

If you have a problem with self-confidence, don't worry, you will learn self-confidence.

WHAT YOU HAVE OR OWN DOES NOT DETERMINE WHO YOU ARE

Let's get used to the fact that there will always be superficial people. The adjective is apt, because their opinions begin and end on the surface. They are not interested in what is within a person, in the character. They judge others only according to their property, fashion, status. In this way, they suggest that you are only of value if you own something expensive. But if you arrive empty-handed, you are an outsider. Of course, this is not true. Financial status is no indication of success. Ingvar Kamprad, one of the richest Europeans, founder of the IKEA furniture giant, flies only economy class, eats in a canteen and drives a run-down 1993 Volvo 240.

Investor Warren Buffett, one of the richest Americans, lives in a house which he bought in 1957 for USD 31 500. His favourite meal is a hamburger and Coca-Cola.

Real wealth is not based on possessions. It is based on a fulfilled life, lived according to your own ideas. After all, even if you have all the wealth in the world, you do not automatically win the esteem, respect or smile of a single child.

If you have a problem arming yourself against the opinions of others, don't worry, you will learn how to arm yourself against their opinions.

NEVER REGRET ANY EXPERIENCE

Nothing in the world is permanent. What you have today, tomorrow can be something you had. Nature is changing, so are we. The Earth does not stop turning for anyone. Every second is an opportunity and every decision made or not acted on is a rejection of something.

Keep in mind that whether you stay together or split up with a partner, every loss is a gain. What you gain in any case is called experience. Whatever it is, something new is learned.

Through this book, the reader will get to understand that every step taken and sincerely decided on, is the correct one.

Because it is exactly what is required at the present time.

PART 1 | CRISIS

HOW TO SOLVE DILEMMAS

To reliably identify the best as well as the worst inner qualities in yourself or a partner, experience a crisis with him/her.

At such a time, do not rail against life, thank it. Life is a gargoyle of unanticipated events. You are unable to control many of these. But what you can control is the way you react, how you cope with events.

Life in itself is neither good nor bad. It all depends on attitude. If you decide to perceive life positively, you will understand that the obstacles are put in your path so as to verify the immediate readiness and ability to work on yourself. That is why you should not condemn complications in a relationship. After all, there is no better way to get to know someone than in a crisis.

A RELATIONSHIP WORTH FIGHTING FOR

Imagine a heavy barbell. A barbell has the ability not only to check your strength, but also to increase it. In the same way, a healthy relationship is able to surmount problems, be strengthened. Often, a proper word at the right moment is sufficient to solve a problem. And it reveals everything about one's partner.

I once witnessed a bad accident. A girl, aged 10 years, was hit by a car on a pedestrian crossing. Her condition was serious and she needed to be given blood immediately. A rare blood group.

The doctor on the scene did not have the correct blood type. Then, near the distraught parents who had paid so terribly for a moment of inattention, he saw the girl's brother, obviously a twin. The boy was sitting and weeping on the pavement.

"I might need your blood for your sister," the doctor knelt down before him, after verifying with his parents that their son had the same blood group. The boy looked up at the doctor, with his eyes like two pools filled with tears.

"It is a matter of life and death," the doctor told him plainly.

The boy's heart seemed to stop, he grew pale and gasped. Then he silently looked at his parents, stood up, went to them and hugged them affectionately. *"Don't forget me,"* he whispered. Everyone looked at him in wonder.

The boy returned to the doctor and in a shaky voice told him: *"Well, we can do it. I am ready to die."*

He thought he was exchanging his life for his sister's.

And he was willing to die for her.

THE MOST IMPORTANT WORDS SPOKEN BY PARTNERS WHICH REFLECT THAT THEIR RELATIONSHIP HAS A HEALTHY FOUNDATION DESPITE PROBLEMS

The average man speaks thousands of words a day.

The average woman speaks tens of thousands of words a day.

As in other areas of life, it does not depend on the quantity, the number of words, but whether one says the right words to the other person, and in the correct order.

To make sure a relationship has a really healthy foundation, it is unnecessary to say or hear many words. There is a reason a human has two ears, two arms and two legs, but only one mouth. So that one can speak less, but listen to, hug and walk more with someone else.

Any problem which a couple experiences is an opportunity to work on it, and to help each other. Precisely because people are different, one person can provide what is currently lacking in the other person. In this way, even if you seem ordinary to yourself, you can be extraordinary to another person.

Not much is needed. Just a few sentences from the Laws of Love. All of them start with the most soothing potion in the world, unfortunately much neglected. With the two words: "*Thank you*".

It is irrelevant on which side you stand – whether uttering or listening to the words. They heal in both cases.

26

TELL THE OTHER PERSON AS OFTEN AS POSSIBLE:

"Thank you for transforming so many ordinary moments into the extraordinary."

If you are alone, unusual moments are special because of something.

If you are in a relationship, unusual moments are special because of someone.

In the second case, these moments are extraordinary. Because extraordinary people create them. For us.

TELL THE OTHER PERSON AS OFTEN AS POSSIBLE:

"Thank you for motivating me when I need it."

Life is sometimes like a car, the possibilities of which you misjudged. In short, you run out of fuel on the road. At such a time, you usually can't push the car by yourself; the petrol station is too far away. This happens when somebody unjustifiably knocks you down, spits on you and leaves you crushed. Perhaps you even feel like remaining in such a position. Resigned and remorseful. The support of a partner is invaluable at such a time. When you are at your lowest strength, the ideal partner can inspire you to get up and be who you always wanted to be.

The ideal partner will force you to stay on course despite your imperfections. Not by violence, shouting, although hands and words are used. A helping hand and words of encouragement. A partner can remind you that many problems would disappear from the world if people talked more to others and less about others.

Your partner is the first person to whom you should speak in a difficult situation. The perfect partner wants to hear the truth, even though it is uncomfortable and uneasy. He requires a truthful relationship. One where partners do not have to be ashamed of the truth, whatever it may be. The same applies to sincerity.

TELL THE OTHER PERSON AS OFTEN AS POSSIBLE:

"Thank you for meeting me halfway."

It is not easy for two individuals with entirely different genetic characteristics, education, past, desires and experience to get on well in life. A permanent presence of incongruities is natural. After all, it is known that a relationship is enriched by problems that two people are able to solve together. It is not important exactly how they solve them, but that they do. Perfect partners solve problems on principle at the halfway mark. What does this mean? Whenever they disagree on something, they work on a solution which makes sense to both sides. It's called compromise. Because if only the need of one side is fulfilled, the other party feels disparaged. Mature couples find a solution on this basis:

- *"Today, we'll do what you wish."*

- *"No, let's do what you wish today."*

Compromise is always sought more easily if it starts with absolute openness to the other person.

TELL THE OTHER PERSON AS OFTEN AS POSSIBLE:

"Thank you for thinking of me as often as I think of you."

Do you feel this? Again, meet your partner halfway. It is necessary. Because there is never one winner and one loser in a relationship. There are always either two winners or two losers.

That is why the perfect partner pays in advance. He provides kindness, empathy, compassion without calculating or expecting something in return. And there is one more thing: the perfect partner gives space to the other person. Give space to the other person when it is needed, before he/she actually feels the need.

Perfect partners can be far apart, yet feel as if they are right next to each other. Indeed, such partners understand that sometimes it is healthy to spend time apart. There are moments when one needs to clarify who one is. That is, without being defined by someone else. In short, sometimes one needs to be alone, to be oneself in a relationship.

TELL THE OTHER PERSON AS OFTEN AS POSSIBLE:

"Thank you for making time for me."

If you are as important to your partner as he says, he will find a way to make sufficient time for you. Without excuses, lies or unfulfilled promises. For that matter, white lies are permitted in a relationship in only one area – compliments. Do not omit the opportunity to tell your partner what he means to you, how wonderful he is, although you cannot see under his skin. Especially when he is feeling down, such a sentence will please him more than anything else. Sometimes it is even unnecessary to say it. Just express it by your actions.

Especially by one particular action:

The most precious gift which you can give someone else is your time and full attention. Perfect partners exchange this gift every time they are together. They are here and now. Without thoughts about work, or with eyes fixed on the phone display.

If you have the perfect partner, he is with you when most needed. Not only when it suits him best.

TELL THE OTHER PERSON AS OFTEN AS POSSIBLE:

"Thank you for knowing when something bad is happening to me."

Even though partners are basically two strangers, thanks to time spent together and attention focused on each other, the one who really knows and loves the other, can see pain in the eyes even when everyone else believes the artificial smiling facade. One is not born with this ability, but gains it through getting to know each other.

The perfect partner makes the effort to understand you, although it may be simpler and easier to ignore your pain. Understanding requires something extra – special kindness and patience. Yes, it requires extra effort. But in a relationship, something extra always counts.

TELL THE OTHER PERSON AS OFTEN AS POSSIBLE:

"Thank you for being willing to admit your mistake."

In a relationship with healthy foundations, a partner does not treat you as if he knows you better than you know yourself. What you want is support. Not to know who is right or wrong.

That is why the perfect partner can admit a mistake even when not at fault. Not because he is aware of it, but because the value of a partnership is always greater than any personal convictions. Never require a partner to listen to your clever prognoses and accusations, what he should or should not have done. In the most difficult moments, be one of those few people who, if they have to talk, encourages the other person to do what he alone intuitively knows is best for himself, but for which he perhaps lacks the courage. This may be a change of job which is worrying him, or anything else. And then stand by him, whether he manages to take the step or not. Because success in a relationship is only measured by a combined front.

TELL THE OTHER PERSON AS OFTEN AS POSSIBLE:

"Thank you for standing by me in the good as well as bad times."

A similar phrase is used in wedding vows. Understandably. People who share the worst with us, also deserve to share the best by our side.

For this reason, appreciate the difficult times. They enable one rarity – to see what the people closest to you are really like. After all, ideal partners can be defined in a mere thirteen words: They help each other in bad times and laugh together in good times.

TELL THE OTHER PERSON AS OFTEN AS POSSIBLE:

"Thank you for understanding that I do not always have the strength for everything."

She is hysterical. He is egoistical.

People utter hurtful words, without realising that nobody is perfect, everybody makes mistakes. So, on certain days, you just need to take some time out. Because you do not have inexhaustible strength to deal with everything.

It is unnecessary to hold the hand of the depressed partner and want to lift him to his feet immediately. After all, he will usually resist this. It helps far more to allow him to calm down. Because *"I cannot lift you up"* does not have to mean *"I don't love you"*, but *"Wait, I will help you to deal with this"*.

In relationships worth struggling for, accept your partner's problems as your own. Not because you do not have enough problems yourself, but because a problem shared is a problem halved.

Therefore, a reasonable person does not require a partner to solve problems on his/her behalf, but a person to solve all the problems together.

TELL THE OTHER PERSON AS OFTEN AS POSSIBLE:

"Thank you for believing in me."

Perfect partners do not primarily voice criticism or advice, but encouragement. Because a single word of encouragement at a time of failure is incomparably more important to a person than year-long flattery in times of success.

Encouraging words are miraculous. They heal and do not hurt. Always treat your partner as if any bad word will burn a mark on your tongue. And remember that a scorched tongue does not look good...

TELL THE OTHER PERSON AS OFTEN AS POSSIBLE:

"Thank you for accepting me as I am."

A partner is a person who knows everything about you and yet accepts you. He does not need to change you in order to make you more attractive to him. He understands that you are unique and supports you to be yourself. And if you go off the rails and stop being yourself, he puts you back on track, emphasising that he loves you the way you are.

In relationships with unhealthy foundations, one partner points out the mistakes of the other, without appreciating the good points. The reason is not that the person being criticised only has faults. But the critic only sees the faults in the partner. Let's not forget that nobody is perfect. So let's also seek out the good in a person. Appreciate the time and energy your partner spends on you. There is nothing more valuable in a relationship.

Also, do not waste time and energy on bad people. Surround yourself in all relationships, including those at the workplace, only with people who are grateful for having you in their lives.

If somebody accepts you the way you want to be, it provides the most amazing power needed in life – to make your dreams come true. And in so doing, enjoy life and yourself to the full. If a person is generously allowed by a partner to primarily love himself in a relationship, he will bring a balanced and loving person into the relationship. Yes, himself.

TELL THE OTHER PERSON AS OFTEN AS POSSIBLE:

"Thank you for your patience and forgiveness."

We are all human. Only people. That is, we make mistakes. One of the mistakes we can make in life, is to hurt someone else. The strength of a relationship then depends on the reaction of the injured person, and whether he reminds the guilty party of the mistake or misuses the corrected mistake. After all, you get to know the character of your partner best if you yourself make a mistake.

If the mistake is acceptable, the perfect partner can be generous, because he knows that if the other partner leaves him, he would lose not only a loved one, but also all the little things experienced with the partner. Mutual laughter and embraces – everything that is free, and yet which surpasses all worldly treasures. In relationship with healthy foundations, partners therefore define patience as the ability to shine a light on someone whose flame is fading, and forgiveness as the ability not to use unchangeable past against the other person. The total of patience and forgiveness brings about a detached view, the ability to be at ease with what cannot be changed.

Do not expect a partnership to be easy. A healthy relationship does not fall from the skies. Just like success in any other area, it requires time, patience and people willing and able to build something meaningful and long-lasting.

Despite problems.

Or, more precisely – because of problems.

JEALOUSY

This is often a mere assumption.

A fantasy. Speculation mistaken for intuition.

Intuition, the inner counsellor, can easily be defined. Because intuition does not paralyse – does not immobilise with a fixed idea which destroys everything around, as well as primarily and especially also the jealous person.

Jealousy arises from the same chemical ingredients as the fear that "I am not good enough," "I can't do anything," "I never succeed," and so on.

Jealousy belongs to the family whose siblings already are: Malice, Envy, Hatred and Inferiority.

My grandfather while alive once read to me from a letter he had written when he was 19 years old and had decided to give up on life. Because of Mary, who was beautiful. That is why he had loved her. That is why he was jealous.

His jealousy had nothing in common with reality or her actions. Grandfather suffered from the feeling that she was being unfaithful to him.

When he was at the peak of his conviction, Mary appeared in the doorway of his bachelor's den. Supposedly, just a minute before he was going to poison himself. She called out:

"Why are you lying here like a lazybones? I have great news for you. I am expecting a baby. Actually, we both are. I am happier than I've ever been before!"

She squeezed him in her embrace.

Grandfather crumpled the suicide note behind his back and lived with Grandmother for the next 70 years.

Every week, he brought her one rose. That was his ritual. He only stopped doing this in the '30s. It was during the crisis when Grandfather lost his job. He did not bring any roses for a long four years. And then he got a job at the tram company – *"with pension entitlement"* – which was a very important factor for households at that time.

The next month, when Grandmother returned home, she unexpectedly found 237 roses in the flat.

With Grandfather's message: *"Paying off my debt."*

As a kid, I did not understand the meaning of giving flowers. Once, Grandfather, already retired, was driving me somewhere. Suddenly, he stepped on the brake, turned the car around to face the opposite direction and apologised with the words: *"I forgot the rose for your Grandmother. I'll just stop at the florist on the corner, it will take just a moment."*

"But Grandfather, nothing will happen if you don't take her a rose for once," I objected.

He looked at me in disbelief: *"How come nothing will happen? Your Grandmother loves roses. And I love her smile whenever she smells the flower. If we stop fulfilling the dreams of others, a lot will happen. Both to us and to them."*

• • •

This experience taught me that, regardless of how bad things are, there is always a more positive way in life. It is up to us if we want to build up or pull down. But it is impossible to do both at once.

HOW TO COPE WITH PERSONAL JEALOUSY

You can mistrust, or you can trust.

There is nothing in between.

And it does not depend on the other person, but especially on yourself. Your approach to your partner is your choice.

If you like, you can doubt anyone and anything. Likewise, you can believe in a positive future. The other way means pulling down black roller blinds to obscure your thinking.

Shaking off jealousy is crucially important for a relationship as well as for yourself. Jealousy is destructive. It liquidates. It is the opposite of trust and no relationship can survive without trust.

Jealousy and trust are exact antipoles. Like black and white. Like oil and water. They are incompatible. Jealousy is hopelessness and disease. Trust is hope and recovery.

Our hearts and minds are not expandable. The more jealousy, the less space for trust. The more energy we give to destruction, the less we manage to build.

Jealous people often argue that they love. But their behaviour does not indicate to the other person how much they love him/her. It only manifests how much they love themselves. That they are able to smash the relationship to pieces. Often due to mere conjecture. And to their own detriment. Because shards of a broken relationship cannot be shaken from the heart and mind. The shards will still be there and they will sting. Even in the next relationship. Because jealous persons carry around the main cause at all times. Themselves.

So what should you be aware of in time? What laws should you adopt?

IT IS NORMAL TO BE APPROPRIATELY WORRIED

Jealousy is a vice. If you want to get rid of any bad habit, first you must understand it. Cast a light on it. Probe and analyse it. So, what is jealousy?

Let's start at the beginning: You choose someone who suits you in a relationship. He has something which is attractive to you. Sometimes you can define it, sometimes it is indefinable, yet you only feel it. Jealousy poses a natural fear that you may lose the person who finally suits you, and the magnet towards which you are attracted. Just as you worry about a job, house, children.

Nevertheless, jealousy is a type of worry which only injures. It steals your self-confidence, leads to irritation and uncertainty. It is a weapon pulled haphazardly from a case, with the gun barrel pointed towards you. Jealousy obscures reason. A jealous person behaves irrationally. He forgets that if he has chosen a beautiful partner, his choice may also be attractive to other people. If she has chosen a rich partner, he is considered rich by other people too. Therefore, any asset which attracts you to a partner can also allure others. This is normal. But the mind of a jealous person is adrift. His imagination begins to work against him. Negatively. There is nothing more that happens. And nothing less.

A negative mind is dangerous in that it is able to create catastrophic visions. The jealous person then lives in a coulisse that is unreal. And he also transposes these images into the real world. Then it happens that, out of his mind, he secretly searches in pockets, mobile phone, e-mails. He does not stop until he finds something suspicious. Do you know which word is the most important in the previous sentence? *"Until."* Yes, this process does not end without conviction. Therefore, paradoxically, absolutely faithful partners are exposed to jealousy the longest. Because

their blame is never proven. And the word "*guiltless*" is not in the jealous person's vocabulary.

The jealous person deprives his partner of dignity, not because of what the partner does, but because of his own behaviour. He does not care what he will or will not find. The jealous person invents the missing evidence in vivid colour. Imagination is omnipotent. The less suspicious evidence the jealous person finds, the more nervous and convinced he is of the guilt of his partner.

Right now, my partner is not writing to anyone.

Right now, she is spending time with me.

Right now, she is telling me how much she loves me.

Isn't it fishy?

IF THERE IS A REASON TO TRUST YOUR PARTNER, TRUST HIM

L et's turn it around. Let's not seek the negatives if we cannot find any, despite all efforts. Let's seek the positives. Let's start to build. Let's trust.

Trust is the glue which holds a relationship together. Distrust is a diluent which decomposes a relationship. In the human tribe, it is common to distrust. Many people do not even believe in themselves. In every circumstance, they find a reason not to have faith in themselves. How then could they trust anyone else?

Let's learn to ask in a different way:

- *Do I have a reason to trust?*

- *What would the world look like if people did not trust each other?*

- *Would they pass by each other with Colts on their belts?*

- *How come we walk around unarmed in the streets?*

- *After all, somebody might shoot us!*

This is the difference between negative and positive thinking.

The only way to find out whether to trust your partner, is to trust him. Your reputation is not at stake. If he cheats on you despite your trust, he will especially defame himself as a rat. So start to behave as if everything the partner tells you is true. If he says he loves you, believe it! If you have an obsessive need to check everything he says, stop doing it.

Simply trust him. This is really beneficial. Relaxing, untiring, and especially less risky to the relationship.

STOP COMPARING YOURSELF TO A POSSIBLY BETTER RIVAL

All the principles of success in life are identical. Whenever you intend to improve yourself in some area and grow, you must basically stop caring how somebody else is doing. Because you are primarily not interested in whether somebody else is improving or growing. It is all about you. Focus on yourself.

Jealousy is a daughter of poor self-image. Whenever you are inclined to compare yourself with others and seek in them something at which they are better, you will find it every time. But in so doing, you tend to forget that if you try to find something at which you are better than others, you will also find it. Because every person is a unique individual with distinctive strong points. Each one of us has something another has not.

That is why you should calm down. There will always be prettier, richer, more experienced... (add any adjective) people than you.

And do you know why? Because people will always differ from each other.

Ask your partner what he likes in particular about you. It is simple. If somebody sincerely loves you, the reason is: the way you are. To him, you have no competition. Not because you are perfect, but because you have specific qualities that are important to him at a given time and nobody else has them – cannot have them, because nobody is like you.

If you are unable to accept your strong as well as your weak points as an inseparable whole, and do not like yourself for what you are, you will never give others the chance to love you sincerely. You must not be ashamed of being an original. Otherwise your partner would have to love a false imitation, someone you pretend

to be and who is factually worthless. Whenever you feel inadequate, you decrease your own innate value. Only because you don't see it.

This does not mean you do not have it.

REALISE THAT YOU ARE STRONG ENOUGH TO BE ABLE TO LIVE WITHOUT AN UNWORTHY PARTNER

Yes, jealousy leads to irrationality. It is manifested, for example, in the fear of losing somebody who could betray you. Please read the previous sentence one more time. What logic do you see there?

What is worse than an unworthy partner betraying and deserting you? If you think about it, you will find that the worst thing would be if the bad partner stayed with you. If you get rid of somebody who does not value you and cannot be trusted, the change is indeed positive.

As a practical exercise, take a pen and sheet of paper and write down five facts that would immediately improve your life if the current relationship ended. How could you use the time gained? What could you do or not do without your partner? (Beware, it is just an exercise, do not indulge in the idea of a lonely life...)

Jealousy is a negative element. It deprives you of the love for others, as well as for yourself. It steals your self-confidence and fools you with the feeling that you are not good enough to survive without the unworthy partner. Jealousy likes to deceive. Especially with the thought that the relationship you are in must last forever. Even without jealousy, no relationship is eternal. In many cases, that is no shame. Some people simply only enter our lives for a short time, to teach us a useful lesson.

STOP RUINING YOUR IMAGINATION WITH SENSELESS POISON

Imagination, like fear, should serve for the good of man. But one must control a servant. You must know the limits of your imagination and where facts start. The fact that Joanne Kathleen Rowling was able to imagine the magic of Harry Potter does not mean that she believes in magic herself. So if jealousy has taken root in you, you must separate imagination from reality.

Example: Your partner is late. The tree of speculations and worries spreads its crown wide. *What is he doing? With whom? What if this is not the first time? What does he find lacking in me? Why is he acting so strikingly differently / the same way lately? After your partner gets home, the assumptions multiply: Why is he silent now? What's he thinking about? He's probably going to break up with me! Or kill me during the night! (These prognoses can go to any length and depth. Because imagination has no limits and can invent in every possible area.)*

Consequence: You start to behave negatively after your partner's late arrival. If you blame him, he will be angry, because nobody likes to be mistrusted. The relationship will go sour from both sides.

Meanwhile, the cause was not in your partner but in your own mind. It was you who explained the uncertain reason of his delay with your own negativity.

Notice, please, the word: negativity.

Why not fill uncertainty with positivity?

Why not accept that he really got stuck working late at his job?

Why, when you do not know, prefer negativity to positivity?

Why rather mistrust than trust?

If jealousy is based only on your assumptions, it has the same value as lies. There-fore, if you stop enabling negative emotions to decide on your fantasies, you will also master your jealousy.

LEAVE THE DOOR OPEN

When a partner confides that he wants to go out with friends one night, accept it. This is a neutral act which can preserve freedom in a relationship. Bad partners turn a relationship into a prison. And the other person into an irresponsible partner. The worst thing is that your negative behaviour negatively influences your partner. It is like a dog. Which dog is more likely to escape – the one always tied up in the kennel, or the one who can run around freely in the garden?

The healthiest relationships are those in which the doors are open on all sides. Because air circulates in such a relationship. It is a fresh environment. If your partner loves you sincerely, he will not run away. And if he does not love you, it is a positive outcome if he leaves as soon as possible and never returns. Because a house cannot be built on unsound foundations, just as the future of a relationship cannot be built on an unsound partner. Leaving the door open means transferring responsibility to the partner. Let him express by his actions how valuable you are to him.

. . .

If you stop being jealous, it is a service you primarily provide to yourself, not to your partner. Because jealousy happens inside. You eat your heart out. If you want to limit or get rid of jealousy, ask yourself:

- *What if everything is all right?*

- *What if I am tormenting myself needlessly?*

- *What if my partner is in fact worthy?*

These are equivalent to the questions people ask when pursuing any success:

- *What if I am all right and can succeed?*

- *What if I am suffering needlessly and can cope blindfold with what I fear?*

- *What if a successful person is dormant within me, and I am only afraid to wake him/her up?*

- *What purpose has my fear?*

Most people have the potential to succeed. They do not succeed merely because their fear does not permit it. Jealousy, like other fears, exists only in the mind. The solution is on the very spot. Keep reminding yourself of these 3 axioms:

1. *Jealousy does not give me anything, it only takes away.*

2. *Jealousy reveals less about my partner and more about me.*

3. *Jealousy is futile. I must not end up the same way – futile.*

BURNOUT

*C*ommunication is the foundation of a functioning relationship. Partners who do not communicate efficiently are like rails that never converge. Individuals all differ significantly; down to microscopic details such as DNA – deoxyribonucleic acid and the carrier of the genetic information of all organisms. We need to understand each other, moderate our original views, be attuned to compromise.

If a barrier is created on one side, the relationship is dying. The signals described in this chapter reveal that this is happening. Then you should instantly discuss with your partner the fact that the flame is dying and seek the reasons WHY and the remedy HOW.

Otherwise you will change into a weather-beaten wall which will fall apart sooner or later. And together with this wall, your entire relationship will collapse.

The father of one of my very first girlfriends was a loving husband, a great dad, he even regularly attended my sports matches to cheer for me. We grew close and so I once pumped him about how it was possible that he was such a great chap who only did the correct things.

In his study, he showed me a framed sheet of yellowed paper. There was an old date on it, exactly one month before my girlfriend was born. I read the following words:

"I am 18 years old, I am an alcoholic who was kicked out of university. I was beaten, abused, have a criminal record as a car thief. And next month one more entry will be added to this list: a teenage father...

But now I take a solemn oath to behave only properly and to do the correct things.

All this for my daughter.

I will be the father I myself did not have."

WHEN IT IS TIME TO GET GOING

About 60 000 thoughts flash through the brain every single day. One can very actively influence their nature. There should basically be more positive thoughts. Because a negative thought starting with "*NO*" just does not need a little sister.

"*NO*" is a word to end everything. With one single excuse, one can ensure that simply nothing will be done. While a positive "*YES*" always needs a little brother. Their names are for example "*HOW*" and "*WHEN*".

One does not have to be behind bars to be imprisoned. You can imprison yourself with prejudice, disbelief and evasion. One merely has to succumb to the belief that something is meaningless.

There is no anatomical difference between people. But as one ages, there is a greater difference between people. Let's learn to write, in the manner of successful people, a semicolon instead of a full stop. Dispute what are supposedly absolutes. Write question marks instead of exclamation marks.

There are two basic responsibilities in a relationship: to the couple and to oneself. Both partners are in the same position, they are primarily responsible for themselves. If a partner cares for your happiness, he is actually following his own agenda. Because, without a happy partner, it is not possible to build a happy relationship, the source of his positive energy. So speak to your partner (it is in his interest, after all), whenever you yourself feel some of the following warning signals of your own burnout:

TALK TO THE OTHER PERSON WHEN YOU THINK TOO OFTEN THAT YOU ARE NOT GOOD ENOUGH

Try not to restrict yourself by thoughts of what you can or cannot do, or what is and is not possible. Realise for once and for all that belief is not a thought controlled by the mind. Belief is a thought which controls the mind.

There will never be a better time to start something you do not believe in, than immediately. You will never be more prepared or experienced, if you prevent yourself from absorbing new knowledge and experience. Belief in oneself does not fall from the skies. You cannot buy it in a supermarket. It is not lying in the road. Your belief does not surround you. Because it is already within. It has been for a long time. You are only not using it. It is like hopping willingly on one leg, cursing the world, politicians and neighbours for being faster than you, while all that you need to do is to start using your second leg too. Do not doubt yourself. You are good, strong, courageous and skilful enough to do something today that you have always feared, and thus become better, stronger, more courageous, more skilful. What if you decide to consider today as being the ideal day to move ahead?

TALK TO THE OTHER PERSON IF YOU SPEND TOO MUCH TIME FULFILLING THE EXPECTATIONS OF OTHERS

Do you know what destroys the foundations of a relationship the most? The gnawing feeling that you are not living the life that you wish for. Or that you are living someone else's life, but not your own.

You wake up unmotivated in the mornings, only to fulfil the expectations of somebody else. You receive a salary, but the money is meaningless to you, as it cannot pay for what you really need. At home, it also seems as if you are living according to somebody else's script. Often you ask:

Where is my own life?

How much time do I devote every day to what I really want to do?

Why don't I have the strength to fight back?

This usually happens when you are so preoccupied by living according to the scenario of others that you lose control of your own life. You are not yourself. And it even seems inappropriate to you to do something according to your own wishes. You fear that somebody else will slander, leave, condemn you. You are afraid that you may lose something by being yourself. And so you prefer not even to begin. As if you are not living at all. You disappear to yourself in a mist.

According to scientific conclusions, there is only one life. The one you are living right now. You know what makes you happy, what fulfils you, what you desire, what you need. Your feelings give you the indications. You know when you feel good and when you feel bad. Please do not forget who you are. Because your partner loves

you as you are. Do not also become lost to him. Ask your partner to give you a hand at such times. You will find that everything you need is already in your hands. And if you are particularly lucky, the everything that you have is your partner.

TALK TO THE OTHER PERSON IF YOU HAVE COMPLAINED ABOUT SOMETHING FOR TOO LONG

Changed people, unexpected situations, unpredictable events. Sometimes in life, you feel that everything is conspiring against you and is to blame for your bad luck. This is a mistake.

All the oceans of the world cannot sink a boat unless water enters it. Nobody and nothing in the world can make you unhappy if you yourself do not allow it. It is not the people, situations or events which drown you. But your outlook on these people, situations and events, and your attitude to them. This is clear with problems: either you control problems, or the problems control you. There is nothing in between. How can you also control circumstances that cannot be influenced?

Most people and experiences do not have to be labelled with specific words. Often they do not have to be understood at all. All that is required is to accept them as facts. Then life will be as you want to see it. Sometimes you only need to change the perspective from which life is judged, and life will automatically change.

It is actually easy to move from the place where you are rotting. You just need to move ahead. This is done by putting one foot in front of the other. And begin to smile. After all, most "*unbearable*" moments can be viewed in a detached manner and with humour in retrospect.

TALK TO THE OTHER PERSON WHEN YOU START TO FOCUS MORE ON YOUR FAILURES, RATHER THAN ON YOUR SUCCESSES

It is much more convenient to settle for one's own mediocrity than to try to rise above the average.

It is much more convenient to talk about what we should learn, than to really start learning it.

It is much more convenient to say that everything is too difficult and complicated, than to find a way to simplify things and to achieve what is supposedly impossible.

It is much more convenient to complain about a bad job and to stay in it, than to seek or create a better one.

How sad that people grumble at the life they are living and, at the same time, avoid change. They do not progress, due to a fear of trials, mistakes and experience. The desire to succeed must always be stronger than the fear of failure. Of course, everybody is afraid. But one must not be too scared even to try.

What you aim for is merely up to you. As the pioneer of the motor industry, Henry Ford, said: *"Whether you think you can, or you think you can't – you're right."*

TALK TO THE OTHER PERSON IF YOU ARE LETTING YOUR FEAR PARALYSE YOUR FUTURE

Every fear is just a feeling. Fear is not a reality. It does not exist, only in your mind. That is why the only thing you should fear in life, is yourself. Only you are able to destroy your dreams once and for all. Only you can ensure that fear is stronger than your commitment. Only you can get stuck and paralyse yourself. Nobody else is to blame. Nobody can decide this on your behalf.

As the saying goes: "*No pain, no gain*".

It is normal that the way ahead will be painful. That strained muscles ache. When limits are overcome is when the muscles begin to strengthen.

That is why the time devoted to growth and pain should never be regretted. On the contrary, those moments should be cherished, because they provide strength, lessons and experience of how to overcome the same problems more easily the next time. No achievement in life is measured by what is achieved, but rather by what has been overcome along the way. The value of the result always grows in proportion to the effort expended.

TALK TO THE OTHER PERSON IF YOU THINK THAT THE BEST IS ALREADY OVER

New experience is gained at each new step. Life teaches one that there is never a time to be so wise that there is not the need to become even wiser. At the same time, at no past moment in life is one as experienced as at the present time. What do these sentences tell you?

That it is unnecessary to be engaged too long in the past. Return to it like to a pantry. For positive supplies. For experience. For nothing else. The past is a period which has no future. The only future is created by what you do in the present. Indeed, your situation can always be improved.

So, try to live. As the Irish dramatist Oscar Wilde wrote, *"To live is the rarest thing in the world. Most people exist, that is all."* To live means especially to open oneself to life.

And life, as we know, is about change.

Open yourself to change.

Seek change, enjoy it, shift your experience and limits. Relish the here and now. All growth is based on new experiences. They comprise the best that you can get. Not in the immature and dead past. The treasure is in the present moment. In what you can do for yourself.

Do not forget that you are the most experienced you have ever been, and the least experienced you will ever be in your lifetime.

. . .

Talk to your partner when you feel confined.

Your partner will relieve the heavy yoke of your emotions.

And do not fear that your partner will mock or reproach you for tormenting yourself with something which may be incomprehensible from his viewpoint.

If your partner is worthy of you, he will empathise with you.

And understand you along the way. Or at least accept you.

LACK OF SUPPORT

There are moments when your partner is busy and cannot be available when needed. Although he is in a relationship, he has his own life with implicit obligations and priorities. Yes, you belong to his life and to his basic values, but there simply is not time for everything.

And you need someone at your side.

Who? I call them angels.

I do not mean the ones with wings. I mean the good souls among people. Substitute, those genuine friends you can lean on in a storm. However strange it may seem, they are crucial for a relationship too. Without them, your energy might start to wane, and so will your entire relationship.

In Prague, I like to sit on the Vyšehrad fortification wall. There is a steep slope down to Vltava River below. There I contemplate the next day.

As I sat there one day, I heard strange footsteps behind me. I turned around – and saw a man. He was quite unusual. His panic-stricken eyes stared at me pleadingly. He slowly tottered towards me, stretching out his hands as if something was holding back the lower part of his body – as if he was falling over an invisible barrier.

He frightened me.

"Do you have a problem, Mister?" I called to him.

"That's exactly my question," he burst out with a dry swallow.

"Excuse me?"

I did not understand his words.

"*You know, I am terribly scared of heights,*" he pointed down to the abyss behind me. "*But I fear even more for you, as I see you sitting in such a dangerous spot. Are you contemplating something bad? Do you want to... jump?*"

His strange deduction that I could be intending to commit suicide made me laugh. I jumped down from the wall and went towards him, frivolously beginning to explain that I was only thinking about something there. But then my laughter ceased.

Because I saw not only relief in the man's eyes, but also tears. Only then I realised what he had done for me. What a barrier in himself he'd had to overcome to approach the fortification and make sure that a stranger, whom he had never before met, and probably never would again, was all right. His kindness, selflessness and bravery touched me.

In the car driving home, I looked at the blocks of flats and wondered why people lived there. *Is it only advantageous economically or do they really need to be close to other people? And when I passed a villa neighbourhood, I asked myself: Do people live there only to show their status, or do they rather want a quieter environment for themselves and their families?*

What do we still do only for money, and what for ourselves? And what do we do only for ourselves and what for other people?

HOW TO IDENTIFY ANGELS AND WHY ONE SHOULD CHERISH THEM

Perhaps, after reading about the meeting on Vyšehrad hill, you wonder:

- *Why should I help anyone?*
- *What's in it for me?*

Such questions are already a handicap. Angels among people do not ask this question. They feel that help on the basis of a barter cannot work. Just because what is a triviality for one, can mean the whole world in somebody else's pressing situation.

So think whether you have any angels around you. Seek them out. And cherish them.

Because they are more important than you think. You will understand when you need them the most.

VALUE THOSE WHO SINCERELY SUPPORT YOU

I emphasise two words. *Sincerely and support.* Both words are equally important.

One of the best ways of taking care of oneself is to take care of others. After all, this is the first law of business. The most successful entrepreneurs started out by assisting. They solved a problem they had, and offered this solution to others. That is why we light our homes with bulbs, communicate by telephone, move around in cars.

Whenever we look at the past, we find that the most important people who had the most influence were not those who answered all the questions or solved all the problems on our behalf, but those who let us find the answers to our questions and the solutions to our problems, while sitting nearby and protecting us. If needed, they lent a shoulder to weep on, and understood that not everyone is experienced. And yet − or just because of it − they stood by us. They taught us that we do not know the answers to our questions for most of our lifetimes and that is why we need to find the answers − and continue on our way with confidence.

It is not important to angels where your pathway leads. It is important to them that you yourself think about it. Because, in any case, it is yours. So they try to *sincerely support* you on your way.

VALUE THOSE WHO GIVE YOU FOCUSED ATTENTION

Angels do not need to repeat or even hold against people how much they care for them, how much they sacrifice for them. They do not need to speak. Merely doing is sufficient. Nothing is valued in relationships as much as focused attention. To be with the other person, to listen to him without looking at your watch, without preconceiving conclusions or the words that should expressed to avoid being considered unsuitable or despicable.

Attention given to somebody does not cost anything and yet it is priceless. It is as if you breathe new life into the other person. This is why the feeling is powerful: *Somebody is here for me.* Due to this, angels have the strength to heal wounds and support the growth of others. Their focused attention is more valuable than any material gift. Human kindness cannot be broken or lost and the recipient will always remember it.

VALUE THOSE WHO GIVE YOU THE FREEDOM TO BE YOURSELF

It sounds natural, but when did you have absolute freedom to be yourself? From childhood you had to do something demanded by others. Parents, teachers, professors, employers. There was a whip above you all the time. If you disobeyed, you could be beaten, complained about, fired. When could you actually be 100 percent authentic?

Some people are not themselves for their entire lives. Courage is needed to be oneself. People feel anxiety, awkwardness, worries. However, more than anything, they wish to be themselves. Angels never blame others for deciding to be authentic. They do not define others according to how they wish to see them. On the contrary, they let others reach their own definitions.

Thanks to angels guarding the path, you have an opportunity to show the world how amazing and unique you are. In addition, in a way which is the most appropriate and convenient to you.

VALUE THOSE WHO ARE WILLING TO ACCEPT YOUR TRUTH AS WELL AS YOUR MISTAKES

Friendship is like an umbrella. If it is not opened entirely, it does not work. What does absolute openness mean?

Firstly, it is normal to disagree with the opinions and actions of others. Because it is actually very rare for two persons to agree completely. They have been brought up differently, followed different life paths, taken different crossroads and acquired different experience and perspectives.

Disagreement is natural. That is why it is senseless to bad-mouth others for what they think or believe in; to reject their dreams only because you dislike them personally. On the contrary, learn to appreciate the grace of other people's opinions, of different views of the same thing. This might mean that you have to swallow your pride and superciliousness and think beyond what is natural or convenient for you. Angels know that real friendship is not a struggle for power or truth. There is no conflict. Friends are not competitors. They stand on the same side under all circumstances, willing to accept the truth as well as the mistakes of others.

After all, one's understanding also deepens with every experience. So do not deprive others of the strengthening opportunity to realise their mistakes for themselves, and to learn to correct them.

VALUE THOSE WHO INSPIRE AND REINVIGORATE YOU

Every step on life's path contributes in some way. Regardless of whether the experience is pleasant or unpleasant, it enriches you. You become wiser. To grow, you need to progress. And to advance, in addition to courage and commitment, you also need some kind of a dynamo to supply increasingly more energy for every move you make. Angels are that dynamo.

A separate section is devoted to angels, because they are indeed special. In what way? For example, they appreciate and praise others. Unfortunately, this is not something which is practised by many today. And angels are capable of reinvigorating others only if they are sufficiently positive. It is not their problem to specify what they admire about others. They can see it in the eyes. At such moments, it is like emitting positive energy by registered letter. After their infusion of positive energy, one has more of it. And thanks to their help, one is positively attuned and able to behave positively in return towards the angels. Yes, those who we encourage will also start to encourage us. That is why no angel ever became poorer through giving.

There is one basic rule for these special beings: praise in public, punish in private. They never mock others publicly if they have the opportunity to do so. If they do not understand someone, they question him. If they disagree with someone, they tell him. But they never condemn him behind his back, never vilify him in front of others. For that matter, there is no reason for doing this. Those who are unafraid of mistakes deserve to be appreciated. And those people will grow with every new experience.

VALUE THOSE WHO MASTER COMPASSION

Even the best of friends are only human. And people make mistakes. It happens that sometimes they go berserk and say something in an emotional moment which they later regret. In the end, it is a bigger problem for them than for you.

Angels learn to prevent this awkwardness. When someone who is furious pushes them into a corner or becomes unpleasant unintentionally, they divert their attention in another direction. They try not to listen. Why? Because – when the angry friend calms down – they can behave as if nothing has happened. On one hand, they enable their friends to rage when they need it, on the other hand, they do not later throw it in their face.

Not returning bad conduct to friends might not seem the most reasonable action, but it is the most compassionate. In a real friendship, the heart is more than the reason or a momentary truth.

Angels can understand that people sometimes behave badly, simply because they are stressed. They give vent to their thoughts by irritation, without any direct connection to the other person. Angels do not occupy themselves with that. They assume that they only turned up in an ill-timed moment. But that is no mistake. It is good. A lightning conductor also helps by receiving shocks.

. . .

If you wonder what angels actually gain from this, think about Nature. Every day, Nature opens millions of flowers all around the world and nobody has ever heard of Nature demanding anything in return. A dog also welcomes his master more warmly when he comes home late. You can be such a ray of sunlight to your friends. Offer them light without expecting reciprocation.

70

Do not doubt for a single moment that this is worthwhile in the end. Finally, the distance you walk in life always depends on your ability to be:

- helpful to the young,

- respectful of older people,

- considerate of the hurt,

- tolerant of the weak

- and supportive of the strong.

UNLOVING MURDERER

---

*T*here are people who judge their partners only with their eyes.

The eyes see a lot. But not everything.

They overlook something. Specifically, something that can only be felt.

Close your eyes and you will understand.

And you will have a more precise opinion of your partner.

You will discover whether he loves you for real.

Not only for the sake of appearance.

My French friend, Melchior, is blind. He has a beautiful relationship with his partner. It must be. Because he does not see her with his eyes, but only with his heart.

The eyesight of his Jeanette is good. Paradoxically, this has handicapped her for a long time. Because she could see everything except Melchior. She judged the book by its cover, not by its contents. Today she already knows how important it is to see with the heart. After all, why do those in love close their eyes when kissing?

There are different laws in force in a relationship than in ordinary life. The blind are not at a disadvantage in a relationship. On the contrary, because evil cannot be seen in the partner's intentions. Evil can only be sensed. We cannot see the impact of infidelity either. And yet it hurts tremendously. So does betrayal, jealousy, distrust, insincerity, mental torture, blackmail, fraud – all these can have a likeable face, designer clothes for the eyes, in addition diverted by luxurious gifts.

The eyes betray. Thanks to them, you can judge blindly as well as trust blindly. Just because a soldier wears the same uniform as yours, you allow him to cover your back. Without actually knowing him. If he disappoints your trust and sticks a knife in your back, it was not he who betrayed you, but your eyes.

The eyes overrule the heart which cannot see, but feels.

That is why my friend Melchior is living happily. He follows his heart and his eyesight can never deceive him. Yes, be happy that you are able to see, the eyes mediate a lot. But always give priority to your heart. This is your radar. It works on a finer frequency than your eyesight. It even perceives qualities that are crucial for life in the long term.

WHY YOU SHOULD NEVER JUDGE A PARTNER ONLY WITH YOUR EYES

Have you also already had the strange feeling (i.e. in your heart) that your partner was betraying you, but you could not find (i.e. with your eyes) any proof? Did the truth eventually emerge and you collapsed, although you had the correct suspicions all the time?

Think why it is the heart which is in pain at such a moment.

I know: because the heart weeps much more than the eyes.

Too often it weeps over its own weak voice.

Whenever you have any doubt regarding a partner, seek solitude. The maximum isolation, a quiet space where you can listen to your heart and take into account his hurtful comments which could not be understood by your senses. Perhaps then it will be easier to see that somebody bad is wasting your time. And not only your time. Especially your hope, faith in a relationship, life in general.

What signals can your heart observe?

BEWARE OF A PARTNER'S EMPTY PROMISES

He was supposed to be here on time and is not. He promised something but did not keep his promise.

The eyes do not see this. Eyes can always be bribed.

Not so the heart. Already, at this moment, it is crying out with all its might. But you do not hear it. How could you, if its voice is suppressed? What dominates are two eyes and two ears accepting your partner's apologies.

More precisely, excuses.

The difference between apology and excuse is that an apology is followed by the fulfilment of the promised condition. An apology is therefore based on a correction, an additional fulfilment of a commitment. On the contrary, an excuse is an empty sentence, manipulative energy without any positive value, without real action. Those who trust an excuse, believe only in words. And words are nothing, until they are accompanied by actions.

Broken promises are as empty as shelved ideas. There is a fundamental difference between talking about what one wants to do, and really doing it. It is the same difference as between somebody who is lying and somebody who is telling the truth. Between somebody who really loves, and somebody who only speaks about his feelings.

English dramatist George Bernard Shaw stated that what matters the most in a book is not the first, but the last chapter. It is not important what a partner promises, but how his promises end. Do not get swamped by yet another empty promise

time after time. Close your eyes, block your ears. So that you can finally perceive only actions. Because actions always speak louder than words.

Words vanish. So do gestures. What remain in a relationship are only actions. Actions are true every time, whereas words are often a lie. In a relationship which has a future, no commitments are expressed by mere promises. Only by their fulfilment.

BEWARE OF A PARTNER'S EFFORTS TO CHANGE YOU

Every person can be original and special only when he can be himself. Therefore in a relationship with prospects, partners mutually respect their differences and appreciate their similarities. The value of a person can never be increased by changing him into somebody else's image. Whenever you cause somebody to lose face, you only decrease his uniqueness. Because you are taking away a piece of him.

When you close your eyes, you will also sense in a bad partner what cannot be seen with the eyes. Manipulation. The effort to force you to be someone you are not.

Do not listen. Do not become your own parody. It is wiser to break off the manipulative relationship but to remain yourself, than to play an embarrassing role your whole life, for an audience who cannot see or even less appreciate your value. Believe that it is much easier to find a new partner than to create an entirely new identity which will never be your own. It is easier to fill an empty place outside with somebody else, than to try to fill an empty place inside where you used to be yourself.

Each partner brings out the best and most meaningful in a relationship. Let's not forget that compromise does not mean the sacrifice of yourself for the other person. On the contrary, it means meeting at the strongest point.

BEWARE OF A PARTNER'S NEED TO TORTURE YOU AND MAKE YOU FEEL GUILTY

When you feel miserable in a job, you can change it relatively easily – simply by resigning.

When a miserable circumstance occurs in your life and it is impossible to change it, you can at least change the way you think about it – view the same thing positively.

When your partner deliberately causes you to feel miserable, it is hard to leave or to view it positively. Because if you love (i.e. need) the other person sincerely, but he is mainly tormenting you, it is similar to your own heart failing.

Most senses can still be deceived at that moment. Because they are reaching for happy past memories. For example, the eyes can see the cabinet which your partner assembled. Your hands touch an old gift he bought you. Your ears still hear your friends and colleagues praising him. And all the senses shout in chorus: *"He can't only be bad!"*

But the heart never participates in the game of self-deceit, because it clearly feels the negative energy and pressure. Negative energy is very powerful. Its power is definitive. When negative energy rules, everything positive is paralysed.

All the plans, conceptions and objectives you ever had do not matter. When negative energy leads, simply nothing happens. And, moreover, if something does happen, the negative energy causes you to doubt that you have ever done anything.

This negative energy can be emitted from a partner who unilaterally enjoys emphasising everything you have ever lost, and, on the other hand, disparaging everything you have ever achieved. He reminds you of all your failures and ignores all the achievements you should be proud of.

You can never see this evil with the eyes. The ears even confirm what you see. But the heart painfully perceives the destructive force. It knows that the partner is trying to make you feel guilty. So that you succumb to the feeling of being worthless. After such a negative attack, you always feel worse, often with a lack of energy. Suddenly you cannot appreciate his strong points – your partner deprived you of a belief in them. He crushed everything about which you felt confident.

In such relationships, people lose self-confidence, become exhausted and paradoxically are dependent on the person who hurt them so much. How is it possible? They simply get used to being defined by him. The partner informs them who they are and what they are incapable of. Understandably, such a partner is lying. Because all of us have not only weaknesses but also strengths. Together, they make us whole. And weaknesses are not to our detriment, because what we are worth is based especially on how we overcome our inadequacies.

Each person has some. That is also why each relationship has its imperfections. In a relationship with a future, partners work on the elimination of drawbacks. It is not important who is better paid or educated in a relationship. One person with a higher social status is not superior to the other person in a relationship. On the contrary. To some extent, the stronger partner is responsible for the weaker one. In a relationship we must support the other person, lift him up when he falls, or even lie down with him if he cannot yet stand up on his own —your partner should never be left alone on the ground.

BEWARE OF A PARTNER'S EFFORTS TO OBSTRUCT YOUR GROWTH

The growth of every human being starts with the feeling that he is deserving of more. The unloving murderer, who is killing the relationship as well as you, deludes you into thinking the opposite. What you have achieved is the ultimate. You are incapable of achieving more. Your present role is what suits him best.

The unloving partner sees your growth as a threat and a risk. He talks about it that way. When you want to try something new, it is a leap into the unknown for him. He points out how badly it may turn out, warns you that it will be the end for you. At such a moment, your heart is pounding in alarm. But this is what a partner is for! He is there to support you! Or did he only say that he would support you?

An unloving murderer likes to rage, and does so often. Enforcement of his opinion is more important than the integrity or support of the couple. He rages to make you succumb to the fabricated speculation that your growth could lead to a mistake and the mistake to a lifelong problem. Yes, he only mentions the negatives. But a positive partner sees problems as challenges – sources of learning and growth. According to Winston Churchill: *"A pessimist sees the difficulty in every opportunity; an optimist sees the opportunity in every difficulty."* Discovery, learning, and even making mistakes, are experiences which are always beneficial.

If you review your life, you will discover that you achieved everything really worthwhile in life only once you accepted the challenges. Only challenges result in personal success. Trying new, untested paths is never a waste of time. If a partner tries to block the way, he is not the perfect partner for you. He is merely another envious enemy who hates the growth of others. Avoid such people, do not tolerate them near you. Time goes by quickly, you only have one life to live.

The heart feels pain under the sphere of influence of such people, because an un-loving murderer depletes all its positive energy. The heart needs positive energy to live. The heart is nourished by everything which fulfils and satisfies you. Do not be deprived of what gives you meaning. Otherwise your heart will stop. You will no longer be really alive. An envious person says that if you do nothing, nothing bad will happen. But the heart knows too well that if you do nothing, nothing good will happen either.

BEWARE OF A PARTNER'S EFFORTS TO DIRECT YOU

T he ears interpret such efforts as pleasant music. *"How nice of him to want to control me. It's right, because he knows what's best for me."* The brain is even happier: *"He intends to work on my behalf! So I can rest! I no longer need to think!"*

The heart cannot believe how stupid the senses can be.

Why do you get deluded so easily into thinking that your own efforts will lead nowhere? How can another person know what is best for you? How can he assess your decision in a specific situation, if he is not in your shoes and also has no experience of such a situation? It seems to be another wonder of the world – you do not yet know the right path for yourself and can only discover it by experience, while your partner reputedly knows how to deal with everything.

Well, not everything. But he is able to deal with you.

Despite being unable to deal with his own life in many cases.

The eyes do not see this. Whenever a partner is too close and comforts you, your vision obscures the overall picture. Like in an art gallery. If one wants to better understand a painting, the brain commands: *"Go nearer to see every detail."* But the heart advises you to step back, so that you rather see the whole picture from a greater distance.

That is why the heart, when it does not understand something in a relationship, advises you to step back. To calm down. To comprehend all the implications – and the whole.

BEWARE OF A PARTNER'S PRESSURE TO LIVE MORE IN THE PAST

A partner whose betrayal or other misdeeds have been revealed, usually blusters in order to deceive your ears, and bribes with material gifts to pull the wool over your eyes. He caresses, kisses, satisfies all the senses. Only one weapon has any effect on the heart — recalling the past when you felt good together.

The argument of a pleasant past is usually a bitter pill to swallow. So bitter that your reason thunders: "*You are right, partner. Those were the best times. Which implies that the best is behind us in our relationship.*" The heart must be resistant. It must not be drawn into the past. The past is an abyss. Something which was, but is no more, and will never again be. Just as the future is something which is not yet, and may never be. Decide on principle according to the present. If your partner bamboozles you into thinking that he has learnt his lesson, fine, give him a chance. But let him prove it by his action and not by words. If he intends to make excuses that he wants to prove it later, fine, wait a while. Indeed, every near future becomes the present. Now, now, now... has he changed his ways?

FERRYMAN

There are relationships that have a slight catch. Or rather a bait. Your partner somehow forgot to mention that he does not intend to stay long. He only came over for a brief fling.

Unfortunately, without being aware of it, like a ferryman, you are only there to transport him from the bank of "Disappointment"— where he is stranded after a former relationship — to the bank of "Satisfaction"— where he will start a new relationship. But not with you.

As a ferryman, you always stay in the boat. You have to learn to live with and carry on amidst all the dirt which your passenger washed off himself, and which remains in the boat.

The loudspeaker in the Tube train had already announced: "*This train is ready to depart, please stand clear of the doors, mind the closing door!*" when a young woman stumbled into the carriage. Her young daughter quickly followed her, and some large bags were thrown in after them. Their personal belongings burst out across the floor. A staggering drunk was seen outside the closing doors. He had just got rid of a burden.

The passengers watched in astonishment as the woman knelt down amidst the havoc of the scattered clothes. Together with other persons nearby, I rushed to help her on to her feet and put the belongings back into the plastic bags. The woman was shocked and shaking. Incoherently she tried to explain: "*I only wanted... him to stop drinking... He beats us up when he gets drunk.*"

Her daughter hugged her tightly and began to sob: "*But Mom, why does he beat you when you're the kindest mother in the world?*"

84

Tears flowed from the mother's eyes: *"Natalie, how do you know I'm the kindest mother? You don't know all the mothers in the whole world."*

The girl looked at her earnestly and hugged her even closer: *"But Mom, you are my whole world."*

. . .

Never, really never think that you are alone with your problems. There is always the opportunity to make a positive difference. And that makes all the difference in the most difficult moments.

WHY IT IS IMPORTANT TO RESOLVE A PAST RELATIONSHIP

The scenario is always the same. Only the cast changes.

Person A is suffering. Her boyfriend broke up with her in a nasty way. She finds what is momentarily lacking in another's arms. She makes person B feel valuable and happy. Suddenly life is full of self-sacrifice, joint plans...

But then – cut! A break-up.

Self-pity, remorse.

"Where did I go wrong?" person B searches his conscience. "Why did person A inform me one day that she no longer loved me and was leaving? But we were so happy together.

"How can I reverse what happened? How can I get back what has vanished? And especially, how can I understand it?"

Simply speaking, a ferryman is a person who accelerates the transport from point A to point B. Were it not for the ferryman, the journey would be longer for the passenger and would require more of his strength. In relationships, a ferryman transports others from a sad past to a happy future. Unfortunately, he always remains alone in the boat as soon as the passenger disembarks on the happy bank.

Ferrying in love is the hardest profession in the world. The service is not paid for by the passenger, but by the ferryman himself – by a broken heart and destroyed faith in people and future relationships. He harvests bitterness in return for his goodness. He eliminated the passenger's bitterness – and was left with it himself.

Unintentional ferrymen ask what good there was in such an experience. There is always something positive, even if somebody makes you his ferryman. Next time, you will be more careful not to repeat the same mistake out of compassion.

Ferrying is a deserved punishment for those who quickly, almost rashly, start a relationship with somebody who is not totally free of a previous relationship. If the person's heart is elsewhere or midway to you, it is not wholly with you. It is always necessary to close the door on the past. If this does not happen and the door to the past remains open, any effort to open the door to the future will cause a draught. And many rotten things will blow in from the past to the present. The memories of a previous relationship keep returning unwittingly to the transported person. Sooner or later, his words begin to be darker, his sight more absent-minded, his embrace colder. His mind is elsewhere, not in the here and now. Even if he wished only for the best when with you, he cannot properly achieve this. Because the only correct way he can (or even must) do this, is to ask you for sufficient time to go aside and slam the old door shut.

It is particularly obvious in a ferrying relationship that doing the right things is more important than doing any other things in the right way. A partner with a heart lost in the past perhaps knows how to kiss properly, how to embrace properly, how to enjoy mutual time together properly, but in his situation, none of those skills is sufficient. Because none of it frees him from the past hurt. What he needs is time. To heal the injury. It is insufficient to pretend that there is no complex defect of the heart — because it exists. An unhealed wound is still painful. And even if it appears to be healed, the new scar tissue is still forming. This also takes time. It pays to wait. The scar will remind the partner how somebody else treated him. And he will appreciate your attitude all the more. But only if he has time to close the door to the past.

Without insistence.

Without reproach.

Without suppressing the past experience.

If somebody you care for is suffering due to his own past, stand by him and support him. But never drag him into your boat. Let him cry his heart out on the other bank, let him curse, release all the evil left by the previous relationship. Do not plug up the rotten feelings inside him. On the contrary, hold out a helping hand to him. Assist

him if he asks you to do so, hug him when he feels alone, answer the phone if he calls you.

It is good for him to know that you are there for him.

But only if he himself wishes it.

Those five words are crucial. He must know it himself. His step towards you must be his own personal choice. Let this option be known to him. But let him decide responsibly and of his own free will. He must not be forced into this step – like in a prison. Because one escapes from a prison at the first opportunity. And to the first person who lets the prisoner into his heart.

Be warned that ferrying is horrendous. If one hurts a dog, he stops trusting people. If one hurts a person, he loses more – he stops trusting in love. Despite the fact that love as such never betrays anyone. Only people betray each other. Such an experience is like an old fracture of a limb. It may be healed, but it always reminds you it is there in bad weather; it aches.

As a ferryman, you tend to reproach yourself for the past, seek the fault in yourself or others, remain alone because that is considered as the easiest solution. It seems that when you are alone, you only have yourself, there is no disappointment, no break-up. But, sooner or later, you discover that solitude is unhealthy. You need others. You need relationships.

That is why you have a mouth with which to speak to someone. You have ears with which to listen to someone. You have arms with which to hug someone. You cannot really hug yourself. And most importantly, you have eyes, a memory and a heart. To see and remember well, and not ever again to be so badly disappointed.

Abused ferrymen can become bitter about the whole world. Or hope that somebody better will save them. No. Nobody can make you as happy as you yourself can. Moreover, you cannot make others happy if you are still filled with negativity. Just as practising certain professions is conditional on a medical examination, so entering a relationship should be conditional on a thorough examination of the heart. This should include the confirmation that there are no remnants from the past in the heart, that the patient is sufficiently free of previous relationships to start a new relationship with a clean slate. Unfortunately, global healthcare is not yet so advanced. Therefore, your responsibility is to enter into a relationship only with

somebody with sufficient closure of a previous relationship. And the other person's responsibility is not to lie to you. Otherwise, he is committing the most heinous emotional murder of a relationship. Of somebody who has actually come to his aid.

If it has ever happened to you that you gave your heart to somebody who ran off with it and that is why you feel so empty, please take note of the following recommendations:

DO NOT ALLOW YOURSELF TO BE DEFINED BY SOMETHING BAD THAT IS BEHIND YOU

Yes, perhaps you ask yourself questions such as:

- *What am I worth?*
- *Do I have any future?*
- *What is left for me?*

It would be a mistake to use the past for the answers. Nothing that has ever happened to you in the past predestines a bad future. This only applies if you do not interrupt, terminate or change something that happened to you previously. If you wish to know your future, there is no need to go to a fortune teller. Just look at what you are now doing. Because your present creates your future.

The fact that you met a bad person in the past can lead to a bad future only if you stay with such a person. In the case of the bad partner no longer being a part of you, there is no factual reason to believe that your future will be equally bad.

And are you still afraid that a bad relationship will be repeated next time? Realise that there is one positive aspect in every bad experience: it teaches you, albeit in harsh ways, how to prevent a repetition of the bad experience. Life is patient. Its lessons are long and intensive, until you stop repeating the mistakes. The most effective understanding comes after difficult lessons.

Do not despair. You have the same chance of finding an ideal other half for a lifetime as hitting the jackpot at the first attempt. It sometimes happens, but more often you must first gain experience and learn from it. There is one advantage. The longer you have waited for the dreamed-of partner, the more you will appreciate him.

DON'T BELIEVE IN DEMONS, THEY DO NOT EXIST

What is done, cannot be undone. What has happened, cannot be changed. Just because something was created in the past, it does not have to continue in the present. You already know that the door to the past must be closed. That is why what was in the past is also going to stay there. Realise two important facts:

If somebody hurt you badly in the past, he need not be part of your life ever again. And if somebody new enters your life, he need not have anything in common with those who isolated you in the past.

In brief, demons are simply in your power. If you do not want to, you need not return to something which did not previously work. Just leave the door to the past closed with a big bolt.

The past and future, as we have already mentioned, are two times that do not exist. So there is no reason why they should trouble you. Actually, nothing ever troubles a human being. Man torments himself. Your suffering is not the fault of other people, circumstances, events. The fault is specifically yours. You do not love yourself enough.

So: you must love yourself more.

Although you are wallowing in self-pity, realise that nobody has stigmatised you, nobody has condemned you. You are the one creating your own life. At every instant, you have everything you need to build a better relationship. Most importantly, you have experience.

Learn to deal with past demons. If a photo of somebody who turned you into a ferryman falls from a photo album, do not throw it away. On the contrary, exhibit it.

Get used to looking demons straight in the eyes and thanking them. There really is a reason. It was they who taught you to be more cautious and not to repeat the ferrying mistake in relationships.

DO NOT CONSIDER PREVIOUS RELATIONSHIPS AS FAILURES

An infant does not know how to walk. As he learns to walk, he falls. He learns to walk by falling. So, is the fall of an infant who is learning to walk, a negative or positive experience?

Likewise: if you leave a relationship which has turned sour, is the event negative or positive?

If you look at your life to date, you find that only one relationship has been a success. The latest one. All previous relationships were fiascos. So historically all of us appear brutally unsuccessful. Like children, who fell down time after time, until beginning to walk on their own.

The nature of people is such that whenever they are learning, they tend to consider the time of the acquisition of useful experience as being lost. They suppose that they do not know what they are still learning. But even the popular children's dodgem car keeps banging into surrounding obstacles until it finds the way out. Every accident had its purpose, it is not futile. Through every experience gained, you find that that is not the right way. With each failure you get closer to your goal, not further away.

That is why there are no futile relationships. Each person who left a trace in you, taught you a crucial lesson, thanks to which your future relationships will be wiser and more functional. Those people who suffered in previous relationships the most, usually have the happiest current relationships. After all, a similar principle apples to financial success. People with an average salary have far fewer reasons to seek better wages than those with miserable earnings, or even the unemployed. Which

is why so many global billionaires originate from poor beginnings. Average people have far fewer reasons to strive for exceptionality.

So be grateful for bad relationships. Only because you found the strength to discard them did you get the opportunity to establish a better relationship. Those who have been burnt, appreciate solace the most. Somebody who has been affronted by a dishonest partner, appreciates an honest partner the most.

DO NOT JUMP INTO A NEW RELATIONSHIP TOO HASTILY

If you want revenge, turn him into a ferryman. Warm yourself up in his arms, let him pull you out of the bog, and when he washes you of all the dirt, dries you and dresses you in clean clothes, depart in another direction without thanking the ferryman.

Ferrymen are people punished by other persons for the misbehaviour of third persons. They resemble butterflies. They do not cause harm to anyone. And still people tear off their wings.

If someone has deceived you, it is imperative to stick to two important principles: do not believe the person who deceives you, and do not deceive somebody who trusts you. Partners who trust you under all circumstances are rare and vulnerable. Indeed, like butterflies. Which is why, when bitter and perhaps even vengeful, do not seek another ferryman to free you. Wait until the heart has shaken it off. Do it for your heart. Give it time. The heart will shake off the dirt. It must shake it off. After all, it beats continuously. Just do not rush it.

Rather weep, than make others weep. It is better to weep alone temporarily and later to laugh for the rest of your life with someone else.

NEVER AVOID POSITIVE PEOPLE AND HAPPY COUPLES

This is probably the most important methodology of the thought process:

- *Negative feelings create negative thoughts.*
- *Negative thoughts spur negative deeds.*
- *And negative deeds lead to negative results.*

Whenever you desire a positive change, you must let positive energy into your body.

There are many sources.

Firstly, joy. From the most ordinary things. Already thanks to them, you can become convinced that joy still exists, that it is all around you and you are capable of feeling it. So seek opportunities for distraction. Open yourself up to a positive life. If somebody has pushed oodles of gall and dirt into you, and you cannot wash it from your body yourself, ask your friends for help. It it best to ask those who are happier and more positive than you. They will know what to do.

You are flooded by negativity and feel that positive people rather provoke you. Unhappy people suffer when they see others happy. Not because unhappy people are bad. The evil is only within them. They would like to be happy, but there is only limited space within. One must get rid of the bad things first, so that the good can fit in.

Positive friends are infectious with their different world views. With a snap of the fingers, you begin to laugh at your missteps. Laughter is powerful. By lifting facial muscles, you lift the floodgates of happiness. Hormones that do you good are released. Laughter, this chemical process, accelerates time. It enables a detached

96

view of even tragic events. The reason is not that events have changed. Only your perception of the events has changed.

Only strong people can uplift others. And strength does not fall from the skies. Strength is built by experience. The strongest person is not the one who has never encountered any obstacles in life, but the one who has overcome as many obstacles as possible. Friends who are in strong relationships understand what you are going through. They have usually previously experienced the same things, which have made them stronger. Thus they provide both courage and a positive example. If they could find the strength by ferrying, so can you.

We can either breathe a carpet full of dust forever, or dust it outside in the fresh air. The same happens in a relationship. Outside with friends. Do not doubt that if you dust out the past, you will breathe better.

BE GRATEFUL TO THE PEOPLE WHO PUSHED YOU FORWARD BY BETRAYING YOU

When you realise that the relationship which once was, is no more, usually in the first instant you regret the time wasted on this relationship. Secondly, you begin to value the time saved. For that matter, Dakota Indians have a saying: *"If you find that you are riding a dead horse, dismount."*

The relationship with people who made you a ferryman has already been dead at the outset. It existed only in your fantasy, in your blind faith, through error. Realising the truth sometimes hurts. But not as much as a life lost in a lie.

WEAKLING

When the Roman Emperor wanted to demonstrate his power, he pardoned those who had been condemned to death. He well knew that if he had them killed, he would only be demonstrating his fear of them and his own weakness. Application of a destructive strength against weaker people, especially those who cannot defend themselves, is always a demonstration of weakness, not of strength. If you want to show your strength and magnanimity in a relationship, then it is paramount not to hurt others, especially if you have the ideal opportunity for doing so.

In the last year of Primary School, an unusual classmate arrived in our class. We could see that her face, neck, hair area as well as her bare limbs were scarred with burn marks. When younger, she was supposedly trapped in a barn which was on fire.

We laughed at her. Children are cruel. And teachers can be even crueller. When the girl did not know an answer to a teacher's question on the board, she had to hear taunts like: "Why don't you speak? Is your tongue also burnt? Are you waiting for a good mark just because your face is scarred?"

She was sad and hung back, lonely.

Then a weakling turned up. That's what we called him. He was from the next-door class and he began to defend her. He found out where she lived and every morning would place a dandelion, which he had picked, on the threshold of her flat.

After a month of this, he included a hand-written note with the meadow flower:

"One flower for each flame that hurt you. Write on the other side how many flames there were."

I knew his mom. She brought up three boys by herself and never complained. And I surmise that her son behaved towards the girl as he would have towards a princess.

Because he was being brought up by a queen.

WHY WEAK MEN HUMILIATE WOMEN

When a man does not give up his seat for a woman in the waiting room or means of transport, he is a weakling. If he cannot hold the door open, move back a chair, help her into her coat, he must be a weakling, because only a weakling does not have the strength to do something like that. If somebody is reluctant to honour the rules of ethics, he is definitely no strongman.

In a relationship, this type of person works with three tools:

- a feeling of guilt,

- a feeling of inadequacy,

- and with a feeling of inferiority.

He dominates a woman with all his weaknesses.

Feeling of guilt: For example, a man who is unsuccessful in his career blames the woman for his failures. He always finds some pretext for her being responsible for his inadequacies. The deserved punishment of the specific man for this behaviour is his own future which is not improving. Because the first precondition of a change for the better in any area, including the professional, is to accept responsibility for one's own mistakes. A man who does not accept his own mistakes keeps repeating the mistakes, so cannot correct them either. No wonder he harvests the same results if he keeps repeating the identical mistakes.

Feeling of inadequacy: On the other hand, a man who is successful in his career makes his partner feel that she is inferior to him. This can take the form of comparing salaries and contributions to the family budget. But this might not apply only to money. The man can remind the woman that she is getting old and losing her grace and sex appeal, that her body is deteriorating. Thus he creates an inferiority complex in the woman. What is worse – he forces her to change somehow and not

to want to be herself. This pressure on the inadequacy of the woman does not last forever. Often only until another man turns up who will restore her self-confidence. He does not need to lie at all. This woman is exactly what he needs. Then the woman will understand that what her former partner said about her rather concerns himself and his world view than who she really is.

Feeling of inferiority: For example, a man can feel threatened for various reasons by a more capable woman. This inferiority complex keeps growing in him, as well as his negative thoughts. Such a man must realise that negations do not create any real growth. A negative man can be superior to his more capable woman, only if he decreases her value. Imagine, for the sake of simplicity, that a man has a level 4 of success. If the woman's degree of success is a 6, the man, who does not have a chance of increasing his own success, will become "*more*" successful only if he decreases her to a level 3. His abilities will not increase in any way, but his ego will rejoice that the woman has been degraded to below his level.

These are some of examples of masculine weakness. Other examples are jokes about women. Do you know why women do not tell jokes about blonde men? Because they do not need to degrade men. But men use labels such as "*gold-digger*" or "*careerist*" for women who are more capable than them.

That is why unfaithful women are "*sluts*" while unfaithful men are "*Don Juans*". Men need words to repaint reality. Why do they do it? We cannot imagine how degrading the feeling of being useless is to an unsuccessful man. Contrary to a man, a woman can be useful very easily. Because she gives birth to children and takes care of most of their upbringing. Even if the woman has achieved nothing else in life, she is useful to mankind. But an unsuccessful man is degraded to the role of a mere inseminator, who is useful to civilisation for just a few minutes and then, as in the case of an insect, he feels more of a handicap than a help.

It is therefore necessary to understand men. They are like diamonds. Seemingly the hardest in the world. And yet, one only needs to cut the fissile line which holds the entire structure of the diamond, for the gem to disintegrate into dust.

Yes, seeming Samsons are in fact the most fragile. Many men in relationships are aware of the fact that women have men in their hands in their own way. And that women can cut one of the ten fissile lines that are listed in the following text. That is why men are irritated and able to be cruel – like very weak creatures.

BEWARE OF A PARTNER WHO IS HAUNTED BY PERFECTIONISM

For the aforementioned reasons, some men become workaholics. They want to be maximally valid and useful. To provide a home, subsistence, be a perfect partner, father, lover. Desire for perfection leads to the destruction of a man. Because there is no perfection in human life.

Moreover, men are handicapped by their own egos. They like to measure themselves against others, they like to compete. Young men are jealous of older men, older men of younger ones. Because both old and young men are lacking something all the time. Both groups notice that the others have something they do not have. This intensely torments and provokes men. That is why they love action movies. They want to be perfect heroes and yet – imagine the paradox – they feel inadequate at every age.

They feel inadequate, either in the past, or the present.

At the same time, ego prevents such a man from seeking the fault within. So he searches for it all around him. And he does not hesitate to blame a woman, who is not to blame, for his inner struggle and who cannot defend herself.

Those are the weak men. What about the opposite?

Strong men are well aware that perfection is unattainable – and they do not torment themselves with the illusion of perfection. But they realise that improvement is possible.

Strong men admit to themselves that they are the creators of their own future. That they can improve themselves in every phase of their lives. But this means in par-

ticular putting ego aside and accepting present imperfections. Which is something only a few men can do.

Most weak men choose inaction. Instead of working on themselves systematically and thus increasing their worth, they lie on the couch or sit with a beer and insult others to diminish their worth. They believe that then their own flaws are not as noticeable, because they are decreased by the derogatory words uttered about others. But those weak men forget who they are and that they will not grow by using verbal abuse. And they remain small.

A wise man attempts to work on his own improvement. But a foolish man resigns himself to his imperfections.

BEWARE OF A PARTNER WHO CONSTANTLY NEEDS APPROVAL

It is said that quality goods praise themselves. So men praise themselves whenever they have the opportunity. Weak men suspect that their inferior worth cannot be seen, so they seek other means of seeking approval. Over a bar counter they beef about sportsmen, without knowing anything about sporting action. They do not need facts and only care that their own opinion wins. Those men are laughable. But there is another category which is very dangerous. The weakest men.

They need to showcase their imaginary successes. They want to arouse envy and are able to get themselves into debt to achieve this. Just to astonish others with the latest model car, gadgets, luxury holidays. They are unable to acquire status by their actual conduct, so they have to buy status (on credit). Like a fake university degree.

These people are devoured by their own envy. They are sick and desperate. Even when they have a new car, they are still pitiful, albeit with the new car. It is important to realise that nobody is born strong. One becomes strong. One must grow through one's own courage, patience and persistence. That is why strong men are so generous, thoughtful, helpful – without these characteristics, they would never have grown to such a level.

You can deprive those men of their new cars, gadgets, holidays. You can take away their influence on others in their careers. But you can never take from them what they have created within themselves.

Women call it charisma. This word has no definition. Because charismatic men are not made by definition but by action.

BEWARE OF A PARTNER WHO HIDES FROM THE TRUTH

Weak men must hide from the truth. Their egos do not allow them to accept where they are. To accept that there are areas of possible improvement. So weak men cannot even learn. It is naïve to expect a weak man to improve if he does not want to hear the truth.

Weak men are their own worst enemies. Men who are strong today, were weak in the past. Everybody is born weak. But contrary to the men who remain weak, strong men are not afraid to confess their failings. It is the same with GPS navigation. If you want to reach a certain destination, not only do you need to know the point of your arrival, but also the point of your departure. If you refuse to confess where you are, how can you orient yourself on the map of life?

Weak men do not like to hear that they have failed at something. Strong men have no problem with this. They are aware that every failure is temporary, until it is subsequently corrected. They remind themselves of the strong points they are left with. Strong men never count what they have lost to date, but what they have gained, what they have. Because it is only possible to build with what one has.

Weak men behave like fish on dry land who believe that everything is actually all right, as long as the other stranded fish are also gasping just as desperately for air. A strong man primarily tries to find the nearest pond in which to save himself. He does not align himself with the other dying fish.

This implies that a weak man is a risk to his whole family. He is able to drag it to the bottom with his own ego. By pretending to be someone he actually is not.

If you want to work on yourself effectively and tangibly improve something, firstly you must be yourself.

Look the truth in the eyes. Weak men are incapable of doing this.

BEWARE OF A PARTNER WHO DECEIVES AND HURTS ONLY BECAUSE HE HAS THE OPPORTUNITY TO DO SO

A man can hurt his partner at any time. Beat her at any time. Indeed, he is stronger physically. He can devastate her on a daily basis. If he is a weakling.

Such behaviour is normal for a weak man. He tries to refer to history, genes, biological needs. Note that weak men never want to be alone in disputes, they like to hide in a crowd. A crowd provides anonymity. They can hurt anyone without risking detection or punishment. Yes, this is how a weak man thinks. On the contrary, a strong man knows that misuse of strength and deceit are not the result of opportunity, but basically a personal choice. The infidelity of specific men have nothing in common with history or biology. The fact that a man decides to hurt a woman does not reveal anything about the man as such. And neither about the woman he deceives. It reveals only what he is like.

Deceitful men like to argue that the woman was to blame because she was unable to meet his needs. No. The deceived woman has only one drawback for which she pays. The drawback is: she trusted the wrong person. That is why women do not want weak men.

Deceiving others is a manifestation of weakness.

Fidelity requires strength, self-renunciation, patience.

Fidelity means doing the right thing in a relationship.

And the right thing requires the right man. A weakling is not the right one. Hurting others has nothing in common with strength, but everything in common with the inability to master oneself.

BEWARE OF A PARTNER WHO DOES NOT HAVE ENOUGH EMPATHY

Empathy is the ability to understand the feelings of others. To empathise with them. But weak men are insensitive. Without compassion, they beat, shout, exploit, stalk.

Empathy is not a product which can be purchased in a shop. Empathy must be learned. This is not difficult, as soon as people convince themselves that in a relationship they always achieve more by kindness than by violence.

For example, empathetic people know that everybody is entitled to privacy. Even as a couple. Everybody should have time for himself, his desires, dreams as well as secrets. He should have a private zone where he can be sure that nobody will disturb him without his consent. His telephone, email, bank account – should be things which are his alone.

It is impossible to breathe freely in a relationship which usurps the basic freedoms. A person who controls each step of his partner may feel powerful. However, instead he is powerless.

Respect the boundaries of the other person. Do not push yourself beyond the borders. Behave in such a way that your partner invites you over them. If he wants to.

BEWARE OF A PARTNER WHO IS PREJUDICED

Weak men lack the strength to keep their emotions under control. Their irritation has victims – women and children. With their inability for self-control, they destroy everything that is living. They behave primitively because they act faster than they think. Or, more precisely – they do not think sufficiently. We can see it from their habit of judging strangers at first sight. To what extent does this speak about others, and to what extent about themselves?

Judging others is a waste of time, among other things, because everything is changing. Other people, their moods, feelings, motivations, stress and suffering are not constant. We change as well. Any judgement about any other person is valid only at that specific moment, and might not be true at the next. And when we mature, we might even be ashamed of how we thought in the past.

A weakling who acts before he thinks, should not be punished, ridiculed or subjected to revenge. On the contrary, he needs help. If we are unable or unwilling to provide such help, then the best service we can provide to this weak man is to let him go. To give him the opportunity of finding someone else who will be able to help him. Do not waste time with gossips.

BEWARE OF A PARTNER WHO IS OBSESSED WITH NEGATIVE THOUGHTS

Weak men incessantly speak about alleged injustices that happened to them. They despise others and keep repeating how "*unfair*" life has been to them. They cannot be a support either in a private or professional sphere. It is not possible to build a relationship with people who only destroy.

But every coin has two sides – the positive and negative side. Positive as well as negative aspects can be found in everything. This is up to us. It is our personal choice whether we are positive or negative. We can never persuade a weak man that the things he complains about can also be perceived positively, as a challenge. Drive. Motivation. And what can be perceived positively, can also be improved. However, it is unacceptable to the ego of the weak man that the condition he is complaining about can be corrected in the long term – and even just as simply as changing his point of view. A weak man is convinced that he is unable to positively influence anything fundamental. This is his problem. He condemns himself to ruin. You do not have to feel sorry for him. Because he has a right to free choice. Even this kind. It is all up to him.

BEWARE OF A PARTNER WHO HARBOURS OLD INJURIES

Everybody makes mistakes. All of us have taken some steps in life that led nowhere. This is normal. And nothing is easier than leaving behind what is not working. Weak men, controlled by ego, take a long time lamenting over spilt milk. They stand over it and weep at how the sour milk smells increasingly bad.

On the contrary, strong men do not lament for a long time. They take a cloth and wipe the floor. Weak men could also do this. But they would have to cease their wailing and start acting. Problems will keep piling up until they do something.

Weak men always pose as victims. Everything that happened to them has been a conspiracy, someone's evil intention, a fatal accident. It was beyond their power to influence anything. As long as they believe this, their personal catastrophe is inevitable. Because they demonstrate that they are unable to make their own decisions.

Strong men do not remain standing in the spilt milk. They are prepared to pay for the mistake. The higher the price, the more pleased they are. Because what we pay for dearly, we never forget. The harder the lesson, the more it is enforced. Paying for a mistake and correcting it is the fastest way to get rid of suffering. It means leaving behind the place which tormented us.

Not relishing in it.

BEWARE OF A PARTNER WHO TAKES EVERYTHING PERSONALLY

Strong men know that when somebody says and does something, it is the result of his upbringing, character, knowledge and experience. Every letter tells more about the writer than the recipient. If somebody considers you amazing or intolerable, it is not so much a reflection of you, but of the person who perceives you in this way.

Weak men are touchy about praise as well as criticism from others. Compliments send them into seventh heaven (*"That's so true..."*), criticism irritates them (*"shameless lies..."*). The most anxiety and frustration enters a man's heart in this way. He takes other people's judgements personally. Strong men are able to filter the opinions of others. What remains is the feedback and useful information. They are grateful for all comments, because they can use them for their own improvement. So they try to take positives for their personal growth from every sentence. And they throw the rest to the winds.

BEWARE OF A PARTNER WHO ENVIES EVERYBODY ELSE

Every man was once weak. There is no difference. Strong men only differ from those who remain weak. For example, he did not keep his orientation towards a specific objective. He began to compare, peek at others. Ego led him astray and never allowed him to return. Envy is the powerful weapon used for this.

Envy is the tendency to count other people's strengths rather than one's own. This empty inclination does not produce anything positive in a man, it only hurts. That is why a strong man rejects envy as much as possible. He does not try to compare himself with others. But because all men are competitive, he still continues comparing himself in one battle. He competes with himself. He tries to be better today than he was yesterday. His rival is his best possible self on that day. Because this is a competitor with whom it is always possible to catch up.

For weak men, the own self is an unbeatable adversary. And this greatly annoys them. How is it possible that I am worse than I should be? Who is to blame? The government? My neighbour? My wife?

. . .

Learn to shake off people who let you down in the long term. And remember: it is no wonder that you are desperate, if you cannot reject those who make you feel desperate.

VAMPIRE

He sucked her dry and tossed her aside. Not for the first time.

But every time was the last time.

At least that is what he said.

"It will never happen again," he begs on his knees.

But it will happen again, time after time. This is what vampires are like.

People who suck energy, trust and money from others, while making them dependent on them.

Everybody asks: Have the abused lost their minds? But reason has no place in love. And suffering is part of love, in a way. Moreover, women have a maternal instinct, they naturally tend to rescue others and tolerate even the intolerable. Not forgetting that they are trusting. And patient. Even for more than 18 years when bringing up children.

"So hopefully my adult vampire will grow out of it too," they comfort themselves in the depths of their souls.

Dependence has two faces. Vampirism can even be beautiful. I saw one such vampire couple in Asia – a husband and wife in their declining years. They sat at the best table in the beach restaurant. Every evening. Each time they had the same celebratory meal. And every evening, after the same toast, he knelt down in the sand and, kissing the palm of his wife's hand, pronounced words I could not hear because they faded in the murmur of the waves. However, it was obvious from his

eyes how moved he was. I point out that this was repeated every evening. Always the same scenario...

The old man had Alzheimer's disease. He had problems orienting himself. Obviously his memory was not good. When I met his wife by chance in the resort, she told me that her husband sometimes could not recall where he was, why he was there, sometimes he could not even recognise her...

"When his memory began deteriorating," the woman said, *"he was confused and irritated. When he wakes up and looks around fearfully, it is not easy to repeat all the associations to him. But I am addicted to him, and I decided to enjoy being here..."*

Enjoy? How?

"As he cannot recall why he is here, every morning I tell him: 'But darling, we are here to renew our marriage vows! Don't you remember that it's our anniversary today?' And his masculine ego does not allow him to confess that he does not remember anything like this. So he behaves very chivalrously and in the evening decides to surprise me with the reservation of the best table, where he always asks for my hand... Every evening."

They spent three weeks in the resort. For the whole time the husband behaved 'extraordinarily' – that is, as if the present day was the last day of their lives.

With reverence, respect, attentiveness.

"I am addicted to her," he once commented in the lift. He did not have to say it. He was proving it. It was the most beautiful mutual addiction I have ever seen.

• • •

That was an example of positive addiction. But dependence, like everything, has a murky side. Let's hold in high esteem all who can live with negative vampires. They prove that it is also possible to find something good in those who deliberately hurt them, whether physically or mentally. People often stay in a vampire bond for the sake of children for whom they thus sacrifice their lives. But the cup of patience has a rim too...

BORDERS OVER WHICH EVIL MUST NOT BE ALLOWED IN A RELATIONSHIP

Of course, the borders of tolerance and intolerance in a vampire relationship are individual. Everybody has a different pain threshold which indicates what can be coped with, and what is unbearable; to what extent he can sacrifice himself and when he becomes aware of a wasted life; where children survive a dysfunctional family, and where family emotions and violence harm children. Because a bad example can benefit as well as harm. For that matter, do you know the story of two separated twins?

Both brothers were brought up in the family of a notorious drunkard. When they met years later, the first brother asked: *"So, how did you end up?"* The second brother replied: *"I'm a drunkard. What else could I be, after daily watching a heavy boozer? And you?"* The first brother: *"I'm a teetotaller. What else could I be, after daily watching a heavy boozer?"*

To find a proper border in a vampire relationship, it is important to understand that true love does not involve finding the perfect person. Indeed, there is nothing like a perfect person. On the contrary, true love is about finding an imperfect person and working together with her on the most perfect relationship possible. True love does not only concern storybook romance, but hard, daily work. It is like success in a career or anything else that is worth the effort.

In general, there are certain borders over which one should not allow evil to penetrate:

DO NOT CONTINUE A RELATIONSHIP IN WHICH YOUR PARTNER DOES NOT RESPECT MUTUAL DIFFERENCES

It is said that opposites attract. It is even better when opposites complement each other. Like yin and yang. Two signs that are absolutely different and yet form a perfect circle. This is how partners can be different and yet be suited to each other. The entire secret of their mutual tolerance is in their thinking. To please each other, first they must understand that partners cannot be the same.

We already said that, in terms of microscopic details, there are no two identical people in the world. They have not existed in the entire human history. More than seven billion people walk the Earth today. Seven billion peculiar individualities. Each person a unique original. That is why we can never come to an unconditional agreement, absolute understanding. We cannot avoid feeling a certain friction between us. After all, we are absolutely different in terms of our past, genes, upbringing, experience. Each of us went a different way in our life until now. We collected different insights, formed different desires as well as conceptions of how to achieve our personal dreams. In a healthy relationship, partners not only can agree, but – much more importantly – disagree – with each other. They are able to become dissonant in terms of opinions, and yet respect each other and cope with the differences.

What is then important in the selection of a partner? That you share to the maximum extent life values and objectives. You do not have to profess absolutely to like the same colour, music, fashion style. But you should be willing and able to pull one rope, hold one oar, steer one course in critical moments. In a relationship, it is not possible for one to pedal while the other brakes. Such a tandem bike simply does not work.

118

So a partner cannot expect you to approve of all his decisions, and he of yours. Both of you will always have your own, different views. What is crucial is to honour the opinion and truth of the other. Voting does not exist in a relationship, it is impossible to outvote a partner. Either partners unanimously agree, or absolutely disagree. Which is good. Partners are forced to seek constructive solutions, work on themselves, advance themselves, and thus the entire relationship. Thanks to this, each partner grows faster in a relationship than in any other area of life. Because he has no choice. He must seek the way ahead. It is his responsibility.

And this is the first border over which you should not allow yourself to be manipulated. A partner must respect your difference and personal freedom. He must not intervene in your territory without your permission.

Partners are simply like two neighbours whose plots share one fence. When they need to solve something, they always meet at the gate in this fence.

Because it is midway for both of them.

DO NOT CONTINUE A RELATIONSHIP WITH A PARTNER WHO DOES NOT REVISE HIS PRECONCEPTIONS OF YOUR BEHAVIOUR

Imagine this couple:

Partner A was brought up in a loving family, where everybody openly expressed how much they loved one another.

Partner B was brought up in a pragmatic environment. Energy was not wasted on emotions. And even less on hugs, confessions, gifts.

How will Partner A interpret the colder behaviour of partner B from his point of view? As indifference? Withdrawal? Not love? Or even a result of infidelity?

All of us carry a concept of what the ideal behaviour of a partner should be like. This preconception is dependent on our life history. Under the influence of these subconscious optics, you expect others to behave towards you exactly according to the pattern in which you have lived most of your life and which you consider to be the only natural and correct way. If you want to damage the relationship unwisely, tell your childhood friends about your partner's *"incomprehensibly strange"* behaviour. Because childhood is part of your history, people present in your childhood co-created your ideal example by their own behaviour. It is a safe bet to expect that they will also express astonishment at your partner's behaviour.

"That sure is not normal," they tap their foreheads.

But, what is a norm? Is not 'normal' different for every individual?

If a partner does not match your preconceptions, often he is not to blame, but the target you set in the course of life. Your partner might not be indifferent, distant or even unfaithful. What if it is his way of love? You cannot conclude that his way is less sincere than yours. It is only different. And different does not mean inferior.

Therefore, beware of a partner who kills a relationship with preconceptions of how you should behave — according to him. You were not part of his previous life. You have your way of thinking. If he wants to live with someone who matches his history, he will have to live only with himself.

DO NOT CONTINUE A RELATIONSHIP WITH A PARTNER WHO DOES NOT UNDERSTAND THAT YOU CANNOT READ HIS MIND

Partner A had a terrible day. He returns home exhausted, with his tail between his legs, just longing for rest.

Partner B had a beautiful day. She's enthusiastic, in a merry mood, just longing for fun.

Result: inevitable clash. Partner A accuses partner B, as if she is supposed to know the reason for his bad mood. They quarrel, they bristle, they make each other angry. All because of the fallacy that one partner should be able to read the other's mind and sense his emotions. That he should predict the correct answers as well as the unspoken questions. That he will dispel even invisible anxieties.

You do not live in someone else's head. You are not an oracle. That is why, in a good relationship, partners make the effort to communicate appropriately to make their needs known and to clear up obscurities, although these may seem obvious. They even communicate just because everything seems clear to them.

This is what mouths are for. So that people can express themselves.

It is incredible that people suffer the most often, and the most unnecessarily, because of the unclarified emotions of a partner.

DO NOT CONTINUE A RELATIONSHIP WITH A PARTNER WHO DOES NOT TRY TO GO IN A MUTUAL DIRECTION

Before you met, each of you followed your separate ways. The tracks show your past and create your present. It does not matter when your trails crossed, from that moment both of you should continue in the same direction. A shared path is the foundation of your joint future.

Yes, people differ. They can have opposing views of the same thing. It does not matter. The fact that both of you look at the shared path from different heights or different points of view does not imply that the path should change. Regardless of different perspectives, the steps two people take can be identical.

For that matter, the word "break-up" sufficiently expresses what happens when two people set out in different directions. They part.

Sometimes a mutual walk is difficult. A woman takes shorter steps. A man has bigger feet. Nevertheless, they can adjust to each other. The woman can feel more certain and secure in the man's footsteps, and the man can stop rushing ahead, taking shorter steps more cautiously. This is advantageous for both. The man becomes more purposeful, the woman less vulnerable. But only if they walk in harmony.

Walking in harmony is called understanding. If Partner A did not sleep well and is not himself, is irritated and tired the following day, but explains it to Partner B, then partner B does not take this personally or succumb to assumptions that this is a consequence of something he has done. But if communication fails, the pain is always double-sided — in anger.

As the English dramatist William Shakespeare wrote, *"A sorrow shared is half a sorrow, a joy shared is twice a joy."*

Sharing of pain as well as of joy always strengthens the relationship and reciprocity.

In the above-mentioned story, for example, Partner B can give Partner A a relaxing massage. Although Partner B expends energy, she will receive new energy from a contented Partner A. This is called synergy – creation of a double volume of energy by simple giving. If Partner B turns away and ignores the problem of Partner A, the footsteps of the two will part.

Because partners can go in only two directions in a relationship.

Either in the same direction or in opposite directions.

DO NOT CONTINUE A RELATIONSHIP WITH A PARTNER WHO DOES NOT UNDERSTAND THE VALUE OF PERSONAL GROWTH

Growth is one of the basic characteristics of life. Although an adult man stops growing physically, personal growth continues through experience. Similarly, a relationship only grows when both partners are willing to learn and work on themselves, as well as on the relationship itself.

In a relationship, both partners also grow faster because they can learn from each other. Through living together, they encourage and motivate each other to improve, to change, to try, and to gain experience. And because they are also in love, they support and protect each other. They resemble a parent who teaches his child to swim by secretly holding his hands under the body for the rescue. The parent teaches the child by allowing him freedom to make independent decisions. But he watches over him.

Although you are to some extent bound in a relationship, there are still two individuals who need to be themselves. If you lose your dissimilarity, you stop bringing the added value to the relationship for the other partner to have at his disposal. A relationship deprived of your strong as well as weak points loses its meaning. And your partner will not feel any difference whether with or without you.

What grows, is alive.

What stagnates, rots away.

Stagnant water always putrefies.

And a relationship in which people do not develop, fossilises.

DO NOT CONTINUE A RELATIONSHIP WITH A PARTNER WHO DENIGRATES YOUR EFFORTS

Nobody is perfect. Ever. Whatever you do, you can do it better. Yes, absolutely everything.

At any moment, there is someone who condemns you for not doing something perfectly. And he has a point. Everything can be done better. However, the problem is that love does not entail who is right or wrong. Love entails support. Support for each other, so that one is not afraid to improve, that is, first and foremost, not to be ashamed of imperfections.

Relationships that continuously improve, function on one fundamental principle – every step taken by the partner is perceived as being the best the partner is able to do at the given moment. Yes, the step is never perfect, but corresponds to the knowledge and experience which the partner has at that moment. That is final.

This is the only possibility of preserving a positive view of life and of one's partner. Although a partner makes obvious mistakes from one's point of view, he is still advancing, because at the same time he is gaining the experience which he needs for improvement.

If, on the contrary, a partner denigrates your active efforts, he is a bad partner. It does not matter if his opinion turns out to be correct and you fail to achieve your goal, as he had warned you. No, love really does not entail who is right or wrong. If you are to gain new experience, even negative, you need your partner especially to provide strength, energy and courage. Even more so, if you are not doing well or are afraid.

If your partner does this, your relationship is more than a mathematical total of its components. It becomes something more. It becomes a clear reason for living in a relationship. Because then you are stronger in a relationship than alone. The contrary is far worse – when you are weaker in a relationship than alone.

That is why a partner should respect your decisions under all circumstances. They are always the right ones. More precisely – the right ones for your growth. Regardless of whether they lead to success or failure at the time. In either case, they provide the experience and lesson you need at that moment to learn and improve.

DO NOT CONTINUE A RELATIONSHIP WITH A PARTNER WHO IS UNABLE TO MIRROR

Do you remember what yin and yang look like? These traditional symbols of light and darkness represent two bitten images that precisely fit together to form a circle. Neither of these symbols is perfect. But they are perfect together, because what one lacks, the other provides. In conflict situations, which are inevitable in all relationships, we should behave in the same manner. A model situation:

She, accusingly: *"You forgot my birthday. I'm hurt and upset."*

He, apologetically: *"Please forgive me for forgetting your birthday. I understand that you're upset and hurt. I would feel the same in your place."*

Summed up and emphasised – the man's apology, understanding, compassion. And the same words are said by the two of them, only with contrasting meaning. This is an example of going in the same direction, although it seems that, due to the man's omission, the pair is walking on a collision course towards each other. But here is the point: if you walk on a collision course towards your partner, sooner or later you'll clash. If the dispute is accompanied with an apology, understanding and compassion, eventually there is also an embrace. This is how the method of mirroring works. Instead of disintegrating and weakening, it strengthens a relationship. In this case, by acknowledgement of the mistake on his side, and by forgiveness on hers. Note that there are different manifestations of understanding on both sides.

Unfortunately, vampires are unable to mirror. Their negative approach does not lead to the connection, but to the disconnection of partners. Disconnected partners

cannot be harmonised. Through mutual affront, they anger each other. In the escalating clash, they argue about trivialities that increasingly divide them, instead of searching for a way of reconnecting.

Nevertheless, it can be done so easily, even wordlessly.

Merely with a flower. A hug. A smile. Some humour.

But most importantly, without undue delay.

DO NOT CONTINUE A RELATIONSHIP FOR WHICH A PARTNER CANNOT MAKE THE TIME

If you want to build a close relationship with a child, it is insufficient just to hire a nanny or shower the child with gifts. You must also make personal time for the child.

It works the same with a partner. No man is indispensable in a job and even more so in a relationship. And if a partner behaves as if he is indispensable, he should not be surprised when there is no place left for him in the relationship.

Healthy relationships do not fall from the sky. They are built. There are masses of toil, compromise, communication behind a solid relationship. Plenty of failures, mistakes and lessons on one or the other side. But, as in a funnel, all these are aimed towards increased understanding, empathy and enhancement of a relationship.

In order to survive such a long and demanding process, the couple must be strong. And the relationship will be strong, if both partners strengthen it sufficiently.

To be able to strengthen it, both partners must be strong themselves. Which is impossible in a relationship with a vampire. Because a vampire weakens the other partner. That is why a strong relationship cannot be built with a vampire.

Only a strong dependence on what is slowly destroying you.

POSTPONING CHANGE

*T*hink.

How can you be happy if you procrastinate about what is required for your happiness?

How can you understand yourself if you are your own main obstacle in the path to happiness?

Why do you postpone a step which could bring you hope, and instead continue in hopelessness, although you know that you are running out of time?

Why, through hesitation about the necessary step, do you deliberately shorten the time of your longer future happiness? What are you waiting for?

My neighbour had a Labrador who was 21 years old. The dog could not stand up, was blind and deaf, and no longer exhausted himself by trying to bark. But whenever I visited the neighbour, the dog tried to wag his tail. To express that he could still feel joy. That he was still there.

The dog did not think about the future. He was living in the moment. Dogs are very wise. They live in the now. In the only time which exists. And also in the time in which human joy must be experienced.

FALSE THOUGHTS THAT ELIMINATE HAPPINESS AND ENDANGER THE ENTIRE RELATIONSHIP

As formulated by the Australian writer Rhonda Byrne in her book Secret, the Law of Attraction postulates: *"Your thoughts cause your feelings. Do not think about what you don't want, or dwell on past occurrences, because if you only think about all the bad things that have happened to you, or the bad things that you think are going to happen to you, then you'll only get more of the bad things you don't want to happen."* This seems like a mystery. Can fate see into your mind? Yet it is so logical. You are your own fate.

Every step on which you decide, is influenced by your thoughts. Only fools act thoughtlessly. What you think of, creates your feelings and leads you to action. And action leads to results. Therefore, a positive thought must be at the birth of every positive result. Just like a negative thought is at the beginning of every failure. To make it clear: failure does not mean trying without success. Failure means not trying at all. Because if you do not attempt to make a change, you preserve the present status quo.

Imagine a house with hermetically sealed windows. What happens if you are inside? In the course of time, you will breathe up all the air. Stagnant water putrefies. And a man who does not act, decays. Note: inactivity does not result in a lack of change. There is a change. For the worse. If one does not strive for any change, the world still continues to change. And if one refuses positive change – fresh air, fresh water – everything only deteriorates.

Nature is wise. It forces people to positive change. Only thanks to this, you keep pace with happiness. You actively cause for yourself what you think about.

How can you recognise that you are decaying? By the thoughts flowing through your mind. Thoughts never stop. And if positive thoughts find no purpose in your mind, eventually they decay too and change into negative thoughts.

DO NOT POSTPONE CHANGE IF YOU KEEP THINKING:

"What I haven't achieved thus far, I'll never achieve."

Negative people believe that all the unsuccessful attempts and mistakes they've ever made are the measure of their current abilities and future prospects. They ask: *"If I haven't fulfilled my wishes to date, how can I believe that I'll succeed tomorrow, or at some future time?"*

If you'd thought like that immediately after your birth, you would never have spoken a single word, written a single letter, swum a single stroke. With every mistake, you realise and learn, grow wiser. Failure is the precondition of improvement. Only by assessing his mistakes, can a formerly unsuccessful man, which includes new-born babies, gradually achieve success.

Nobody is born successful. One becomes successful.

Failure is temporary. Giving up is permanent.

Therefore, if this passive thought pursues you, it is time to start acting as quickly as possible.

DO NOT POSTPONE CHANGE IF YOU ARE EATEN UP BY THE QUESTION:

"What will others think of me?"

It is paradoxical that often you realise that you need change, but are afraid to step out in a new direction. Just because of the reaction of others. You are afraid that nobody will support you, or will even slander or condemn you. You count what you might lose by the considered change, rather than what you might possibly gain.

However, just at the moment when you step out towards a change, you will see most clearly the real faces of those around you. You will understand who is a real friend, and who is only posing as one. Do not fear that somebody will slander you behind your back. Indeed, this is where such a person belongs. Behind your back. He deserves to be ignored.

Being weak means giving up the war without a battle. Such a war does not provide any new experience. Being strong means going through battle. It does not only have to be on the battlefield. The battle can take place right inside you. But being strong also means not fighting, when it is wiser to leave without a word. This is not the same as surrendering. Those who surrender, do not advance anywhere. But those who retreat wisely, behave like an arrow which moves back slightly at first as it is forced into the bowstring, in order to fly ahead increasingly faster.

Do not preoccupy yourself by considering what anybody else thinks of you. You are not the centre of the universe. You might think you are. But that's the point: everybody sees himself as the centre of the universe. Even those whose judgements we fear. They see only themselves in the centre of the universe. You are not. It is just

your illusion that you are the main topic of all your relatives' discussions. No, the main topic of any person is that person's alone.

DO NOT POSTPONE CHANGE IF YOU KEEP PROMISING YOURSELF:

"Some day in the future I'll eventually do something which leads to my happiness."

Please take a calendar and find a day which is called some day, one day, or next time. Unfortunately, those days are not indicated on the calendar. Because they do not exist.

At every single moment, you are the oldest you have ever been, and the youngest you will ever be. If you seek an ideal day to set out towards your dreams, you will not find a more suitable day than today. Regardless of how many days you have left to live, it is clear that tomorrow you will have one day less for the achievement of your goals.

So, replace in your thoughts all indicated non-specified dates with the word today. It will change your life. Because, from this moment, you will start to pursue your dreams without postponements. After all, every day in the future will at one time be today. And you would be drowning in exactly the same feelings as today, only older and more demotivated.

DO NOT POSTPONE CHANGE IF YOU KEEP DELUDING YOURSELF:

"I can't do it. I'm not good enough. It is too late."

You can delude yourself that you cannot overcome any obstacle you face in life. It is strange that after a lapse of time, the same obstacle that you overcame seems negligible. Just recall: your first exam, first date, first speech before a group of friends or colleagues...

The obstacles that you intend to deal with, make you tougher already by striving to overcome them. Those who seek a way to success will find it sooner or later. However, the basic requirement for finding anything, is to start seeking.

People who are not committed to success, do not succeed.

People who are committed to success, often succeed.

They discover that they can do it. That they are good enough. That it is not too late.

It is always better to try and be wrong, than not to try and be right.

DO NOT POSTPONE CHANGE IF YOU KEEP ASKING YOURSELF:

"What if it fails?"

It is surprising how many people consume negative news – in the press, television, talking to friends. Why do people intentionally worry so much? Because to think negatively is more convenient. If you basically suppose that something will not work out, it will be meaningless even to try. And this is very convenient.

A negatively thinking person does not have to do anything for his opinion to be confirmed. Because what he does not do, really does not work out. And so there are always enough negative people. Because their catastrophic prophecies are always fulfilled. Especially if they relate them to their own lives. They believe that the worst is yet to come, so they do nothing, and the worst really comes – due to their inaction.

What if I do not succeed? A really powerful question. But ask another. It is the difference of only one word, and yet makes the difference between an unsuccessful and a successful life. What if I do succeed? Such a question may sound like heresy to some. Yet, unless you try to overcome a challenge facing you, you will never know if you can succeed. You will find out only by trying. Sure, you might not succeed. But if you learn a lesson from the possible failure, one day success must come.

So, be honest with yourself:

Are you sure you can't achieve something?

Or do you only think so?

And how will you feel when somebody else really does the thing which today you think is impossible for you?

139

DO NOT POSTPONE CHANGE IF YOU KEEP SWEARING TO YOURSELF:

"I'll never trust anyone else ever again."

Perhaps your partner has hurt you a great deal. So be it. After all, it is his responsibility and his problem too. You do not have to stay with somebody who has hurt you. If you stay with him only due to the assumption that nobody better will come along, you are living in fantasy and not in reality.

Yes, your ability to trust may be eroded. But this has nothing to do with the actions of other people who may enter a relationship with you and eventually persuade you that not all people are the same. Sincerely, this will not be hard for them. It is senseless to assume that all people are similar. You already know that the contrary is true and that people are totally dissimilar.

The commitment not to trust anyone else ever again reveals more about you than about others. You close your heart to yourself, not to others. It is not that you do not trust others. You basically do not trust yourself. Because you doubt that you can handle the pain of another possible break-up, betrayal or distressing emotion. No, this really does not concern others, but only you yourself.

Of course, lost trust brings suffering. But it is through suffering that you become aware of your inner strength. If you only stress your heart, you will discover how much it can actually endure. Do not doubt that your heart is stronger than you think. Just make the effort.

In every situation, try to trust one more person.

The next one. Give him a chance.

DO NOT POSTPONE CHANGE IF YOU KEEP TELLING YOURSELF:

"If everybody around me does it, then it must be right."

Maybe you have friends who experienced something similar. A betrayal, for example. One person coped with the betrayal and stayed, another could not bear it and left. But in each case it is the decision of a specific person, made on the basis of his upbringing, experience and momentary methodology of decision-making. The step he takes is always the right one, because it is exactly what he needs at the specific time. And it is never an example for you. You live a different life, and, to be happy in your own way, you might need to take entirely different steps in similar situations.

Unfortunately, there is no universal guidebook to life. Although it may seem that people's lives are similar, this impression is not true. Each individual walks on his own pathway. At every moment in time, you are actually in a place where nobody else has been before. You do not have to wait to see what somebody else does. Because you are always the first in every situation.

Do not be guided by the decisions of others in similar situations. You cannot read their hearts and minds. Firstly, you do not know if they are really so happy, and also you have no idea what they are experiencing and needing. Rather focus on what you wish in life. And do not be ashamed of your ideas. Never behave like the crowd. The crowd is not you.

In a crowd, one is just an anonymous part.

Be yourself instead. Be unique.

DO NOT POSTPONE CHANGE IF YOU KEEP WAILING:

"I don't have the time to dream of something better."

The real tragedy in life is not failing to achieve one's dream, but having no dream. It is never easy to make dreams come true. If it was easy, people would fulfil their dreams easily, sitting on a couch. But dreams are Solomonic – and this is a good thing. They force us to get up from the couch. To leave the comfort zone. To work on ourselves. To seek a way over the obstacle. To rejoice in a little progress. And to grow through all this.

One day you will find that finally it does not matter if you achieved the dreamed-of objective. An objective is not some point at the end of the road. The road itself is the dream. Because you grow, thanks to walking in the pathway. Not only when you reach the goal.

On the contrary, you lose drive and speed at the finish line. Like runners who finally stop sprinting. They have no motivation to continue. They have already reached their goal. The finish line. That is why you should keep finding increasingly higher objectives in any phase of life. Values that give you meaning and at the same time motivate you. Values worth pursuing despite the effort that must be put in.

The most beautiful thing about dreams is that they are yours alone. Just like life. Is there anything more important for the use of time than your own life, and the things that fulfil it?

DO NOT POSTPONE CHANGE IF YOU KEEP DISCOURAGING YOURSELF:

"Oh-oh, the path will be too long."

Every life is as short or as long as the way you fill it. Life is not measured by days, but by actions. If it seems that your dream is so distant that its achievement requires lots of time, you should rejoice. Because you have the drive for a long time ahead.

If a meaningful pathway is long, be happy about it. As the Baptist preacher Martin Luther King said, "*Take the first step in faith. You don't have to see the whole staircase, just take the first step.*" The first step in the direction to change which you need for transformation and which will give you meaning for a long time ahead. Is it not an actually amazing feeling?

DO YOU HAVE A PROBLEM WITH POSTPONEMENT? PRACTICAL QUESTIONS THAT WILL POINT YOU TOWARDS YOUR GOAL

have explained which wrong thoughts must be driven out of your mind. That was the first step.

The second step was to fill the mind with the right thoughts.

Or, with the right questions.

If you do not find the right answer in life, it is often by not asking the right question.

Yes, replies and questions... you need to talk.

To yourself.

Because the right questions can evoke the right answers and these – as far as your life is concerned – do not occur anywhere else around you, but directly within. They are only waiting to be aroused by the right questions.

Without the right questions, you are like a broken compass. The needle leads you in this direction and then in that direction. Your inner dialogue, if conducted correctly, will show you the direction which you should take in life. It will repair your needle. So, have a talk. Not to me. To yourself.

ASK YOURSELF AS OFTEN AS POSSIBLE:

"What do you really want?"

At one time, you wanted something. This seems to have vanished in the course of time. You stopped attributing importance to it. You resigned yourself to your fate. You began to take life as it came. You changed into a weathercock which revolves according to the direction in which the wind pushes it. A weathercock has no heart, no dreams. Therefore it also has no stable needle to point in a specific direction. A weathercock is just an inanimate, passionless item.

Without enthusiasm, one gradually slows down. One lacks purpose, motivation, direction. All people are sailboats, and the worst thing that can happen to them is not a storm, but a state of windlessness. Windless conditions might seem safer. Like a vessel in a harbour. But ships and people are not built to remain in port. And man is not born for inaction. A man who does not act therefore has the feeling of not living at all in the coming years. And, in a way, he really is not alive. He is just surviving.

Life is not eternal, its duration is limited. We regret this fact, but it is actually a positive thing. Many people behave as passively as if they are going to live forever. Therefore, think about how you deal with the time allotted to you. And forget the advance excuses that it is too late or too early for something you really want to do. Because the question of what you really want never comes too late, or too soon. Do not regret in your old age what your life could have been like.

Strive to make your life as it should be, immediately.

Immediately means without delay.

ASK YOURSELF AS OFTEN AS POSSIBLE:

"What do you really believe?"

Since childhood, you have been used to listening to others, adjusting to their advice and evaluation. Some people remain in this mode even in adulthood. Whereas, as far as you are concerned, it is unimportant how others see you, but how you see yourself. Only if you feel comfortable in your own skin, can you feel happy. Because then you are attuned to the way you are living. Why is everybody not like that? This means being yourself. And being yourself requires courage.

You must be sincere especially to yourself and not be afraid to follow your own path. You can feel good or bad on the path. Depending on how seriously you take the reactions of others.

There will always be people who will reproach you for your independent way of thinking and own way of doing things. You do not have to blame them for that. They have a right to form their own opinions and it is normal that opinions of people differ. Their opinions do not have to bother you. You do not live in their skin and they do not live in yours. In any case, you do not live in falsehood, anxiety and pain, only to be somebody whose skin does not fit you. On the contrary, if you act as you feel and your skin fits you, your vibes are healthier and at the same time there is no way that anybody can remove you from your own skin.

People will definitely try. They will claim that your skin does not suit you, that it is outdated, that you are not good enough in it, that your choices are bad.

Anyone can – and undoubtedly will – say that.

146

What they say is entirely their own business.

But what you believe is your business.

Whether that is somebody else's path, or your own.

ASK YOURSELF AS OFTEN AS POSSIBLE:

"What are you willing to sacrifice?"

In principle, it is not so hard to decide what you want and where you want to be, let's say, in a year's time. But it is much harder to clarify to yourself what you are able to give up, to be able to take the necessary steps towards the achievement of your goal.

This is the most important part of a dialogue during which you clear in your mind what level of temporary inconvenience you can bear – what your dreams are worth. You have to realise that you are endangered by dizziness and falls along the path you are going to take, because it will take you through landscapes where you have never before ventured. You will struggle on the way, as well as with yourself. With your own fear, which will keep whispering that you are not strong enough to negotiate the path. And with other people who might not wish success for you, just to prevent you from achieving more than them. People around you are the most common reason for deciding not to act. You are afraid of failure as much as of success. But if you succeed, you will show everybody who doubted you, that there is a way, and that it works. Everybody who had to make the same sacrifice, once had to ask himself the unpleasant question: Why did somebody else manage to do it but I did not?

That is why the path to your own dreams is often lonely. You are only not alone on the path if you have a mature partner. Such a partner will stay with you even if the whole world turns away. Such a partner shares your sacrifices.

Think about what you are willing to sacrifice. And do not economise. The size of the sacrifice expresses what your goal is worth. It shows its value. If you are not

willing to make any sacrifice, your goal is apparently not worth anything. However, if you avoid any self-sacrifice, you cannot expect a good reward. Life is not a social institution, a provider. It is no charity. Life is a rough businessman.

Life requires results, that is, real action.

ASK YOURSELF AS OFTEN AS POSSIBLE:

"What small victories do you enjoy?"

There is no living being in Nature who behaves more mysteriously (with regard to achievement of goals) than man. He wants something, but usually only waits for it to happen. He seldom acts in the interest of his goal. And then he wonders why he does not get what he wants. He behaves like a mountain climber who would like to reach the top of Mount Everest, but only sits at the bottom of the mountain, waiting for the peak to descend to his feet.

There is nothing miraculous about the achievement of a great goal. A great goal is a series of small goals. Unsuccessful people dislike the fact that the achievement of a big goal takes so long. On the contrary, successful people rejoice, because they can celebrate small victories more often. Have you noticed how these two groups of people differ?

The first group sees a big goal. Too distant, unattainable. The other group focuses on small goals and is led by them to the big ones. Both categories live on the same planet. They have similar situations. Yet they achieve different results. The first group cannot achieve any goal. Because the only goal they are able to set for themselves, is big. Such a goal behaves like rails meeting on the horizon. Whenever we get closer to the point of convergence, we find that the point has moved a bit and the rails converge again on the horizon. A big goal is like that. And when we fulfil a smaller task, we realise that it actually does not suffice us.

On the other hand, small goals are all around us.

They fulfil us daily.

Taking the first step can already be seen as a small success.

Some might consider the step small. But small is better than nothing at all.

ASK YOURSELF AS OFTEN AS POSSIBLE:

"Where do you obtain energy?"

In the real world, no positive things happen by themselves. No helping hand will appear out of thin air, not even a smile is conjured up without a reason. We cannot be successful and happy without invested effort. This is arranged well. The more effort we put in, the sweeter is the achievement of the goal.

But there is a hitch. Sufficient effort is conditioned by a sufficient store of energy. To obtain energy, you must get it from somewhere. The best way is by being positive. Because physical laws do not apply to positive energy. When we obtain positive energy somewhere, it does not mean that somebody else has to lose it. Do you remember the example of a massage (66th Law)? Even though you put in your energy, both you and your partner obtain more from it.

Synergy works both ways, positively as well as negatively. If you radiate positive energy, both you and your partner feel better. If you radiate negative energy, both of you feel worse. Because energy always multiplies in a relationship. It is only up to you with which type of energy you work. But be careful, it is like dynamite. Firing up positive energy means allowing encouragement, admiration, appreciation, assistance to explode. Synergy multiplies exponentially in a society of positive people. The more positives we give to others, the more we get from them.

Well, do you know where you obtain energy, and whether it is positive or negative?

ASK YOURSELF AS OFTEN AS POSSIBLE:

"What makes you happy?"

Although many people refuse to admit it, one is actually equipped with everything necessary for contentment. Yes, you already have it within, it is only hidden under the silt of mud, stress and anxiety. It is not necessary to wait for someone or something to make you happy. Nobody and nothing can organise your happiness, if you alone do not find and name what makes you happy.

Your feelings fortunately do not depend on the incompetence of people around you. Nobody can know what you need at a specific moment. For that matter, how can anyone else know if you yourself do not know it? No, nobody sees within you. But you can see into your own heart. You feel exactly when you are being yourself. You have reliable advisers – your feelings. You know the situations in which you feel good, and in which you feel bad.

Happiness is especially a state of mind. Nothing is needed. Start noticing the little things that you tend to overlook. Just concentrate on what you already have, and stop dealing with what you do not yet have, or what you've already lost.

This is called a positive outlook.

Let's think about what we will do, not what we will not do. Let's think about what we are, not about what we are not. To think positively means to build. To think negatively means to destroy. They are two sides of the same coin. Two sides of the same choices you have. And you express this choice by the way you view your daily life. Do you see opportunities to whine about or to smile about in your life?

153

The answer is not a problem of life or your surroundings, but of your decision to see primarily the good, or the bad. Let's not forget that we usually find what we seek.

Pay more attention to new beginnings than to old endings. Do not say that you want a new life, if you keep doing old things. Do not wait for years for the moment of realisation that you should have lived your life in a better way. A better life starts precisely at the moment you decide to live it.

INFIDELITY

N o other betrayal evokes such contradictory feelings. You want to scream and be silent at the same time. To attack as well as to weep. To run away and also to beg for return. This because infidelity hits two sensitive spots with one blow. Both sides of self-respect. On one side, you do not wish to see the unfaithful partner any more; on the other hand, you need him to assure you that you have not lost your worth. That you are still valuable.

Infidelity is malicious and disgusting. And the person who is punished more is the one who did not sin.

I met two different beings in two days.

The first was positive, smiling, resolute.

The second was negative, frustrated, resigned.

Yet it was one and the same woman who turned around 180 degrees in a mere 24 hours.

The cause was clear. It is said, behind every disappointed face, seek the man who caused it.

There was somebody behind this face too.

The woman had gone through a break-up. Heartless, breathtaking, undeserved. It paralysed her so much that it disqualified her from any positive activity. It was use-less to advise her. "*Do not preoccupy yourself with it, forget and move on.*" Because one is buried in concrete. One cannot move from a place, and the only thing working is the brain – unfortunately reliving memories and remorse: "*It was my fault. I am worthless. My life will never have any purpose.*"

Unfaithfulness is a symptomatic word. One loses faith. Love is like a snowflake. When you think you are holding it tightly, it melts. That is why it is important to shake oneself off with the following laws:

HOW TO SURVIVE A PARTNER'S BETRAYAL WHICH DERAILED YOU

W*arning: All the following laws will seem extraordinarily hard and uncompromising to you. It is the only way out of hell. Because whenever you go through hell, it is important to keep walking. Without compromise. Because, otherwise you will burn in this hell.*

UNDERSTAND THAT THERE ARE PEOPLE WITHOUT WHOM YOU ARE UNHAPPY, BUT THEY ARE HAPPY WITHOUT YOU

Every person in this world has a right to live life as he chooses. He has a right to be with whoever he desires, and not to be with whoever he does not desire. If you accept and honour this fundamental right, you should paradoxically be the first to support an unfaithful partner. By his action, he has made it clear that he is able to betray your trust at any time, so enable him to leave, even more so, if you sincerely love him. After all, his happiness is unconditionally important to you in such a case.

Does it sound hard? In the following lines, I will explain why letting go is the best service you can provide both to an unfaithful partner and (especially) to yourself.

The problem for too many people is that they love conditionally. By their approach they say: "*I love you, BUT ONLY as long as you are with me. Otherwise, I wish the worst for you.*" If you love someone, then your primary concern should be that your partner is happy, regardless of the circumstances. That is, whether he is with or without you. If a partner lets you know that he is happier with someone else, simply because you love him, you should support him on his way to happiness, and prove that he can rely on you. Even if this means he is leaving you. Otherwise, you are only pretending that you care, while in fact behaving possessively and selfishly.

I do not believe that anyone wants to live with a possessive egoist. Or with somebody who does not wish to stay in the relationship.

Therefore, do not hurt yourself. Let him go, if he wants to.

This is necessary in your own interest.

REMOVE THE BARS

We like to delude ourselves: He is mine alone, she is mine alone. But the reality is fittingly expressed by the anecdote:

"I asked the magic mirror who in the world is prettier than me."

"And what did the mirror say?"

"It is still belching out names."

Reconcile yourself to it. There will always be somebody younger, older, richer, poorer, slimmer, stronger. You can do all you like with your figure, but this is not what a successful relationship rests on.

A partner does not have to find a perfect match. It is enough if he finds a match which he perceives as perfect. We all seek a person to make us happier than anybody else. But happiness is not to be found in a stifling relationship. What is valuable about a partner who must return home every evening? Is not the partner who wants to return home every evening, more valuable?

Let's try not to make an obligation out of love. If obligation is eliminated, sincerity remains. So don't be afraid that your partner will not return. At least, start creating an environment to which he likes to return. At least communicate and together find compromises that are acceptable to both, not only to one.

Yes, removing the bars means risking that he will leave at any time. But if your partner leaves, it is never necessary to wonder whether the relationship with him had any prospects. By his action, he has saved you time. To remove the bars means to eliminate all speculations, assumptions and gloomy visions. The one who returns to a relationship to which he does not have to return, answers the assumed question very clearly. And only one remains: Do I have the certainty that he will never leave? In a healthy relationship, partners do not have this certainty. That is why they

work on the relationship. Without bars, we very quickly discover to whom we are sincerely valuable, and to whom not.

As long as your parents are alive, you do not need anyone else to take care of you. As long as you have friends, you don't need anyone else to comfort you. But regardless of parents and friends, you need somebody to lean on. Just like that, without any reason. Such support is provided by a partner who stays with you, despite being able to leave you at any time.

DEMAND OBLIGATION AS WELL AS RESPONSIBILITY FROM A PARTNER

A person older than 18 years is officially mature, an adult. Also according to the authorities, he is responsible and able to think about the effect and consequences of his actions. That is why people in a relationship do not make mistakes – at least not in the definition of what we understand as mistakes. In a relationship, each person does what he considers to be the best or the most advantageous. For himself, of course. If something affects him later and he comes to the conclusion that he has made a mistake, he should not apologise. Because there is no reason. He did what he believed was the best or the most advantageous at the given moment. That is why you should not accept any apologies after infidelity. If you are already an adult, you well know what you are doing at every moment, and what can be caused by it. "*I'm sorry*" is said when you bump into someone in the street. Not when you break somebody's heart.

Any person older than 18 is responsible for his actions. But the fact that somebody is responsible does not mean that he behaves responsibly. To behave responsibly in a relationship means to behave at all times in such a way that you do not have to apologise for anything. That is, do not deny or trivialise what you have done. When you stop accepting your partner's apologies in a relationship, he will get to understand that he must behave like an adult. Responsible people do not need second chances. Because they always stand behind their actions, whatever they are.

If you start accepting apologies, you will hear them a million times. An unfaithful partner can say what he likes. But if his actions do not match his words, it is a waste of time listening to him. If he cannot make his words come true, they do not mean anything.

"*Action speaks louder than words but not nearly as often,*" as Mark Twain so rightly said.

For that matter, love is just a word too. Until somebody arrives who gives this ordinary word an extraordinary meaning.

Remember in principle that a relationship is simple:

If somebody is really interested in you, he likes to be with you.

If somebody really wants to see you, he will find the time.

If somebody wants to hear you, at least he will call you.

All else are excuses.

ONE WHO LOVES, DOES NOT HURT A PARTNER

People mistakenly suppose that being kind in a relationship means not leaving. But that is not true. An unfaithful partner hurts the most by staying in the relationship. Then it is the case that your priority is somebody for whom you are just one of the options.

Loving often rather means leaving and letting go. Leaving means not hurting a partner, if you sense that you cannot give what he/she needs. Openness is the foundation of a functional relationship. Anybody can undress and have sex. But to sincerely open your heart to someone, show your weaknesses, fears, hopes as well as dreams means really being naked and vulnerable.

Understand that people keep changing and developing. Only because your values once intersected with your partner's does not mean that your paths will keep overlapping in all the changes people go through. This is surely a romantic perception. But sometimes the mutual pathway is unsustainable, even with the best communication and compromise. It would be a beautiful concept if this were not so. But beauty is not always true. Just like truth is not always beautiful.

Remember that it is not only the one you care about who deserves your understanding and love. But especially the one who cares about you. Do not emotionally blackmail an unfaithful partner, do not behave like him. If he has decided on a different path, he has not done anything other than express that he only has one life to live and does not want to live it with you.

Do not descend to blackmail, and especially not if there are children involved in the relationship. It is not in the interest of any parent, and even less of a child, to turn

a home into a pressure pot. On the contrary, open the valve, let off the steam, and everything bad with it.

Yes, rejection in the form of infidelity hurts.

Terribly. But it has to be like that.

It is the best school for the future.

A lesson you will not forget and rejoice over.

Because you will start appreciating faithful people even more.

DO NOT TAKE REVENGE

The end of suffering is better than suffering without end. Rather have a non-functioning heart transplanted, than existing in the delusion that everything is absolutely fine.

Of course, you will be taken by surprise if a partner in whom you put so much trust, does something like that. It is a shock, I know. That is why you should never take someone else's feelings, words and attitudes as a matter of fact which does not change. That's life. Life is change. And change is life.

At first, many deceived people think of revenge. Do not do it. Concentrate on positive steps. Negative actions do not lead to anything good, because you are not breaking out of the negative core. You are suffering by concentrating on the person who deceived you. You are behaving like somebody who is rummaging in droppings and wondering why he himself smells of droppings. A positive step means trying to see a partner in colour, not only in black and white.

You basically cannot imagine what the other person had to endure and how much courage he had to pluck up before telling you something which would probably break your heart. Appreciate the sincerity which your partner expresses, although it leads to the parting of your ways.

Yes, it hurts. Every memory torments you. In times of despair, no pain endured is worse than memories of happiness. However, there are two kinds of pain. One wounds you. The other changes you. The pain of infidelity does both. So try not to be changed for the worse by the wounding pain.

If you concentrate on negative steps, you will never get out of hell. But you need to leave the past behind. Every effort to remind the partner how great things were before, or any revenge taken to show him what it was that especially hurt you, is

not doing anything constructive. You are only suspended in a time and space which existed in the past. But it is possible to leave hell only in the present time.

Yes, it is undoubtedly challenging to survive the first moments. You can forget the bad words the partner said, even the bad deeds he did, but never forget the feelings of hurt within. This is a bitter path. But you have to bear it.

The only way ahead is not to beg. In the course of time, you will understand that when you do not get in life what you long for, perhaps the reason is not that you do not deserve it, but on the contrary, that you deserve much more.

DO NOT WRITE A COMMA WHERE LIFE WRITES A FULL STOP

Unfaithful people often try to glue together broken pots. Think twice about this. Rather be with someone who appreciates what he has when he has it. Not only after he loses it.

Deceived people are also vulnerable, because they have so much pain in their hearts and the only person to ease the pain is the one who caused it. Only in the course of time will one understand that there is a reason why a bad person from the past is not in one's future. What a pity that, through all those tears, one does not hear life saying: "*Don't be angry with me. I just want you to learn something.*"

One of the lessons infidelity teaches you is not to worry about those who do not worry about you. And to stop always being the one to take the first step. Life teaches one that it is no miracle to have 1 000 Facebook friends. It is a miracle to have one person who will stand by you when 1 000 people on Facebook are against you. That is support. That is a Partner with a capital "*P*". By the way, do you know why a perfect partner will never return? Because a partner who loves you sincerely, will never leave you.

Do not try to dilute a mess, or to write a comma where life writes a full stop. Do not grovel with text messages: "*I love you, I miss you.*" These words are so powerful that they reveal how weak you are at such moments. And weak people cannot be a support in a relationship. Weak people forgive. But if you forgive too often, others will get used to hurting you. The more you show an unworthy partner that you cannot live without him, the more reasons you give him to take you for granted.

Like an old rag, which can be thrown away and picked up at any time. That is, if he graciously wants to.

LEARN TO VERIFY PEOPLE

Being deceived is also a useful experience, because you learn to know people better. Because infidelity is usually a consequence of some lasting problem in a relationship. A partner lacked something, so he sought it elsewhere. This is also where the share of responsibility lies. Indeed, you cannot see into somebody else's mind. If a partner lacks anything in some phase of a relationship, he has a tongue with which to communicate. Problems exist to be solved. Not to run away from. When a partner runs away, the problem is not solved. Often he carries it right within himself. Because the problem could actually be himself, and his approach to resolving inconsistencies.

Therefore, a partner who has deceived is primarily to blame. Not only because he deceived. But especially because he did not resolve a problem which was evidently relevant. Give thanks to this school. It enables you to understand that there are people who get to know the best of you and still deceive you. However, what you need are people who get to know the worst in you, and yet never leave you.

Why keep giving a second chance to someone, if many others are waiting for a first? Do not cry over spilt milk. Tears prevent you from seeing the beautiful stars. A future which will open up before you. It would be a mistake to forget about the past, but an even bigger mistake to allow it to paralyse your future. That's how life goes – we get to choose our friends, and partners are to a considerable extent selected by time and experience. Thanks to that experience, you will stop accepting apologies such as, *"I am sorry for not calling you. I was busy, too far away."* Distance, not only geographic, can prevent a physical embrace, but never emotions. This applies to friends too. Verify who you can really count on in a crisis.

ENJOY TRANQUILLITY

When a yacht lowers the sails, there is nothingness. The Captain experiences calm and has the amazing luxury of deciding which direction to take. Solitude is a precious change for us too. We have the exclusive opportunity of sorting out our entire lives. Remorse, accusations, all the pros and cons disappear in the calm. The relationship between former partners also changes. At that moment, they really get to know each other. Because they are not obliged to do anything else. They can only, in total nakedness, begin to understand one another. Maybe you will discover somebody interesting, and realise that, while you were sorting through stones for years in private, you were merely overlooking a gem.

Tranquillity is the time to clear up many things. During stocktaking, you will always find somebody who disappointed you, and somebody who helped you. But the result is never in balance. Because you get rid of those who hurt you, but surround yourself with those who helped you. So every betrayal actually cleans out your surroundings. You will find that, after a betrayal, you are better off in terms of human resources, than before the betrayal.

The evil has gone. The good has arrived. What more could one wish for?

REMAIN POSITIVE

Even if a partner leaves you, you should not start believing that love is not beautiful, and turn away from the sun. Try to be positive. Turn your sight towards the sun. Because then all the shadows are cast behind you. Of course, nothing will be as before. But it can never be as before. Because if somebody bad has left your life, he has opened the door for somebody better.

Smile. Stop tormenting yourself with questions about who will be the next one, and what he will look like. Well, for example, like a dog. That is, the only being who loves a human being more than himself. A being who will give you his heart if you give your heart to him. Do not doubt that in future you will meet someone who will make it clear to you why the relationship with your former partner failed.

Someone who understands the core principle of love: Love more than yesterday, and less than tomorrow.

Somebody whose reply to the question *"Do you love me or yourself more?"* is *"Myself"* – because you are his life.

Perhaps he will not be perfect, but he will suit you perfectly. Perhaps he will not be exceptional, but you will discover his exceptionality for yourself. Then you realise that you have encountered two important types of people in life. The first ones knock you down, while the second help you up. In the course of time, you thank both sincerely.

CHAMELEON

L et me give you a riddle: It was here and is no more. And yet it lives on. What is it?

Naturally, a chameleon. A being able to change its colours according to circumstances. But beware, we are not only speaking about the animal...

People can change colour even more unexpectedly.

They can change beyond recognition.

With their new, changed action or inaction, they reject their own past. Contradicting everything you ever knew about him, or what he told you about himself, suddenly he deceives, cheats, ignores you – as if you are an entirely different person.

You do not recognise him and just keep wondering:

Was it your mistake, naivety, blindness?

Which of his two versions can you now believe?

In the hospital where I went to see my mother, I met a man who could not have been a chameleon. It all started with a woman who was hospitalised and artificially kept alive after having had a sudden stroke and going into a coma. Her condition was stable, but serious. The doctors were unable to predict whether there was any hope of her ever waking up. But with each passing week, they grew more pessimistic.

Despite everything, her boyfriend, who had been with her for a brief time, came to the hospital every day. He had no idea if the woman was aware of his presence at

all, but he sat by her bedside for long hours, speaking to her. With every passing week, his efforts seemed more futile, more foolish.

The woman awoke from her coma 48 weeks later. She kissed the astonished man sitting by her bedside, and said: *"Thank you for being with me all the time, for talking to me, for never ceasing to believe in me. And yes, I want to marry you too..."*

WHAT IS POSITIVE ABOUT PARTNERS WHO PORTRAYED THEMSELVES NEGATIVELY?

How is it possible for a man to turn around 180 degrees?

How is it possible to be negatively transformed?

Is it your fault that you were so naïve and trusting? How do you say goodbye to Mr Hyde, who is hurting you, if you still remember Dr Jekyll who, on the contrary, always stood by your side?

Which of the two faces can be believed?

And if you reconcile yourself to the negative side, how do you accept the wasted time which nobody can give back to you?

Such questions, aftertaste, wrath and remorse are left behind by chameleons who are transformed for the worse in their careers, personal lives and social position.

Everything such partners evoke in you is negative. And that is bad. It is important to keep a positive outlook in a relationship, and to deal appropriately with the past. You must realise that it is pointless to expect anything from other people. That everybody changes according to what suits them at any given moment. And if you want to get to know people, place banknotes in front of them. Because money does not ruin character.

Money reveals character.

How can you handle the destructive transformation of your partner and ever again believe anyone else after such an experience?

174

DO NOT REGRET LEAVING AN UNWORTHY PERSON; BAD EXPERIENCE IS ALSO POSITIVE IN THE LONG RUN

A best friend steals your partner.

A popular colleague betrays your team and company.

A relative turns into a hyena during inheritance proceedings.

Regardless of the manifestations of chameleonship, one always feels bitterness. Yet it is often sufficient to bite one's tongue to sense sweetness. That is the case of the mouth as well as of life. Whenever life knocks you down, the intentions are good.

Although at first you do not have to understand or see the good aspects, undoubtedly every experience is necessary. A negative experience is doubly positive. How so? Firstly, you get rid of a bad person in your immediate vicinity, and also you improve the sensitivity of your radar system for future similar types.

DO NOT REGRET LEAVING A BAD PERSON; AT LEAST THERE IS ONE LESS AROUND YOU

D o you know what is worse than being left by a bad friend?

Still to have him nearby.

Because that would mean that he has not hurt you enough for you to be able to do without him. Giving a second (or further) chance to a bad person is like loading his pistol once more because he has missed you with the first shot.

Disappointment is almost always perceived negatively, but it is actually one of the most effective ways of opening the eyes, mind and heart to a blind person, and to return her to the right path. We function like satellite car navigation, when it is surprised by the new data and announces: "*Updating...*" It is disoriented for a moment. But then it takes you to your destination much more precisely. Because it has been updated with new facts, about which it had no previous idea. Likewise, we also begin to perceive positively that we have unmasked an individual. Although transformation hurts, at least we no longer have to live a lie.

Everything ends well in fairy tales. Real life is just like that. Evil serves the good. People knocked down to the bottom re-evaluate their lives. They start from zero, from their fundamental values, and build a much more stable future. This is the blessing of every fall. It heals, it liberates. When a pond is cleaned, not only is the dirty water sluiced out, but the mud is also removed. The inventory we take within has the same effect.

DO NOT REGRET LEAVING A BAD PERSON; YOU WILL APPRECIATE A GOOD ONE EVEN MORE

The quality of every relationship depends on the willingness and ability of both partners to work at it. A successful relationship is built faster with the aid of quality people. If you drive an unreliable chameleon out of a relationship, you will find that a boulder has disappeared and it is easier to rebuild your life. It is always better to be alone, than to be with a partner and yet alone.

For every person who has ever betrayed you, you learn to appreciate the people who have not betrayed you. In so doing, you yourself grow. One who has had to call for help can better understand the SOS call of others. In short, anyone who has encountered a chameleon has a chance to be a better person. Because, through the negative experience, you have received one of the most valuable human gifts: the ability to empathise with others.

Unfortunately, many people are unable to break up with a partner. They live in the assumption that, although he is bad, the next partner could be even worse. This is only half true. The next partner could also be much better. Why do we rather believe in the negative? We suffer from the syndrome of a mountain observer. If we focus on one mountain as a solitaire, we lose perspective. It astonishes us by its size and we do not realise that there are far higher peaks. Without a comparison, some people give the impression of being a mountain, and yet are like a molehill next to a real mountain range.

So find a better partner. But to be able to find somebody better, you first of all have to start seeking. Be courageous and take a step away from a chameleon-like relationship. You will not regret it. It is a move from evil towards good.

DO NOT REGRET LEAVING A BAD PERSON; AT LEAST YOU HAVE THE CHANCE OF A BETTER LIFE

Yes, you weep. And when you want to wipe away your tears, you have to remove your spectacles. Whether dark or rose-coloured. This is the crucial moment. Stop being a pessimist or an idealist. You have to see things as they really are.

Only in this way, can you name your starting position as precisely as possible. If you want to go somewhere, you have to know where you are going. The end of coexistence with a chameleon is automatically a new beginning. A new page. You have learnt the lesson. So you can justifiably believe that the next answer you write will be better.

BEGGING AND A LACK OF ATTENTION

This is one of the paradoxes of many relationships.

Those who give the least, get the most.

And on the contrary, the most self-sacrificing people are also sacrificed the most often. However illogical it may seem, it is understandable.

Those who love without reciprocal feelings, are able to conduct themselves without dignity, and yet are ignored by others. More precisely: they are ignored just because of that. Hardly any feeling is more frustrating than the one expressed with these words: "I give everything to you, and yet it is not enough."

A woman arrived for her first lesson in sign language. Her vocal cords had been removed as a result of a very serious health complication. She needed to communicate somehow.

She did not come alone for the lesson, but was accompanied by her husband, three children, two sisters, brother, mother, father, and nine best friends.

Although she had lost the ability to speak, they did not want to lose the ability to communicate with her, which is the most important thing in any relationship.

The ability to communicate with each other. In any way. But without interruption.

HOW TO REMIND A PARTNER, WHO HAS CEASED TO APPRECIATE YOU, OF YOUR VALUE

Almost all relationship problems can be resolved if there is a mutual will to communicate. And in contrast, any relationship can collapse due to a trivial cause. Because whenever partners stop communicating with each other, they lose the meaning and value of each other. Then it is impossible to create compromises, build the relationship and move ahead due to their differences. If one of a couple gets stuck and boycotts communication, he simply lets the relationship fade away.

If you are indifferent to the fate of a relationship, you often tend to react to further pressure. If you want to drive away a partner, increase the time spent together, do even more for him. But this rarely helps. Because the more you impose yourself and emphasise that you cannot live without him and that he is as precious as the air you breathe, the more mockingly your partner will let you know that you are like air to him too. Only air.

The roundabout of bootlicking has its limits. You can descend below your worth only as long as you have any. Then you have no value to your partner. You are perceived as worthless.

This sounds crazy. How is it possible that a person who gives the maximum to the other can be worthless? You will understand this when you realise that, out of everything you now own, or out of all the successes you have ever achieved, you value most dearly those for which you have sacrificed the most.

Victory in a sporting game is more valuable to you if you have sweated for it, than if it just fell into your lap because the opponent was accidentally injured, gave up or did not arrive at all. Similarly, you jump into flames for something which has personal value for you, rather than for something of value which has no specific bond to you. Indeed, the perceived value is almost never determined by the nominal price, but what you've had to give up for the specific thing or person.

Imagine yourself as a thing. If you want others to notice and appreciate you, you must have a value to them – that is, they must fight for you, sacrifice themselves for you. You must not depreciate yourself before them. Such as by enabling them to have you without a struggle.

Many employees know this from their jobs. Whenever they agree to a lower salary, they hear how easily they can be replaced. At the same time, they are more dependent on the employer, because it is more difficult to scrape by and so they also need their next salary. They are unable to save much from a small sum of money, so they cannot gamble with ideas of leaving the company, even though they are dissatisfied and humiliated there. They would not be able to survive the transitional period before finding another job.

This applies to love, just as to a job: if you are to have any value, you must not lose it. People whose work or love is available cheaply, unfortunately appear cheap. It is not necessary to fight for them, to sacrifice anything extra for them.

So how do you wake up your partner?

How do you regain your original value in his eyes?

How do you begin to start impressing your partner again?

BE YOURSELF

The fastest way to lose your self-worth is to start living according to the ideas or requirements of others. To be managed by them. To submit yourself to them. To stop being yourself.

If you indicate that you depend on another person in a relationship, you switch off your added value. Added value is the reason why you yourself enter into a relationship. Because you come to realise that together, two people are more than one, and thanks to the other person, you will have something you do not have by yourself. I have already mentioned yin and yang.

To retain your added value for the other person, you have to constantly retain what he does not have without you. This is simple in principle. After all, we are all different. We have different characteristics, knowledge, experience. So it should be in a partner's interest not to try to imitate, duplicate him, or overlap his abilities. You should bring something unique into the relationship, something entirely your own. Because it is an added value for your partner.

If both partners retain their own identity to a healthy extent, both are incomparably more resistant. They are less dependant on each other, as well as allowing their relationship to flourish. Because if you have one leg and stumble, you are more likely to fall than if you have two legs and one of them stumbles. If your experiences differ from a partner's concerning your own life, the partnership is more stable. An example: Partner A returns home after a bad day and Partner B is in happy mood after a good day. The sourpuss can then be freed from negations more easily than if both of them shared the same fate to come home either happy or sad. If one wants a partner to become a carbon copy of himself, he is his own worst enemy. Because sooner or later it will seem to him that the other person is useless in the relationship.

Such a relationship can turn nasty. It is paradoxical that the person who submitted himself to the partner is indicated as the culprit. Communication worsens unilaterally, because the more dominant partner will think that he is doing everything in the relationship, while the other one is just going along for the ride. He can be so firmly convinced about it that he refuses to discuss anything else.

To maintain a certain share of independence and privacy means to be yourself and, thanks to this, also to complete your partner if he coincidentally fails. In other words: you will be a reserve battery for him. That is why the wisest partners are those who allow sufficient freedom to each other in a relationship.

TRY NOT TO BE TOTALLY DEPENDENT ON EACH OTHER

Dependency has one undesirable effect. Almost nobody in a relationship cares for a weakling. A person who behaves as if deprived of his own freedom to decide, pulls the entire couple under water as if tied to a stone. That is why it is so important for a relationship to be formed by responsible people who are aware of their freedom and do not back down.

If you let your partner know too often that you are unable to live without him, you give the impression of being a weakling. Weaklings do not have sufficient strength. And without sufficient strength, one is not able to build a long-term relationship.

If a partner who decides to sacrifice himself totally to another, thinks that he is the good one, the one who gives more to the relationship, he should imagine himself in the role of the person on whom he depends. Because this person thinks the opposite. He must carry the whole relationship. So who is actually sacrificing to whom?

So if you look at dependency from both sides, you will understand that both sides must work on a healthy relationship, and are best in balance. This is not possible if one labourer only sits on the kerb, praising his hard-working colleague who is doing everything: "*You do it so well. I couldn't do a better job myself. Just carry on. I'll only spoil it...*", while thinking how much he is sacrificing.

A weakling in a relationship is like a non-swimmer you are responsible for in the sea. If the non-swimmer depends on you, both of you will drown, because you will have a lot of trouble with him as well as with yourself. It is very naïve to believe that dependency of one on another deepens a relationship. What is actually deepening is rather the abyss between them.

BE CONSTANTLY AWARE OF THE RESERVES YOU AND YOUR PARTNER HAVE

Every person is like a statue. Every individual was born as an uncarved piece. One is shaped by every experience. Every day, one's form is shaped into the form of who one wants to be. Paradoxically, one is fortunate not to be what one wants to be. Because this forces one to work on oneself constantly.

Losing the reason to live is real suffering. A dream, goal, work, motivation. Desires motivate people. Whenever you tend to become lazy, not living but merely surviving, your partner comes to assist your sculpturing. He does it in two ways. Firstly, by tactfully pointing out the imperfections you still have. Secondly, by supporting you to eliminate those imperfections.

If a partner pretends that you are perfect (which is naturally a lie, because nobody is perfect), he is not the person needed to motivate you. For the same reason, do not treat your partner – in his own interest – as perfect. You would be lying. Nobody is perfect and everybody wants to be better than he is at the present time. But this does not come free of charge. It hurts, it requires work.

On the contrary, you will be useful if you eliminate your mental obstacle to express that you are aware of your partner's imperfections. Do not trivialise them, but at the same time make it clear that you will support him to become better than he is at the present moment.

Understandably, you also have to be aware of your own imperfections and equally committed to working on yourself. Do it not only for your partner. Do it for yourself.

That is, for both of you.

Because as the quality of the partners increases, the relationship grows.

185

DO NOT TRY TO CHANGE YOURSELF TO SUIT YOUR PARTNER

One of the basic human needs, to which you have already been accustomed since childhood, is being appreciated. But it is even more important to deserve appreciation. A long-lasting solution never consists of altering yourself to suit another person and harvesting false praise for doing so. Because sooner or later you will realise that the praise is not for you, but for the model you imitate. And you begin to feel awkward. It is no wonder, as you have stopped being yourself in the meantime. You begin to lose your own uniqueness, your self-worth.

You are beneficial to a partner if you supplement what he lacks. You can find this out by observation or — if he is willing to communicate with you — by asking him about it. This is the best way to discover what your partner lacks, what he desires, and whether you are able to fill those empty spaces yourself. "*Being able*" reflects not only the current situation, but all your possible future improvements — your willingness to work on yourself.

Every "*yes*" for the benefit of a relationship is a meaningful promise which you should keep. It is nothing less, but also nothing more than a word which must be supported by a deed. If you do not fulfil what you promised your partner, or at least if you do not sincerely try to make it come true, you signal to your partner that your word has no value. Actually, just like you.

A partner does not need you to change yourself to suit him. On the contrary, he will appreciate you more if you are yourself. Because only then can he achieve what he might not have without you.

GIVE AND TAKE IN A RELATIONSHIP

A healthy relationship is balanced in energy. What you put in, you should get back. It does not have to be in the same form (lent money), but it must be in some form (feelings).

To make it clear: a relationship is not a trade. But everything in Nature must be balanced. Whenever you are willing to give too much, your partner is in an unpleasant position. He senses this imbalance and is aware that he is unable to pay back such a big loan.

Therefore, do not be hasty to give, particularly at the beginning of a relationship. There is always time enough for giving. If you meet a fair partner, he will even reject a relationship in which you shower him with benefits, or he will take a reserved stance towards it.

This is the problem of all people who give in an exaggerated manner, and then even blame a partner for it. What can a partner do, if he cannot express emotions in such a splendid way, if he is not used to it and refuses to devalue his compliments by this approach? Understandably, he recedes from the scene or disappears entirely. And keeps on being surprised. Because the person who got him into the embarrassing position even rails at him from a distance.

RESPECT EACH OTHER

Understandably, mutual respect is one of the essential preconditions of a successful relationship. Keep your differences in mind. Reconcile yourself to the fact that your partner needs more time than you for the same issues, or that he holds a different opinion.

In the case of you reaching the conclusion that you deserve the partner and that you could form an amazing relationship, first give him the proof that you are sufficiently mature and have adequate added value: respect his differences and all his wishes.

Build your own as well as his life. Shape the sculpture together. And most importantly, be yourself. If you manage to do this, your own self-worth, as well as the worth of the relationship, will never depreciate.

LOW SELF-ESTEEM

This is actually only the converse of the previous problem. Your partner has low self-esteem, but it is not your fault. For example, it is simple to destroy a person who wishes to be successful in his job. Just deprive him of his self-esteem. Then he is unable to apply even profound knowledge and skills. He feels like a zombie. Good for nothing. He turns into a weakling whose nihilism can destroy the entire relationship. Your test is whether you can empathise with him and restore his self-esteem. Because it is your duty, and also your obligation as a partner.

It is easy to condemn somebody. But before you do it, rather think twice. Some things are not what they seem. Like the story of the man washing his new car.

His young son was playing nearby, before obviously finding something of interest on the other side of the vehicle. Then the man realised that the sound he could hear was that of a nail scratching on the car's body.

At that moment, the son's eyes met his father's furious glare as he immediately ran around the car, with the sinister belt in his hand. *"But Dad..."* he only managed to utter before the father beat him until he was bleeding.

He remained injured and crying in the road. The man plucked up the courage to return to the car to evaluate the damage done to the vehicle body with the nail.

Indeed, there was something scratched on the door by the boy:

"Dad, I luv you very m"

• • •

Your partner is your *"better half"*. If you allow yourself to be controlled by emotions, ask questions and communicate before you attack.

SIGNALS THAT MAKE IT CLEAR THAT A PARTNER NEEDS HELP

The human body can be imagined as a *"fuel tank"*. The fuel drives the body. If there are holes in the tank, the contents will leak out. The contents are self-esteem. Without it, all planning, education and capital are suddenly worthless. Because without self-esteem, you cannot apply any of it. You are afraid to take any steps.

Anybody who tries, can achieve success in any area. Success can be achieved, but does not necessarily have to be. It is not a certainty. Nevertheless, what is certain is that if one does not try to succeed, nothing will ever be achieved. Imagine that your partner is in the best situation to succeed, but does not apply his strong points. The more he suffers, the longer he makes no progress, the weaker he becomes. Until he totally gives up. The surrender of a man often tells less about the obstacles he has to overcome, and more about how little he thinks of himself.

A person who believes in himself, finds the most stable support. He is able to continue sailing even with torn sails. He is able to see some constructive possibility in every circumstance. *One who believes, desires. And one who desires, can do it.*

The person who does not believe in himself, needs the support of a partner. Let's not forget that you are a reserve resource. Whenever your partner is frustrated by the hellish problems he is experiencing at work, present a positive mirror: explain to him that this is actually an advantage. All successful people have been through some kind of hell. The times when nobody believed in them taught them to stand on their own feet, to rely especially on themselves and not to expect their self-esteem to be boosted from the outside. In that way, people find a way to regain their self-esteem. Because they rediscover the value in themselves. They never lost it

– in fact, nobody loses self-esteem – but only accepted the opinion of others that they had none.

Please keep an eye on your partner. Unfortunately, there is no warning light signalling that self-esteem is dwindling. However, you can sense the moment, if you learn to adhere to the following laws:

HELP A PARTNER WHO INCREASINGLY SEEKS THE APPROVAL OF OTHERS

D o you know the scathing comment: *"He's just being himself."*

Yes, somebody who is mocked by others is being himself.

For that matter, what else should he be?

Every self-confident man is being himself. Because he is living a life which does not belong to anyone else. Nobody else is responsible for the mistakes in his life. Only he himself is.

That is why, if somebody is being himself, he does not feel obliged to please anyone else. Anyway, it is not in his power. There is no person with whom everybody agrees. It is impossible to please everyone. In order to make everyone agree with you, you would have to constantly change according to the attitudes of the individuals you encounter, one by one. With each new person, you would have to focus on that person and never on yourself.

On the contrary, whenever you free yourself of the tendency to please everybody, you narrow down the important persons within your circle only to the few individuals closest to you, the ones you care about most in your life. These are called friends and family. You easily know that they trust and respect you. Because they do not really care what you aim at or what you strive for – as long as it is your ambition, your wish, your path, and you really want to have that experience. Then they stand unconditionally behind you. In any case, close enough to provide rescue in case something bad happens.

They have no need to manipulate you. To change you. To solve your problems. And yet they are always at hand, supporting you. Not so that you can do things ac-

cording to their ideas, but because you do things according to your own. Which is exactly what your partner should hear in the first place: support your partner on his path, whatever that is.

HELP A PARTNER WHO CONTINUOUSLY MAKES EXCUSES

An excuse does not tell anything about the circumstances you apologise for, but about your ability to cope with them. Every obstacle can be overcome, more easily when faced by two people together. Your vision must always be bigger than your excuses. There is never a point in life when it is useless to strive for more. As long as one is alive, there is something to be achieved, created, experienced. There will always be someone in the world who you can help.

You must take ownership of your thoughts and actions. Do not blame anyone in your surroundings for your failure. Admit to yourself that you did not manage to achieve something. Do not nurture your weaknesses with falsehoods such as, "*I had no time,*" "*I'm not good enough.*" Learn to make the time and work on the elimination of areas that can be improved, until the desired results are achieved. Even a small step forwards is more than a big excuse.

Tell this to your partner. Help him to stop seeing every obstacle as a signal for making an excuse. Instead, let him find a solution, see obstacles as an exercise machine for personal growth. Obstacles are not what are encountered in life. Obstacles are life itself.

194

HELP A PARTNER WHO CONTINUOUSLY DISPARAGES HIMSELF WITH DEROGATORY WORDS

Words are an invisible weapon which one must learn to handle. The basic skill is not to turn this weapon either against others or against yourself. Be aware of the destructive force of words. The difference between the rhetorical questions *"Why SHOULD I succeed?"* and *"Why SHOULDN'T I succeed?"* can mean the difference between an unsuccessful and a successful person.

Motivate your partner to constructive discussions. Explain to him that the derogatory sentences he uses in his own defence are futile. Indeed, negative sentences uttered about oneself, have no recipient other than oneself. They are like the ball in a squash court. When alone in a fierce contest, you either defeat or injure yourself. No other outcome is possible in the game.

If a partner makes the effort to formulate some words, let him rather utter positive words. In terms of expended energy, it takes the same effort. However, the result is entirely different.

HELP A PARTNER WHO CONSTANTLY NEEDS TO WIN IN DEBATES WITH YOU

Your partner made a mistake. So what?

He had an idea which did not turn out well. So what?

Let your partner speak unhesitatingly about everything that is running through his mind. Let him not be afraid of his opinions. Discuss them. From your different points of view, arrive at boundaries and compromises. Argue with a smile, persuade, prompt. Do not adopt a posture just to be right. On the contrary, talk simply because you are not afraid to be wrong.

Small-minded people are very irritated when others disagree with them. Under no circumstances will they admit that they can be wrong. They insist on always being right, even when they are obviously wrong. Their ego wants, and even needs, everyone around them to confirm this. However, such behaviour is close to folly and far removed from self-esteem.

Explain to a partner who, like a child, insists on his own viewpoint, that it does not matter if he finds himself in the wrong. Finding out what is right is more important than being right at all costs. Whenever you discover that you were wrong, be pleased about it. Change your mind as far as is necessary, and correct yourself. Nothing will happen. Well, something actually does happen.

Something very fundamental happens. You are incomparably better off than when sticking to a false conclusion. Indeed, you are wiser.

HELP A PARTNER WHO CONSTANTLY SPEAKS JUST TO HEAR HIS OWN VOICE

I f somebody strives for attention by incessant talking, it is as if he is wearing a mask over his insecurity. Self-confident people are often silent, because they are certain of their opinions. They listen rather than speak. They know what they think. And they do not need to repeat it aloud. What they need far more is to know what others think about a specific matter. By their silence, they give them the space to formulate their opinions, and thus present new views on a matter. That is why, instead of replying to questions nobody has even asked, rather ask others:

- *"How did you manage to do this?"*

- *"What did you learn during the process?"*

- *"What would you do differently, if you were to try again today?"*

Ask, in order to learn something. Because each of us knows something, but none of us knows everything. The only way to learn more, is to listen.

So remember: Whenever you wish to improve a relationship, ask questions. Or reply to questions the other person asks. But in no case just speak to hear your own voice. You will not learn anything new in that way.

HELP A PARTNER WHO IS INCREASINGLY OBSESSED BY SUCCESS/FAILURE

If success makes one arrogant, it is definitely not the achievement of real success. Perhaps you have earned some money, but continue to be an arrogant person, and not only with regard to money. Even failure should not change a man for the worse. This is no reason. Failure forces a man to re-evaluate what has been achieved so far, which is beneficial.

Regardless of whether life goes well or badly, try to accept it in the same way. Resting on one's laurels has deplorable consequences, because one stagnates. Succumbing to anxiety backfires too, because one also stagnates. Try always to learn a lesson from failure. Analyse why you succeeded or failed at something. In this way, you will adjust your strengths as well your weaknesses. You can strengthen the strengths, and weaken the weaknesses. So always learn both from success and failure.

Victory and loss are two poles with the same contents – both contain a detonator as well as a treasure. It is only up to you which one you choose. Winning or losing can either destroy you or motivate you. If you remain positive, you can be better tomorrow than you are today. If your partner does not have his feet on the ground, he is heading for disaster.

HELP A PARTNER WHO IS INCREASINGLY AFRAID OF NEW EXPERIENCES

L ife has quite defined pitfalls. Motivation can be a painful experience. However, in retrospect, one always evaluates new experiences as beneficial. Experiences give one the appetite for trying further offers life has prepared.

The chasm in society is opening and deepening like an abyss between people who are afraid of change, and those who enjoy it. They have a diametrically different way of thinking. The first ask: What if we make a mistake by changing? Even people who are very dissatisfied in a relationship, in work, and in life in general, then hesitate as to whether they should make a change. Because they can get used to even bad conditions, and the certainty of the bad is more acceptable to them than the uncertainty outside the comfort zone. They do not want to leave what they know intimately, although it does not suit them, because they are afraid of what else could happen. They defend the bad, instead of striving for better. These people either do not leave bad partners, or enter relationships with similar types. They always go to the same vacation destination. Although they admit that nicer locations might exist, this is enough for them. Man is a creature of habit. He tends to repeat identical scenarios and stick to his own established ways. The most comfortable way of life that he knows.

These people are also attached to their past. They are stuck emotionally in it. The past gives them certainty. They worship today, even after it becomes yesterday. They live in regret over what was. Yet, what is, flows through their fingers. They cannot cope with today, but are unable to do away with the past (because they

199

know it). They wake up with worries. And in the evening they go to bed, surprised that the day has turned out not to be as bad as expected.

This is because most worries never materialise. And the few that actually do materialise, do not end up as horribly as in the imagination. In most cases, fear obstructs man unnecessarily. The tragedy is that fear of a mistaken decision paralyses the decision-making ability so much, that one rather does not make any decisions. Support your partner not to fear new experiences and mistakes. Let him rather worry about the day when it is too late for any experiences or mistakes. When all he will do is regret.

KNOCKOUT BY LIFE

Death is the only certainty in our lives. We correctly call it shattering, because it virtually shatters the person whose dear one has died. Death can take a partner from one, but also an integral part of a relationship, like a child. If any important pillar disappears, the whole structure is shaken. At first, one only counts the loss. In time, as one grows wiser, what is left is also counted. One begins to realise that one can start rebuilding on what one has left. Death puts life in a different light. Nevertheless, the light is always the right one. How is it possible? Because it illuminates the most fundamental values that have long-term meaning. About which we tend to forget in the bustle of events. So also death, if we can rise above it, can be evaluated as positive. But first we must understand it.

"I called the hospital again on a Sunday morning. Like every previous day. But this time, the nurse told me that she would call the doctor. This was unusual and I anticipated something terrible. Then the doctor told me over the phone something I will never forget: 'Mr Passer, we are sorry but your son died last night, at a quarter to four.'"

Radim Passer was 36 years old. Imagine yourself in his skin: the value of his company, which he had built up from scratch, was tens of millions of dollars. He was living the American dream, as he had always desired. The only missing piece in the mosaic of absolute happiness, was a son to take over his father's life work. *"In our family, as the first child had been a boy five times in a row. I also wished for this. My wife and I waited for a long time for a baby. Then she finally got pregnant. And indeed, it was a boy. We named him Max, after my father! However, he was born several weeks early and was put in an incubator. I stayed in the ward with Jana. We held each other's hands and experienced incredible, yet ordinary, human happiness. Whenever I drove to them from the office, tears of joy welled up in my eyes.*

Every day I looked forward to bathing little Max, I never wanted to miss it. After bathtime, Jana fed him and put him to bed. But it seemed to her that the boy was not drinking much lately."

They took their son, only a month old, to the hospital. Doctors found that the cerebrospinal fluid was not flowing from one chamber to another. At six weeks of age, Max underwent a neurosurgical operation. The operation itself was successful, but the doctors wanted to discover the cause of the whole problem. Magnetic resonance imaging resulted in a devastating sentence. *"They announced to us that Max had a tumour in his brain which could not be surgically removed. That he had no chance of survival. I would have given up everything I had for the ability to help him. But NOTHING could be done in this uneven duel."*

After Max's death, Radim Passer did not know how his life would continue. He was a successful developer, but what was it all for? He knew how to make money, but what is money worth if it cannot be exchanged for what is really important?

Nevertheless, whenever life collapses, fundamental values still remain and give one a reason to live again fully. After this experience, Radim Passer began to think more about life, death, God (*"It is interesting that even the obstinate infidel begins to pray on a sinking boat..."*) and especially about helping other people. Thanks to this experience, his life obtained a new meaning.

Today, he is among the forty richest Czechs and has two sons to whom he can leave his empire one day. But he stopped caring about money after that fateful event. *"It is no longer important to me if my sons are successful entrepreneurs. What counts is that they are good people."*

HOW TO GET UP AGAIN IF LIFE KNOCKS YOU DOWN

Not everybody believes in God. But everybody needs to believe in something. In something to lift you back up on your feet if life collapses around you like a house of cards and everything seemingly loses its meaning. These moments come even though one hates them. They have a precise and positive purpose, which one usually does not see or appreciate.

How do you cope with initial bitterness, devastation and pain?

Where do you find the motivation to carry on again?

And what steps do you take to make it come true?

Firstly, everything begins in one's thoughts. One finds the most important issues there. Answers and laws that can lead you, like shining lights, out of the dark tunnel.

203

WHAT YOU FOCUS ON, YOU CAN CHANGE

The whole process of success and happiness starts with your thinking. It is impossible to lead a positive life with a negative approach. So how do you switch your attitude from negative to positive in hard times?

In a hopeless situation, one most often feels impotent, because you do not know what to do, you are in shock because you did not count on something like this, and you feel pain because suddenly all you see are closed doors. It seems as if the world has conspired against you, that you are nothing, and can see no future. You are filled with the fear of the unknown, certainties are an empty concept. Time does not heal injuries. On the contrary, the burden is increasingly heavy. Day after day, your position as a victim is confirmed. You are dejected and eaten up by feelings of injustice. You lose faith, strength as well as willpower.

Everything can change if you admit that every crisis has a positive message and solution. What is that? Firstly, it is necessary to find out what has caused your mental downfall. Maybe you made a mistake, maybe you did not. Perhaps you had some warning signs and ignored them. All such thinking is painful. It is like chafing at an unhealed wound. But you chafe at it so as not to hurt yourself, but to help yourself for the next time. Indeed all crises are beneficial for giving a clear indication that life has not proceeded in the right direction. When you realise this, you start seeing crises as useful opportunities for change, for a better and more functional life. You stop being crazy about looking obsessively back in time. Why return to it? Was not one mistake one too many?

Every crisis, if correctly understood as an opportunity, can lead to revolutionary personal transformation. Transformation of your behaviour, attitude to life, discovery of new possibilities. Simply, a transformation of your life as a whole.

Of course, you must forget the bad situation.

Not succumb to it.

Use it as a kick-start for new decisions.

WITHOUT OCCASIONAL UNHAPPINESS YOU WOULD NOT RECOGNISE HAPPINESS

If it were not for winter, we would not notice the arrival of spring. If it were not for bad times, we would not appreciate the good ones. Diversity of life enables us to be grateful for times when we are doing well, and to be patient in moments when we are not.

Bad luck returns us to the basic phase when one again answers the questions preceding every new beginning and positive forgetting. Such as:

- What will fulfil me?

- What is my real dream?

- What do I still want to achieve in life?

Why are these questions so important? Our goals define us. They tell us who we are and what is important to us. Goals give our dreams a clearer and more specific contour, and a direction for us to follow. We must also ask these questions, because in the hardest knockouts we often do not know what we really want. When we formulate it, we do not dare to follow it. We drown in the negative feeling that we do not even deserve to be successful. Yet the contrary is true.

People who manage to outgrow negative goals, recognise the positive ones. So build on your fundamental values, strengths and everything you like and enjoy. Somewhere out there you will find your goal, your joy of life, your happiness. Although what you long for seems huge, do not be afraid. Every huge goal can be divided into many small, more easily attainable goals. So what, if it takes a long

time to achieve the big goal? It does not matter, because it will be aligned to your happiness the whole time.

All goals that are related to your inner desires, are more easily and quickly fulfilled. In due course, you will no longer care about the obstacles in your path, because the pathway already fulfils you. The primary objective you should have is to fill the emptiness inside, the inadequacy you are currently experiencing. Such a goal will charge you with commitment, energy, as well as reconciliation to life. And as for life, it sometimes must turn you upside down to force you to go on straight ahead.

A LESSON CAN BE LEARNT FROM EVERY DIFFICULT MOMENT

What do I want less of and what do I want more of in life?

What have I managed to do already, and what do I still want to achieve?

More questions which one should not forget to answer. Their magic is based on the fact that one cannot answer them without experience gained along the way. Experience that can be equally good or bad.

Experience is not what has happened to you. Experience is how you have dealt with what has happened to you. Whether you succeed or not is an opportunity to learn. Every evening, whether successful or not, you can praise yourself for the progress. Yes, you can conclude every day with a smile on your face and a feeling that you are closer to your dream. Does it sound strange that you should not blame yourself for not fulfilling all the tasks? Tomorrow you can correct it, and do much more. Even today can be regarded as a useful and encouraging lesson. Because tomorrow's success is up to you.

Your life is comprised of what you think, say, do.

Your life is the people you keep around you.

Your life is your priorities and the time you devote to them.

Yes, we are a combination of all these. We embody every experience we have gained along the way. After all, it is perceptible in our thoughts and deeds. Negative experiences can shape us for the better, make us more humble and considerate.

But – do not forget – anything is only possible if you allow it.

EVERY MOMENT IS A NEW BEGINNING

Whatever happened to you is over. That is why it is called the past. Wishing for a different past is a waste of time. The past is unchangeable. You only need to do one thing: take it as a fact. Reconcile yourself to it. You have no other option anyway.

However, what you can change is the present. Every present moment offers a new beginning. Your previous joys as well as mistakes remain in the past. It is important to understand this. You are not who you were. You are who you decide to become. But for this, you need to change your habits, stop running along the same rut — because the rails leading from the past have brought you right here. To the present station. And what you do today, builds the rails to tomorrow's station.

Life is very merciful to people. Whenever they survive a fatal crisis, it provides them with lots of energy. However, people waste this energy on weeping, escaping from reality, taking revenge, kicking themselves. Imagine using the same energy positively — to cut off the past and build something new. Crises occur merely to enable you to pause, re-evaluate the existing process and change the stereotype. This is the only thing that can lead you out of the vicious cycle. Yes, life sometimes uses tough methods. But, let's be frank, what lessons other than the tough ones can really wake you up?

Every new experience increases the probability of you becoming who you want to be. But you have to learn your lesson, carry on and never give up. Regardless of how hard the period you have been through is, you always have the ability to change.

IF YOU LEAVE THE PAST BEHIND, YOU DO NOT LOSE IT

Your past is an archive. A large vault of experiences found within your mind. Depending on the quality of your memory, you can return to the past as often as you like. The past is a useful aid with which to confront the present thoughts and actions. It enables you to recall what did not work before, and thus to find the way to what can work.

It can be painful to leave behind old memories, actions and people in the past. However, the pain of remaining in something non-functional is always bigger than the pain of leaving it. Departure from bad people hurts less than remaining in a relationship with them. Because prolongation of a relationship with a bad person will never create a good relationship.

Some departures impart the feeling that you have lost something. That you have wasted time on something that eventually turned out to be dysfunctional. However, reality is the exact opposite. You did not lose anything and only gained – experience, as well as all the time that is yet to come. Starting from scratch is no shame, but a manifestation of strength and courage. After some time, you will appreciate this period and the experience gained and be grateful for it. It is always cleansing to return to living in compliance with one's own values. And somebody who forgets his own values, needs a regular slap from life. In his own interest.

BE KINDER TO YOURSELF THAN YOU HAVE TO BE

Failure is accompanied by a search for culprits. One seeks someone to blame externally as well as within oneself. In so doing, you are negative, and feel the same. Change this. Try to be kind to yourself, especially at this time. Accept yourself with the mistakes you have made. Treat yourself with respect. Even if you think that you cannot do anything positive for yourself, at least do a little. Every step in the right direction comes in useful.

Every pain is related to the process of recovery and healing.

And doctors recommend rest for every disease.

So rest. And do not harm yourself. This is how the rebound from the bottom starts.

DO YOU HAVE A PROBLEM WITH REBOUNDING?
WHAT YOU SHOULD STOP DOING WHEN YOU FIND YOURSELF DOWN, THROUGH NO FAULT OF YOUR OWN

The wife of my foreign business partner was diagnosed with a fatal disease. The news devastated not only his spouse, but the entire family. His son, immediately on hearing the news, had a car accident due to his lack of attention. He died when his car crashed into a tree. Thus my associate lost two key persons in his life within a few days.

Now, years later, he is in a new relationship and, although he has two scars on his soul, he is smiling again. He survived the worst times by adhering to the following laws:

STOP HIDING FROM THE TRUTH

This hide-and-seek game cannot be won. The truth will always find you. Many people, as a first reaction, do not want to admit the truth. They believe that it is just a bad dream or that everything will somehow change. They know from films that every story must have a happy ending. But life does not have to give us anything. Life owes us nothing. That is the first point to remember.

Secondly, just by ignoring the truth, does not make it cease to exist. On the contrary, ignoring the truth forces one to live a lie. Lies make every day, every night, worse. Imagine seeing an obstacle in the road, such as a tree blocking the way. Understandably, this does not suit you. So you take a blanket, throw it on to the fallen tree and pretend that the tree is not there. If you even believe this and drive your car as if the road is clear, you'll certainly come off worst. It is the same in life. Any obstacle must be eliminated, not masked.

In a relationship, it applies that ignoring the evil of a bad partner will not transform him into a good partner. Do not avoid the truth. Truth hurts only once – when you learn it. But a lie continues to hurt as long as you live it.

DO NOT REWIND A MAGNETIC TAPE WITHOUT USING THE STOP BUTTON

Life is like an old magnetic tape. Rough treatment damages it. Living in the present means letting the tape play freely, run freely. If you fervently need to return to the past at any point in your life, do it considerately. First stop your tape. Just like when you need to reverse a car which is moving forwards, you first put it into neutral and only then change to reverse. The neutral gear corresponds to the STOP button of a tape recorder. If you want to return to the past, you first have to stop. To understand the difference between the present and the past. To understand that the most intense recollections do not change anything. You do not change either the past or the present. Life can be influenced only in the present, by actions taken now.

We all are products of the past, but not its prisoners. You do not have to suffer for something which is no longer true. Whenever you say goodbye to an old thought, a new one will say hello. Connect to the past only with positive feelings, especially with lessons learnt. Not with negative feelings and remorse. For that matter, neither you nor your past deserve bitterness.

STOP INSISTING ON WHO YOU WERE BEFORE THE STORM

Hard times are like a storm. A storm comes out of the blue sky and prevents one from reaching the original destination. Moreover, a storm has immense power for change. It can blow the hair, smudge make-up, soak clothes, turn all the best-made plans upside down. It is meaningless to wonder retrospectively how you looked before the storm, because this will not change your present state. Time simply cannot be rewound.

An unusual phenomenon exists on Seychelles. The locals do not run from the beach and do not curse the weather when it starts to rain. On the contrary, they relish the rain, as the islands will be greener, the air cleaner and the nights more pleasant. This is not due to the different type of equatorial rain, it is thanks to Nature and the people's viewpoint. Of course, all of us are capable of such an attitude. We know that every storm in life teaches patience, humility, persistence. Thanks to the storm, we are then able to appreciate every sunny moment and enjoy the times of good weather. This is also one of the positives of unhappy times – happier times can be looked forward to.

When my business associate, about whom I told you a few lines above, absorbed the tragic events life had in store for him, he did not start to live less. On the contrary, he began to live more. He valued all the good people more who had not abandoned him, and since then has been appreciating every moment spent with them. He did not want to be as he had been before, because then he had not perceived real values. He had formerly not appreciated his wife and son sufficiently. And he no longer wants to be like that.

If it were not for misfortune, we would not grow any wiser. Even a negative past positively influences our present and future. Whenever life injures you, remember that a day will come when you realise how important those injuries were for you.

DO NOT GO ON STRIKE FOR IMPROVED CONDITIONS

We are no trade unionists, and life is not our employer. It is naive to resign yourself mulishly to a situation, hoping that things will get better on their own. Because if you are resigned, nothing will improve. No flat road leads to the highest points. You must invest effort and endure inconvenience. You must keep walking uphill. There is no doubt that life is worth the effort. Life will reward you – make you stronger.

If somebody has resigned himself to a situation, he remains in the same mess he was in before. He repeatedly worries about an untenable situation. Understand that all thoughts are instructions to your limbs. Man is one big cluster of nerves. What you think about, generates instructions to your body. Nature has wisely arranged it so that thoughts are executed immediately – this is how rapidly information flows from the brain to the hands or legs. However, only positive orders cause movement. Non-action does not change your position. What is worse, non-action only deepens the hole under you.

So stop protesting and think. Likewise, if you want to get out of a hole, first you must stop deepening it.

YOU DO NOT CONTRIBUTE

You may have an amazing partner, and yet the relationship is not working. This happens when you do not contribute sufficiently. For example, you neglect certain activities, or merely neglect saying the words that are important to your partner. Are you surprised that the relationship may burn out as a result of "only words"? However, beautiful words which remain unspoken can hurt just as much.

The long-term girlfriend of my friend died in an accident. Due to the fault of a driver coming from the opposite direction. Unfortunately, this is also part of living in the 21st century. This can happen to any one of us, or to our friends. The friend who informed me of this sad news, commented: *"I loved her more than anyone else in the world. She was that important to me. She was my everything. I am sorry that I didn't manage to tell her that."*

The contradiction startled me. Why does only the death of a beloved person make us realise what we wanted to say and should have said to the person? Are we under a spell, if we cannot tell the people we care about how much we appreciate them? Indeed, they deserve to know that they give meaning to our lives. That they even mean the world to us...

However, we should learn to speak to ourselves. Regardless of what is currently happening in our lives, we should use the sentences listed below – because we never know when circumstances change, when a lifetime opportunity passes us by.

It will not wait for a time which suits you. You need to believe in yourself precisely at this moment. In the end, lifetime opportunities are like the postman. He arrives daily, but never returns with the same mail.

Cherish your partner as well as yourself. After all, you are the only person who is certain to live with you until your last day. You have your share of responsibility for a relationship. You are the person your partner needs for support.

So repeat the above sentences to yourself, as well as those below.

They are so simple that people tend to forget them...

DO NOT FORGET TO SAY:

"I love you."

'll tell you the most horrible fact:

Regardless of who you love, your relationship will end one day.

No relationship lasts forever.

You experience all the amazing feelings only temporarily.

It does not matter if you break up or if death parts you; it will happen. Do not grieve then. Grieve now already if you forget to appreciate these moments. It is meaningless to wait too long for anything positive in life. And it is even more futile to procrastinate about saying kind words. If you love someone, show it to him or her. Right now. Most hearts are broken by the undone deeds of partners.

There are no postponements, no tomorrow in a healthy relationship.

You can only express your love and admiration today.

DO NOT FORGET TO SAY:

"Thank you."

When young and unappreciative, I considered the care of those around me as the norm. It even bothered me.

Today, I miss that same care.

For example, a neighbour once gave me a pair of grey trousers. They irritated me, were out-of-date. Ungratefully, I tossed the trousers on the floor. The neighbour died a week later. It turned out that the trousers were the last thing he was ever able to give me.

Since then, I have thanked him many times in spirit. But still not enough to end the regret that I did not say the simple words to his face.

"Thank you". So simple that it might seem boring and useless. I thank everyone now. For each act of kindness.

Because I never know if it will be the last one.

DO NOT FORGET TO SAY:

"I deserve to love and respect myself."

An average man can survive one week without water, two weeks without food, and many years without a roof above his head. But in seclusion? This is perhaps the most difficult torture. It is a condition which cannot be escaped – when you are lonely and all alone. When you do not feel comfortable in your own skin. A partner or a friend can bring lots of joy to your life, but cannot fill the emptiness you yourself have caused within.

You are responsible for your feelings of happiness. If you do not feel happy, this is nobody else's fault. People can give you tons of sugar, but if you are sour to yourself, no external effort to sweeten your life will help.

The world is full of people. Whenever you feel lonely, you must be in bad company. There are only two possibilities: Either you are in the company of bad people, or you are behaving badly to yourself. Either way, whenever you feel lonely, start with the most important relationship you have. The one you have with yourself.

DO NOT FORGET TO SAY:

"I can't win every time, but I can always learn something."

If you do not know how to do something, it pays at least to try. Even though you do not win, you can still gain something – experience, a lesson. Do not mistake your fate for the inability to decide. Learn to admit your mistakes and to deal with them positively. Although people sometimes curse their mistakes, it is the mistakes which enrich them.

What we like to call Fate, is actually our character which can be shaped. Simply realise that you are responsible for your own deeds and attitudes. This awareness needs not discourage or scare you. On the contrary, it should motivate you, because it means that you are empowered to change your destiny.

Just look back at your past, how stupid and naive you were then. Especially in your youth. Of course, you are ashamed of your actions. And you would not make the same mistakes today. Because you have learned from your mistakes. You are not two different people. Only living proof that you have matured at each attempt.

DO NOT FORGET TO SAY:

"Life is good now already."

There are people who wait all day for the end of their working hours, and wait the whole working week for Friday, the whole year for a holiday, and their whole lives for happiness. Do not be one of those passive expectants. On the last day of your life, you will only realise that all the good times are already actually over.

No, a good life does not start some time in the future. A good life begins when you stop waiting for a better one.

DO NOT FORGET TO SAY:

"It is time to do something positive."

Whenever you catch yourself complaining excessively, ask yourself the question: *"What do I really want – to continue moaning or really to improve my situation?"*

No complaint is strong enough to change the situation. Only actions can result in change. And nobody will take them on your behalf.

Precisely when you are drowning in negatives, it is time to do something positive. Constructive. To start building.

DO NOT FORGET TO SAY:

"I can do it."

No obstacle in life is big enough to stop you. What stops you is your belief that you cannot overcome the given obstacle. The problem is never having too much or too little, we just use this as an excuse to postpone action for another day – a day which is not on the calendar.

If you do not have enough money and do not take clear steps to improve this situation, you will simply never have any more. If you are not successful enough and do not take distinct steps to improve your situation, you will simply never be more successful. If you are unhappy in a relationship and do not take distinct steps to improve the situation, you will never be happier in the relationship either.

You can call it injustice. You can regret the past. You can rely on the future. You can hope that a saviour will come to solve it on your behalf. You can dream of perfection. There is one problem with everything: we live in an imperfect world, one which lacks any perfection or ideal moments. Therefore, instead of seeking excuses to avoid surmounting an obstacle, rather find the reasons why you should conquer it as soon as possible.

The Bible also states that God does not give anyone a bigger burden than what he is able to bear. There is no doubt that you can cope with any obstacle that comes your way. It will be worthwhile. Because by surmounting an obstacle, you will obtain a manual on how to surmount it the second, third time, whenever. Simply, the obstacle you triumph over ceases to be an obstacle.

DO NOT FORGET TO SAY:

"I apologise."

The feeling of guilt festers in every man. An apology is the best way to have the last word in a difference of opinions. But don't bother to apologise if you intend to continue doing what you are apologising for. When you say something, mean it. Be the partner who looks the other person straight in the eye and feels every single word deeply when apologising.

DO NOT FORGET TO SAY:

"I forgive you."

A once damaged relationship which has experienced forgiveness, is often stronger than before. Because the two people remind themselves that they are fallible beings and as such respect each other. Of course, forgiveness need not lead to the healing of a relationship in all cases. Our relationships do not always have to be long-lasting. Some people enter our lives only to provide a short-term lesson. But always forgive.

Forgiveness is not as much a service to the other person as to yourself. Forgiveness is for your own good. Indeed, this internal act enables you to stop occupying yourself with the past and to refocus on the present, or the future. It is like lifting an anchor and sailing from the berth which brought you no happiness.

Without forgiveness, no wound will be completely healed. So learn to forgive. What happened in the past was simply just one chapter of your life. You do not have to close a book because of one bad chapter. Just turn the page.

PART 2 | ALONE

HOW TO BUILD YOUR SELF

Imagine a chain consisting of a hundred links. Ninety-nine are flawless, one has a defect.

If the defective link breaks, the chain is torn apart – regardless of the perfect quality of all the other remaining links.

The same applies to a partnership.

A relationship is only as resilient as the weaker member of the couple. Therefore, if an imbalanced and unprepared partner enters into a relationship, the whole relationship will be just as unstable and uncertain.

Therefore, whether you are alone, again or still, your aloneness is an important part of the preparation for the next relationship. If you are not contemplating a new partner and are focused only on building your self, you are doing the most substantial thing for the resilience of one of the two pillars in a future relationship – your self.

RECONCILIATION TO SOLITUDE

The divorce is over. Primarily, it is time to remember real friends. Obviously not only the partner has disappeared, but also people who, like him, posed as your close friends. Nevertheless, they were only masquerading as such, but never really were friends. A period of cleansing lies ahead, which will be challenging both for you and those around you. Imagine yourself in the skin of your friends: Should they let you be? Or should they distract you as much as they can? What is more important?

A valued guest arrived for a visit. A friend from France. He brought Burgundy wine and spoke the whole evening of how beautiful his girlfriend is. I forgot to mention: George is blind.

When we were 17 years old, we stood at roadsides on the outskirts of cities and hitchhiked throughout half of Europe. We travelled without a plan, dependent on and following the routes of the drivers who gave us lifts. Only in Saint-Tropez, on the Cote D'Azur, did we have to turn back. It was impossible to continue. The road ended at the ocean.

George stayed in France. He became a fireman. He was blinded during one fire-fighting operation. The house was already in a dangerous state of collapse and the commander ordered the team to retreat. George wanted to pull out one more woman. The gas in the house exploded. George lost his eyesight, but grabbed Amelia in his arms and carried her out, blinded.

He did not leave her then; she has not left him ever since. Today she is his partner and care-giver. *"I know it was not sensible, but it was the right thing to do. Her shouts would have woken me from my dreams. Perhaps I would have been absolutely healthy, but not happy. For my entire lifetime, I would always have regretted a deed I had not dared to do,"* he told me five years later.

231

At the time when my mom had just died, I was feeling desperate. Suddenly the phone rang – George was calling. *"I heard what happened. I am so sorry. Accept my sincere condolences. And tell me what would please you the most now."* Knowing that my friend was in France and that there was a distance of 1 000 kilometres between us, I only smiled bitterly: *"If only we could go for a beer, as we used to do when we were young."*

The call was interrupted, but the doorbell started ringing. I looked out of the window and in front of the house – to my astonishment – I saw George. He was still holding the mobile phone in one hand, and Amelia by the other. He enquired of her mischievously: *"Hurry up, describe his face! What does he look like?"*

He had come from France just because of me. How insane.

Tears welled up in my eyes, while his eyes were opaque. *"Petr, as long as I did sensible things in life, I was not happy. Perhaps those whom I obeyed were happy, but I was not. Only when I do the right things according to my own values, regardless of what other people think of them, then I am happy. Because my heart somehow knows best..."*

HOW TO COPE AFTER A BREAK-UP: WHY FOLLOW THE HEART RATHER THAN REASON

Your heartbeat... Can you hear it? If not, be even more silent.

It is not only beating. It is also speaking silently. Although other people do not hear it.

Oftentimes, neither do you. But you feel what you really need. The heart always knows this. No matter whether you are alone again, or still single, what your heart is trying to tell you goes like this:

"Do not doubt yourself. You do not need other people to tell you what your value is. To have your value assigned by them. Everyone already has a value. And it will not increase in the slightest if you live in the way determined by others. On the contrary, your value will decrease. People will naturally be unhappy whenever they try to elicit praise from others – because it is just impossible to please absolutely everyone. There will always be someone disagreeing with you, slandering you or disputing with you. Even if you do the best that you are capable of, there will always be some-one dissatisfied with you, because you do not conform to his life values, desires and the method of their achievement.

"Do not doubt yourself, even with regard to your former partner. If you constantly try to extend the thread of the old relationship and believe that this time the other person will recognise your worth, you will only experience frustration again, because nothing you attempt may be sufficient to satisfy the other person. He will blame you again and you will start to fear, stop acting for yourself, let yourself be controlled by another. But this will condemn you to unhappiness, because others cannot know

what makes you happy. Only you know and feel this. So do not try to live according to others or demand from others to live according to you. This is the advice from me, your heart."

Think about what your heart is trying to tell you. What if you do not try to please other people, as this is unrealistic anyway? What if, instead of others, you try to please just one person? This might be feasible, don't you agree?

Are you asking: which one person?

The one who is the most important in your life.

Yourself.

If you are afraid to think of yourself, you will have an unacceptable feeling when you suddenly find yourself alone. You have been used to being beside someone since the cradle − even at the cost of obeying the other person. Some prefer to remain such children. They are ashamed of their authenticity, personal dreams, different opinions. But humanity lies precisely in vulnerability, emotions, and the minor imperfections that you can work on.

When you look at yourself in the mirror, you are a unique piece, precisely because of your authenticity and individuality. Each of us is 100 % original by nature. So dare to accept who you are. Decide to fulfil your dreams and follow the path your heart recommends. Do not seek only material benefit. No reward is big enough to suffice the soul, if it does not suffice the heart. Perhaps money can satisfy reason, but one can live without reason, not without heart.

Even if you feel like despairing after a break-up, it is because you do not realise the amazing zero point you are at. What should you first be aware of?

THE PERSON WHO IS WORTH PLEASING, WISHES YOU TO BE YOURSELF

Have you had a dispute with relatives or friends because of a break-up? Do they lack understanding? Are they not supportive? Do they make you feel that it is all your fault and that you will pay for it?

"*Joey, all we want is your happiness,*" parents say to the little boy.

"*Excellent,*" Joey replies, "*so what about letting me choose my own way?*", the bitter anecdote goes.

It is bitter, because it often reflects the reality. Think why parents forbid something to little Joeys? Why do they enforce their ways and impose their solutions, as if they had a patent not only for reason, but for the entire lives of their children?

Many parents behave as if they do not really want their children to be happy. Instead, the parents wish happiness only for themselves. These self-appointed directors of other people's lives turn their own children into obedient actors, even puppets. But it never lasts long. Smart kids soon discover that it is better to be criticised for who you are, than to be praised for who you are not. Relationships with friends and partners work in a similar way. That is also why a relationship that makes you feel better without changing you into someone else, works in the long term. How is it possible that you keep improving in such a relationship? It makes you better by developing your strong points. You remain the person you always were. Only thanks to the newly gained experience in areas where you feel good and certain (supported by the people around you), you naturally become wiser, more mature, simply, more perfect.

Real friends do not rope you into something of which you are uncertain. They respect and appreciate you merely for the ability to be yourself and insisting on your own way, with all the consequences, even the negative ones. They stand by you — and doubly so, if other people criticise your way.

Have you ever wondered why people have such a need to comment on and "*solve*" other people's problems? And why, in solving them, do they do so with mostly negative words? Because they do not know any other way of increasing their value relative to you, than by somehow degrading, debasing your own conduct. But do not bother about this. You cannot influence it, and it is not really your concern. After all, it is the problem of those people, not yours. Prove things to yourself, not to others. After all, no one else will live your life.

NOBODY ELSE KNOWS WHAT IS BEST FOR YOU, BUT THE HEART ALWAYS KNOWS THIS

It is sometimes a sad realisation. Even people you regarded as your best friends express doubt and amazement about the actions you choose. Please do not ever demand from others or strive for them to fully understand your choice. It is not feasible. Do not transfer this responsibility to your friends, because they often cannot understand. They have never followed the same path, were not in the same situation and do not have the same future as you ahead of them. Despite all their efforts, your friends cannot judge objectively, or even advise you effectively. Their opinion only has the intention of support for you. Nevertheless, it is just a shot in the dark. If you seek assurance, listen to yourself, to your heart, not to others. No intuition but your own will be with you until the end of your life.

Real friends should not feel the need for an explanation. They should stand by your decisions and support you unconditionally. Allow other people, that you do not rank as friends, to accept or reject your decision. It is their issue and decision which they make on the basis of their experience, ideas and values, and has no connection to your life. Even if your voice trembles when you face others, keep a steady pace. Whenever you follow your intuition, you will not make a mistake. The heart always chooses the best path to the goal. It does not have to be the easiest and it might lead over obstacles which must be overcome. But always trust your heart. It is normal to doubt whether you are on the right path. If you are in doubt, obstacles will seem a bit bigger than those encountered before. You may stumble over them, make mistakes. But allow your imperfection to teach you how to grow and to learn.

This is the only way to self-confidence. Every person grows with the awareness that he can stumble, but also get up again. The most important thing is that you are able to walk ahead, without begging for the approval of others. Yes, this is self-confidence.

YOU ARE THE ONLY PERSON WHO CAN EFFECTIVELY CHANGE YOUR LIFE

If somebody around you lectures you that you should not have left your ex and similar errors, pay no attention to it. This is true for every person: only you can change your life. Either by changing the situation bothering you, or by changing your attitude and dealing with it. Everything you are able to achieve in life is independent of the opinions of other people, on what they think you should do. Everything depends on your management of your time and energy.

There will always be people around you who will be *"absolutely certain"* of what is best for you, who will believe they are more authorised to make decisions about your life than you, who believe that everyone must share the same views of values such as happiness and success. Throw these people to the wind. You have your own values and ideas about life.

Whatever your decision is, it is yours, just like life. There is no dream you cannot attempt to realise. There are no limits to what you can achieve. And there is only one person who can reliably stop you. You.

LIFE IS NOT A RACE

*D*o not break up with him. Your biological clock is ticking. You must... you must not. Do you sometimes hear such instructions from adults? However, there is one truth which cannot be denied. Life indeed gets shorter with every passing moment, although this does not mean that you should fear change. On the contrary, there is no time to be wasted.

Many people mistakenly believe that life is a race. That they must reach the mountain peak as quickly as possible to be known as mountain climbers. They forget that growth and success in any area do not happen at the finish, but along the way. If life were a race, the winner would be the first to reach the graveyard. Neither is a relationship about achieving a goal, but about having a satisfactory journey. You can be happy every day for the rest of your life with the right partner, but you must find such a person.

So let your everyday path become your goal.

Why should you only want to be happy on the last day of your life, if you can already live your life according to your own values now and forever more?

OBSTACLES ARE NOT IN YOUR WAY, OBSTACLES ARE THE WAY

A break-up is an obstacle in life. Overcoming it results in experience and a lesson. With every overcome obstacle, you eliminate one mistaken action in your life. Overcoming obstacles is the meaning of life.

There is no guidebook to life. All of us must attempt to find out what works and what does not. People's preferences differ. But it applies to everybody that trying is part of the process of success. So is failure. To look like a fool is the only possible way ahead. You will feel like a fool after parting with a long-term partner. Loss of time, mockery, taunts, negative prognoses. Smile at those. After all, each overcome obstacle moves you a bit closer to your goal, you gradually get to know the way. Do not be afraid to fail publicly. Because if somebody minds losing in the eyes of others, he probably is incapable of taking the steps needed to win in his own eyes.

Learn to be cool about your mistakes. Understand their message. Mistakes teach you the way over obstacles. To walk more easily through life. To avoid mistakes the next time.

Mistakes do not teach you to discover an obstacle-free path. Indeed, there is no such path. They teach you to overcome the obstacles which you thought would destroy you.

THERE IS NO PLEASING EVERYONE WITH EVERYTHING

A break-up is an effective filter of friends. It teaches you to delete from your life the people who suddenly have a lot to say about what you did wrong, and somehow forget what you did right. Do not try to pander to them, ingratiate yourself or seek appreciation from persons who discredit or humiliate you. Leave them far behind with their assumptions and opinions, because time devoted to negative people is always a waste.

No, you cannot please everyone, and even less can you satisfy negative people. So don't pay attention to what they spit out at you.

HOW TO COPE WITH PEOPLE CLOSE TO YOU: WHY YOU SHOULD BEWARE OF SO-CALLED GOOD INTENTIONS AND ADVICE

Sometimes, the indiscreet word of a stranger makes you feel hatred in your heart. More precisely: In YOUR heart.

Yes, due to outside evil, the evil settles within you.

Try to avoid having any negativity within.

Because negatives are a burden.

They only burden you, not others.

But finally you need to lighten your life.

For that matter, let me tell you about a former classmate of mine.

At first, he obeyed his parents – believing that he had no sense as he was underage. Then he equally consistently obeyed his professors – believing that without a degree he was stupid and inferior in comparison to them. Finally, he doggedly obeyed his employer – believing that he was not entitled to his own opinion or life as an employee.

Unfortunately, my former classmate somehow lost himself along the way. All the time he had taken heed of the people around him, never of himself. Eventually he had a physical breakdown. His body, which he had been neglecting, made out the bill for him. In the intensive care unit, where I visited him, he berated himself for

243

having lived according to others for so long: *"Every morning I got up with a single worry – what is expected from me today?"*

Remember this story well. The man's happiness depended on other people's moods and judgements. Perhaps you have already realised that living according to others means a mere existence from day to day, not a life spent in compliance with your self. But it seemed inappropriate to you to stand on your own legs and to follow the path which appealed the most to you. For the first time in your life actually, without the approval of parents, teachers, employer or partner.

Maybe it is happening right now that you feel vulnerable and the people around you would like to take control of you – under the pretence of helpfulness and good intentions. The following laws will clarify why you should avoid such assistance, for the sake of your own life, as well as that of a future relationship.

YOU HAVE NO MORAL OR LEGAL OBLIGATION TO LIVE ACCORDING TO OTHERS

Now our patience is over. You will do what we say. You are our child.

Sounds familiar? Well, let's make this point clear:

At the moment of birth, you did not conclude any agreement with life, which would force life to continue as you would like. Neither are you obliged in adulthood to live according to another person, regardless of kinship.

Especially in the case of parents and relatives, do what you consider right. You will actually relieve them, as they will not be burdened and stressed by advising you about something they cannot ultimately influence.

Whenever people close to you offer their kind-hearted mentoring, be fair to them and do not expose them to the responsibility for your life. Likewise, do not curse life for being harsh and for things not going according to what you had imagined. Time will show you that life plotted everything well and acted for your benefit.

Be thankful for every experience. And the most dearly paid for experiences contain unforgettable lessons.

YOU DO NOT NEED ANYONE TO HOLD YOUR HAND AT EVERY STEP

Even when surrounded by a bunch of counsellors, you still walk alone. Which is good, because learning to walk on your own steam means learning how to be independent. This comes in useful. People who start running with you might not be with you at the finish. However nice it is to cheer for someone, one must not forget about your own life and path. So remind your advisors that they must take action in their own lives, not in yours. They might use the time devoted to you for themselves.

Everybody is responsible for his own life. In a family too. A family is like a relay race. Runners in relays do not finish together. Everyone is responsible for his own sector. That is, both in practice and performance. Thank your family for their care and willingness to be there for you. But if they are not running in your relay, their place is on the stands. That is, in the part of the stadium which does not interfere in the path of the runners.

DO NOT TAKE CATASTROPHIC VISIONS PERSONALLY

Anybody can hold any opinion of your person and of what you are doing. This is a reality. But their opinion is influenced not only by genes and experience, but also by the moods and the immediate attitude of your critics. These factors are so variable that the same person can view the same thing absolutely contrarily shortly afterwards. It depends especially on how he feels. His thoughts are created according to his feelings. For a person in a bad mood, you will be a hopeless case. For the same person in a good mood, you will be a hopeful case. His judgements are based specifically on him alone.

If a stranger were to evaluate you objectively, he would have to know the whole mosaic of your life. Not just one piece. If somebody knows your current situation, he might not know the whole history. Nobody was present at each and every step and stumble you took, did not witness your dreams and the worries that influenced you, did not go with you through your internal battles that constructed your thoughts, as well as your deeds and experiences.

Nobody but you can know the whole truth about yourself. So another can hardly advise you successfully. Moreover, you do not even need anyone like that. You know very well who you are, what you've been through, what you deserve and what is the best for you at every moment.

ONLY YOU CAN DETERMINE WHAT IS POSSIBLE FOR YOU

Every life decision is in your thoughts. It does not concern what others see in you, but how you feel, what feelings are produced by your thoughts. Of course, everybody falters sometimes, and needs a shoulder to cry on, to receive the support and opinion of another person. But be prepared to hear anything from others. Even that you are a waste of time.

It is up to you whether to believe what others say. Try to draw your own conclusions, rather than being limited by other people's assumptions of your limitations. After all, only you can determine what you can do, by attempting it.

EXPERIENCE GAINED LEADS TO HIGHER STANDARDS

Sometimes people around you seem to enjoy throwing around their opinions about the end of your relationship. Even if the relationship has been bad. They are worried that you are in a vicious circle and that the next relationship will be equally bad, or even worse. But do not fall prey to the same panic, everything only depends on your attitude.

A normal person works on the basis of perpetual improvement. A child who learns to ride a bike and falls, keeps trying until he can ride it confidently. A relationship ended with the wrong partner usually leads to a subconscious setting of the warning bounds beyond which you do not intend to proceed so as not to waste any more time. This means that only such partners who are on a higher level than the former partner will pass through such a sieve. Therefore, contrary to your panicking friends, you need not worry that you will be worse off in the next relationship. This will only be possible if you allow your self-confidence to be diminished by the former partner or other people.

Here is an example from another area: When leaving a bad job, if somebody makes you believe that you are inadequate, that you made a mistake and will not find anything better and should accept anything, under this pressure you might accept even inferior employment or a lower salary than you had before. This tactic is used by numerous employers during negotiations. They put psychological pressure on an applicant for the purpose of decreasing the employee's salary and trying to convince him that there are cheaper applicants for the position. The trick is mendacious, but the end justifies the means.

Beware of what others tell you. And pay special attention to who says it. People who really love and care about your contentment know how important it is to follow

your own path. The chain reaction applies: Stop living according to others = learn responsibility for your own decisions. Be responsible for your own decisions = stop making excuses. Stop making excuses = get nearer to your own goals, not further away.

STOP CONFORMING TO OTHERS, THE HATERS WILL DISAPPEAR

You perceive what you focus on. As long as you care about the opinions of others, you hear those who express negative views. Haters are particularly vociferous, those programmed critics of all who actively strive for positive change.

However, take note of what happens to the haters when you stop monitoring your surroundings and start to live according to yourself. The number and volume of haters begin to decrease until they gradually disappear. They have not gone anywhere. There will always be haters around you – there will be more, the more successful you are. But the less attention you pay to them, the less effect they will have on your actions. It is either – or. Either they overpower and knock you down, or you push them out of your mind and soar ahead. Haters will never disappear. They keep lurking around, hoping for someone's weakness to destroy him. But this does not have to bother you. It is their problem. They do not exist for you.

FIND MORE TIME FOR THE RIGHT PEOPLE

f you erase the haters and those who generally try to manipulate you, bad persons will be reduced to make way for better people. It will not be difficult to find them. A life which unwinds as you choose contains less drama. It lacks the drama prepared by other people's expectations that you cannot satisfy. When you become responsible only for yourself, astonishingly you will register a growing number of like-minded persons in your surroundings. They will accept you for the way you are, and appreciate you for what you have, and not condemn you for what you have not. It seems like magic, but it is not.

Sometimes people yield to the illusion that the world is getting better. But it is only the immediate environment. Every person is the average of the five persons with whom he spends the most time. If you surround yourself with more positive and quality people, you will begin to grow yourself. And in turn, attract even more successful people who appeal to you, or vice versa. The environment has an enormous influence on people, and this again only concerns focusing on the right persons. Their number is not increasing, you have just begun to focus on them more. Just as you have begun to pay less or no attention to the haters.

HOW TO HAVE THE OPTIMAL RELATIONSHIP WITH YOURSELF AND THOSE CLOSEST TO YOU: HOW TO FIND THE BEST FRIEND IN YOURSELF

People around you can help, support, advise you. But ultimately, you must cope on your own with a new situation, solitude. You have to reconcile yourself especially to what are known as anchors.

The past is not cut off at all times. A former partner can call, try to revive the relationship, beg or threaten impressively. This period of fading echoes is your test. Your ex may want you to return to what once was. But it is not in your interest to return to something bad. That would be a step backwards.

You need to move ahead. To build something new, more reliable. For this you must especially take an internal inventory. How do you do this? Firstly, you must discover what is left of you.

And you must refresh the meaningful values trampled on by the former partner. You need to become yourself again. Because only in this way can you be the most important person, the best friend, to yourself.

How do you find the self which you have lost? How do you allow yourself to trust future relationship decisions, if the previous relationship has crashed?

How can you believe in yourself to take at least small steps, if so far you have been used to obeying a partner's wishes? How do you rely on yourself again after a long time?

These crucial questions can devour you.

But you must not allow this to happen.

Firstly, you have to return to the model that you, and only you, are responsible for your life decisions. You are responsible for your actions. This sounds unpleasant, not everybody wishes this. They would rather pass the buck. But responsibility for yourself means realising the strength you have. The strength to control your life. The possibility to set a positive course. Indeed, it is just a matter of positive thoughts and deeds.

The equation is simple: you will be happy if you start doing what makes you happy. And you will grow if you do the best you can. This is not difficult. Just keep comparing your present-day version with yesterday's and strive for your tomorrow's self to be better than today's.

People fear loneliness after a break-up. But this period is useful, as it provides the time and space to think more about yourself. You will brush up the relationship which is the most important and intimate in everybody's life: the relationship with yourself. In brief, you pull yourself together. And then you start seeking out a new relationship. But to be beneficial for the new partner and to enter the relationship with a positive self-image and self-confidence, you yourself must be strong and healthy. It may sound egoistic, but have no doubt: putting yourself first is the best selfish thing you can do for others (prospectively).

Because only someone stable on his own can be a person who is supportive of others. And of a partner.

In order to achieve this, it is necessary to comply with the following laws:

UNDERTAKE NOT TO USE THE PAST AGAINST YOURSELF

Anyone can denounce, denigrate, besmirch you. It is more important that you have one person you can rely on under any circumstances. A person who will not leave you till the end of your life. Everybody can have such a person. Who is it? You, of course.

Whenever you stop seeking the best friend around you and start looking within yourself, life becomes easier and fairer. The first step is to move from the place in which you feel bad. Free yourself from the negative words other people usually use in their efforts to persuade you of what you can or cannot do. These people like to base their judgements on the past. They claim that you may never achieve what you have failed to achieve to date (to find the ideal partner). The contrary is true. If you manage to learn from the past, then all previous failures, weaknesses, regrets and mistakes will help you to move ahead. And vice versa, if you are unwilling to understand the lesson, the past will keep on hurting you. What people like to call "*Fate*" is actually a matter of personal choice.

Bear in mind that your decision makes an immediate difference. The first decision might seem crazy: allow your failures to teach you. Yes, let the mistakes you fear become your teachers – on a daily basis, if necessary. But be careful that you don't use the mistakes against yourself. Do not blame yourself for previously having been stupid. At the time of making the mistake, you did the best you could. You lacked the knowledge and experience you have today. Sure, if you could make the decision again now, you would find a different, wiser solution. But do not forget that it is thanks to these mistakes that you are wiser today. You grow and mature from making mistakes.

Retrospectively, you always seem small and immature to yourself. You frown at your past image. But this is childish. On the contrary, a backward look should please you. Because it shows how much you have grown since that time. You have learned to accept better solutions. Therefore, thank the past for the mistakes made.

It taught you to reconsider and to live a better life.

UNDERTAKE NOT TO RENOUNCE RESPONSIBILITY FOR YOUR LIFE

I do not make mistakes. This is how people speak who make the biggest mistakes. They do not accept responsibility for their lives. They rejoice at how they have outsmarted others. But they did not outsmart themselves.

If you deny the responsibility for your own life, you reduce your ability to move ahead with your life in any way. But nobody else can do it in your stead. Rather learn to behave like the stained glass windows in churches. As long as the sun is shining outdoors, the colourful pieces of glass reflect its glitter and gloss. Like a person everybody is smiling at. However, at nightfall, they preserve the glitter and brightness. Like the illuminated interior of a place of worship.

Your inner light is your faith in yourself.

Your responsibility for your own future.

UNDERTAKE TO LIVE ONLY A LIFE WHICH SEEMS RIGHT TO YOU, NOT TO OTHERS

Whenever you decide to create happiness in your own way, you will strike the resistance of others. Because your ideas will undoubtedly collide with the plans of other people, especially those who have different, their own plans, in store for you.

These people mostly want you to help them create their own happiness. So be it. But ask one key question: Who will then create your happiness?

Do not ask others for formal permission to follow your own path. Otherwise you will be needlessly disappointed. Because you will hear only discouragement from them, claims that what you have chosen is not the right path. These people may not feel that they are lying. It may be their truth, for which they would be willing to take an oath. It stems from their own convictions. If you look at it from their viewpoint, you will understand them. Because logically, your way cannot be the right way for them. They have their way with which they are in absolute concord and about which they feel happy. They must resist, contest and misjudge your way.

Or must they? Of course not.

If they are wise enough, they will understand that, just as your way is not suitable for them, you would not feel 100 percent happy and confident in theirs.

And if the opinions of people who care about you begin to diverge fundamentally from yours, ask yourself this question: Me or them? According to whom do you want to live your life?

I am not thrusting the reply on you.

But assume responsibility for your answer.

UNDERTAKE NOT TO PROLONG A RELATIONSHIP THAT HAS CEASED TO SUIT YOU

Never doubt that everybody who enters your path in life is there to teach you something. And it is for you to learn a lesson from them. Sometimes a person arrives and departs. The difference that remains is your experience. That's it, he was not supposed to provide any more. And he deserves thanks for it. Everyone was definitely not born to remain in your life forever. Many are not able to give you any more, even if they serve beyond retirement age.

That is why not all relationships that you build last for a lifetime. Their duration is limited. Nevertheless, the experience they provided will remain forever.

Do not regret spending time with somebody who turned out not to be part of your future. This discovery is one of the ways of becoming convinced about the end of such a relationship. Everything in life has its positive influence. At any moment, you are exactly where you should be right now, to have the present experience and to learn to deal with it in the future.

UNDERTAKE NOT TO ALLOW ANY SITUATION TO END YOUR SMILE FOREVER

There is one general rule: whenever you are at the bottom, bounce back with a smile. The difficulty of a specific situation actually does not matter. And the most difficult situations form the strongest people. This is because these people start from scratch. So they evaluate what is the most important to them in the long run, their key priorities. They build on those foundations.

The basic priorities of probably all people include peace and quiet.

People recover where they feel good, most often with friends and those closest to them. Our environment is usually the only place in the world where we are absolutely immune to our suffering. This is where we recharge our batteries and realise that nothing is as amazing and strengthening as a smile which was born through tears.

Do not forget about this retreat, even when your situation improves. Do not succumb to the illusion that you are all right. Nobody can be happy in the long term if everything goes smoothly. Because then people stop to revere happiness. Fortunately, wise Mother Nature functions in waves and change. High tide and low tide, day and night, alternating seasons. Human heart, thoughts, blood... are all pulsating. That is why the road to happiness begins with a misfortune. And happiness is appreciated most by someone who has toiled for it.

UNDERTAKE TO REVERE THE LIFE YOU HAVE

Too many people place too high a value on what they do not have, and undervalue what they do have. They talk as if life has behaved unfairly. But life is very just. For everything you lose, you gain something else. That is why you should not only count your failures and losses, but also the lessons and gains. Being positive costs nothing and yet it can change a life immeasurably. How? You realise that you can absolutely control your thoughts. Just decrease your efforts and appreciate the life you are leading right now.

UNDERTAKE THAT YOU WILL IMPROVE

Y ou may ask: *For whom must I do this if I am alone?* The answer is clear: *Both for yourself and the person you will be with sooner or later!*

Everything in life that is worth doing, is worth doing properly. Work you do on yourself is never a waste of time and is beneficial for the future relationship or family. And the fact that you have no one for whom you should get better? Remember: you do not put a life jacket on only after you start drowning.

If you are just not in the mood to improve, then you are in most need of it right now. Follow this procedure: Set a slightly unreachable goal. A goal slightly above your upper limit. It will force you to stand on tiptoes, stretch up, jump or strain your muscles to reach the goal. And when you do, increase the goal some more. Keep forcing yourself to improve.

Do not measure what you have achieved by your present position, but by looking back at the distance you have already covered from the start. This is your development, your growth. This achievement will always please and motivate you, regardless of the starting position. Because success is primarily about advancement and persistence.

Self-improvement can eventually fulfil your whole life. Indeed, after a break-up, working on yourself and enjoying all the little pleasures you had no time for in the relationship is one of the most effective and pleasant remedies.

PAIN THAT IS SO DEEP THAT YOU CANNOT EASILY RISE ABOVE IT

Life is like a book. It has many chapters. One sad chapter does not mean the whole book is sad. In most cases, sad chapters are not at the end either. They are only part of the plot and serve to advance the story.

The only thing you can do when reading sad chapters is to realise that to move ahead in the story, it is unnecessary to read the sad chapter from the beginning again.

All you need to do is turn the page. And start reading the new chapter. To draw a cover over what was, and focus on what might happen.

After all, a book need not be funny the whole time to make you smile at the end. The opposite is true. The sweetest punchline comes after overcoming all the sad chapters in life.

As a boy, I once looked out of the window of our flat. On the street, a couple captured my attention. They were laughing, embracing and enjoying one other's presence.

They were the parents of my friend.

Divorced for three years.

It took them three years to overcome their trivial disputes and start to see and appreciate each other's uniqueness.

They would not become life partners again.

Because they did not need that to understand and support one another again.

. . .

Every step you take means experience. If you maintain a positive outlook, failure practically does not exist. What we usually call failure is just a topic for reflection, to lead to change and perfection. Whether we want it or not, life, which we like to curse so often, does not take sides. Fortunately. It keeps pushing us ahead, to another place. It liberates us from the past with every new morning, each new event. Of course, time solves many troubles. But time is too scarce to leave the healing from our mistakes only to it. Add an additional ingredient to the recipe, your own effort. Respect the following laws, because they will rescue you from the swamp of the four fiercest pains that do not want to leave you...

THE FIRST SOLITUDE THAT IS TOO DEEP: WITH CHILDREN.
HOW TO SET THE BEST POSSIBLE EXAMPLE

It is so easy to break down. To be the victim. To vent your anger on children. To share with them problems they don't understand, or are not their concern. It is necessary to do something with this weakness.

However, this weakness does not erupt only after a break-up. It emerges earlier, and if you care about children as much as you like to say you do, abide by the following laws. If you are ever left alone with the children, you have the opportunity to focus better on these recommendations. This section is for parents who are inclined to preach to their children.

Let's start with the opinion of French writer Honoré de Balzac: "*Nothing hurts children more than life unlived by their parents.*" Yes, it is very easy to issue commands to children: "*Don't be naughty. Don't disturb. Don't talk back. Don't lie. Don't laze around. Don't smoke. Don't drink alcohol. Don't take drugs. Don't attract attention.*" Parents like to issue instructions starting with DON'T, because parents always know best what children should not do. Fine, so the children will not do it. But what next? What should the children do?

Also after a break-up a parent knows well what he should not do. But no movement forward is possible by inaction. In order to set a positive example (especially at times when life is not going well), the parent must first change his attitude. He must realise that life is neither positive nor negative. You control this. In fact, how many times in life has it happened to you that something that had crushed you originally,

after a while brought a smile to your face? The reason is not that the event changed. What changed is your attitude.

A parent should never forget that anything in life can be seen in a positive as well as in a negative context. Our frustrations stem especially from our mood and reaction, not from the nature of the circumstances we are experiencing. If you are in a bad mood, even something trivial can be a serious setback, but if you are in a good mood, you can cope with even the worst news. Any event can be seen as half completed. Nothing is final, only presented for completion – by your approach.

You can always smile at the end. No matter how dismal the present is, it will soon become the past. What is now will soon turn into what was. Therefore, learn to live positively. So that your children acquire this skill too, regardless of circumstances.

WHAT YOU EXPERIENCE COMES PRIMARILY FROM WHAT YOU EXPECT

---

*S*eek cones in the forest.

And you will find fewer mushrooms.

Focus on negatives in life.

And you will almost stop seeing the positives.

The controller of your thoughts and reality is your brain. Your life consists of what the brain focuses on – not because there is no other alternative, but because it does not perceive any other reality. The brain is a diligent worker.

So if you start focusing on pleasant things, life will become more beautiful. And on the contrary, whenever you poison this vision, you will experience a day of constant misery. Everything will collapse around you. You may try to blame the day, while the actual culprit is yourself. How could the negative feelings and thoughts create positive deeds? This is the whole problem. The reason why we are inefficient.

Feelings rule our lives more than we admit. And our emotions are triggered by expectations. Often we feel dissatisfied when we have high demands. But just look around and you will see that things you complain about so often are the same things that most people in this world would love to have.

Try to bring up your children with this attitude. Examples of modesty will definitely do no harm. Especially if you have to cut back on your expenses after a break-up, and also have to be less generous towards pampered children.

So do not spoil your children too much. They should not be rewarded/compensated by gifts just because you are not successful in a relationship. Children are part of

you and must share your fate, even if they have not done anything wrong. Economising will be a useful lesson in life for them too. Not to mention that they will also be helping you to ease the financial burden and the feelings of guilt that you are not making up sufficiently for the problems your former partner caused.

A POSITIVE OUTLOOK ALWAYS PAYS OFF

Under all circumstances, set a positive example for children. Teach them that no ideas are lost as long as you keep them in mind. And no dream ends, as long as you do not give it up permanently.

Men with a positive outlook find it easier to apply this principle – thanks to their ego, which does not allow them to abandon their great dreams too soon. Women find it harder to remain positive; they must learn to relax and to laugh. To laugh (with children) as often as they can.

Laughter is the great medicine that we always carry within ourselves. It changes the whole being of the body. Thanks to laughter, you feel better immediately. You go through the present more happily, regardless of its nature. And you look at the future with more hope and enthusiasm, although what it holds is uncertain.

Imagine negative emotions – especially pessimism, anger, hatred and envy – as a heavy black cloak, which you cannot see through and which does not allow you to do anything positive. However, a positive outlook is the only way to escape from feelings of pessimism, anger, hate and envy. As well as from fear, the biggest thief of time. Fear steals everything, including happiness and joyful expectations, and makes you very busy, doing nothing useful. The mind is only occupied by the imagination, which creates non-existing scenarios.

However, children especially should know that people who have no problems do not improve either. They feel no urge to develop, get better, overcome obstacles. Remaining in one spot without moving, like a sailboat on a windless ocean, means not gaining any new experience, not going beyond anything in the past.

That is why you must not despair when you have had a failure. Do not write complaints, the complaints department of life is already full and does not accept any new ones. Rather learn from the problems. And do not underestimate yourself, even if you feel you can hardly breathe. You can endure much more than you think.

WASTING TIME TAKES AS MUCH ENERGY AS MAKING GOOD USE OF TIME

People can be tired from too much activity, as well as from too much idleness. A sport that uses excessive energy also gives back in excess – in the form of hormones, enthusiasm, a feeling of satisfaction. The difference between doing the right thing and doing the easy thing is seen in the reward.

What fulfils you is usually not easy. Because the way to get energy is first to be drained of it. But we release different types of energy. Positive energy brings you nearer to the kind of person you want to be. Negative energy takes you further from who you are. Therefore energy management is crucial – engage in activities that give meaning and correspond to your values (and to the person you want to be). Give out the best, positive energy, and you receive it in return.

Children know this from birth. They ignore goals they do not enjoy, and do not continue in activities that do not recharge them. They live by the activities that prevent them from falling asleep at night, and make them jump out of bed early in the morning. Children are wise in terms of energy efficiency. Parents would be able to learn from them.

WHAT YOU DO NOT TRY, YOU CANNOT ACHIEVE

Unsuccessful people claim that those who have succeeded must have had a lot of luck, talent, help from others and favourable circumstances. But they forget about the most basic thing: luck, talent or help would be of no use to the man who does not try. Yes, everything we have ever achieved is primarily the result of the effort we put into it. Even children cannot learn a foreign language unless they are exposed to conditions in which they can learn it.

There is a fundamental difference between wanting and acting. Those who act, believe in their success and the value of their intentions. That is why they are successful. Life rewards action, not mere desires. What is the good of an ingenious idea if there is no implementation?

Those who attempt something and are successful are those who are not put off by failure at the first attempt. They know that every effort they put in leads to greater understanding. Whether you succeed or not, you will see the next step. Success is really nothing but the patient overcoming of mistakes, until the last one disappears. If you accept the lessons and persist in your effort, you will stop making mistakes one day. Therefore you must succeed.

So, like children, make sure you always have some goals that keep you motivated. Goals are like fireflies in a tunnel – always one step ahead, so they illuminate your path. Objectives that are constantly set a little higher are a precondition to success. Because if you consider the achieved goal to be sufficient and desire no more, you would have nothing to grow for, and you would stop improving. On the contrary, if a goal is just out of reach, it will not lose its appeal. You will continue to progress toward it, albeit only in small steps.

Therefore, let us teach children that the way to success is like a sport in which you are your own opponent.

OTHER PEOPLE'S OPINIONS ARE NOT THE REALITY

Allow people to give you information, but not to limit you. Be yourself. Give children an example of how to deal with others.

If others call you a fool, remember that is their problem. What is impossible for them can be possible for you. You can achieve things that others cannot even imagine. There are two types of limits you should be aware of. Do not break the law, but do not hesitate to push human limits. Possibilities cannot be restricted. Homo sapiens has already achieved too many impossible things to limit people today. So rather provide opportunities and support for your children, so that you improve their strengths despite a negative environment – let them go beyond the borders of what can only be imagined.

The opinions of others actually only inform you about themselves. Nothing more. Everything in life only has the meaning that you assign to it. What you feel is right, is right for you. What you feel is bad, is bad for you. In simple terms, your reality is formed by the way you perceive it. So respect the views of children for their perception of a world that is different from yours. Guide them on their way, but let them create their lives on their own.

Children are not copies of us, they are originals. They do not have the same DNA as we do. So approach them as partners. Understand and appreciate their unique value. Although they differ from you, you can form an amazing tandem, where the differences complement each other.

So let us be team players with children, despite our different angles of viewing the game. But let us not be adversaries.

IF YOU ACCEPT YOUR IMPERFECTIONS, THEY WILL STOP UNDERMINING YOU

You know it. And children even more so.

Each child has different strengths and weaknesses. Children who are thoughtless ridicule other children who are different from them. Without realising that everyone has something someone else lacks. And everyone lacks something someone else has. Nobody is perfect, nobody has everything.

Even adults feel bad when ridiculed by others. It is much harder for children who are quite aware that they do not have certain things that others have. But the solution is simple: accept your imperfections. When you do this and reconcile yourself with your wrinkles and your scars, nobody will be able to hurt you by pointing them out. These people will have to find something else about you that they think is different – which you will also be able to neutralise.

Accepting your own weaknesses is a process that has never hurt anyone. Nor can it – both our strengths and weaknesses define us. Thanks to them, we learn who we are. We even realise that we do not have to have the talent to do everything. Nobody has the talent to do everything.

Accepting ourselves in this way should especially concern the future – all the mistakes we made in the past and all the decisions we made and now regret are past, they cannot be undone. Simply accept this as a fact and start with a clean slate. Do not give up today just because of what happened yesterday.

Let's teach children not only to enjoy results, but also the journey toward achieving them. Let them appreciate every milestone reached along the way. It will not matter if these milestones are not their goal, the important thing is that they are on the right path.

THE SECOND SOLITUDE THAT IS TOO DEEP: IN YOUR JOB.
HOW NOT TO BECOME AN OBSTACLE

Why is man the most powerful creature on Earth?

Is he the biggest?

Strongest?

Most numerous?

Or the fastest?

No, none of these. Yet he rules.

All animals are afraid of man. Because he is unpredictable. He can destroy any species of flora or fauna he chooses to. He has even started destroying himself. How strange.

He does many things that are not really necessary.

He attacks without actually being threatened.

Man is so erratic that he even does things he does not want to do. He turns weapons from Mother Nature against himself.

Such as thinking and speech.

The problem is that this can harm others when he needs them, and can harm himself too, despite there being more than enough personal catastrophes.

And a job brings its own challenges.

Break-ups are risky because they cause us to lose concentration, to lose sight of the goal. We feel sorry for ourselves, harm ourselves with negative feelings and cannot switch to constructive behaviour. This can have a negative impact on our work. Because nobody pays you for being unproductive. And no employer or colleagues can be found guilty of things you cannot deal with yourself.

And there is another unpleasant fact: if you are to change your life positively, you must learn to make decisions quickly. Not to postpone thorny problems but solve them. But what if you do not have the strength? Work can be an amazing tonic for someone drowning in personal problems. Contact with other people can clear your mind. Look at things in a new light. But if you do not have the right approach, it can lead to you being discharged, because you are unable to perform your job after the break-up. How do you avoid this?

The Gospel of John starts with one of the most famous biblical verses: *"In the beginning was the Word, and the Word was with God, and the Word was God."* Words have immense power. If they are positive, they can evoke positive feelings, positive feelings lead to positive thoughts, positive thoughts give rise to positive actions and positive actions bring positive results. You have to put yourself back on your feet by proper words directed both at your colleagues and at yourself.

Because words are energy too. Positive words dissolve negative ones. Their places can be filled with new positive ones that often flow back in the form of appreciation from the other side.

DO NOT HESITATE TO USE THE SENTENCE:

"Finally I managed to start."

The hardest thing with every change is to overcome the moment when you do not want to change anything. You can have plans, goals, ideas. But if you do not start carrying them out, you will actually have nothing.

At the beginning, there is immense energy contained in zeal, hope, faith. Fear and doubts urge us to be cautious. By going ahead despite fear of the unknown and failure, you require a huge amount of positive energy for your intentions to succeed in the face of the fear and doubts. So do not avoid new beginnings. More so at work, when your personal life clouds the issues. Look forward to the beautiful word – finally. Yes, the first step is the hardest.

It must be.

Because this one is the longest.

From nothing to something.

DO NOT HESITATE TO USE THE SENTENCE:

"It is all my fault."

We are sensitive after a break-up. And when we are sensitive, we are irritated. We tend to take everything as personal and deliberately unfair. Even at work.

The period after a break-up is especially difficult because you do not stop being human. And it is human to make mistakes. On the one hand, sensitive people have a whip at hand to blame and besmirch colleagues for making a mistake at work – just so that a little of the mud and grime of personal life, with which the colleagues have nothing to do, gets stuck on them. On the other hand, you can have the opposite situation when someone waits to reproach you for a mistake. A suitable opportunity will always arise. So how should you react in this sensitive period?

In the first case: Do not blame others.

In the second case: Keep a detached view and learn to admit your mistakes. There is no shame in making a mistake. A mistake is an indispensable precondition for progress. But not every man develops, even though every man makes mistakes. Why is this so?

Because if you are to improve, you must eliminate the mistake.

To eliminate it, you must first be aware of it.

And to be aware of it, you must admit it to yourself.

It is only thanks to this mistake chain that you can focus on being smarter, faster, more creative next time – that is, simply better.

Therefore, in progressive companies, the people who are the most appreciated are those who, in petty matters, can even admit to a mistake that they themselves did not make. By this action, they show that they can rise above the small-minded search for someone to blame and save this time by working on the job at hand. So ensure that the team is made aware that identifying one specific individual to bear the blame is not a necessity. Focus on the positive.

DO NOT HESITATE TO USE THE SENTENCE:

"It was not as bad as I thought it would be."

Man can be paralysed by fear of the unknown. Logically. If it is a familiar situation, you know how to face it. In that situation, you are not afraid in the real sense, you are only nervous about whether you can do it, or can do it even better than before.

The biggest paradox is that most of the fears of the unknown are never realised. And if they are, in most cases the consequences are not as bad as the catastrophe you imagined. To overcome the fear of the unknown, you only need to step up to it. The fear will disappear, and you will be like a bobsleigh rider who rebounds from the top of the wall and has no time to face fear because he must act. At that moment, he usually finds his natural abilities, and he learns quickly from the situation.

If you do what you were most afraid of, it almost always turns out to be not as bad as you expected. And, often, the reality is even exciting. Not only because of the actual experience, but especially because of the fear overcome. Internal satisfaction strengthens our self-confidence, which is one of our most essential qualities. The new self-confidence can even lead us to repeating the attempt or to finding other fears to conquer.

This is a very effective medicine after a break-up.

DO NOT HESITATE TO USE THE SENTENCE:

"Wait, I'll show you."

This is heard jokingly among friends as an overstatement, but it can also be used seriously. After all, competition ('competitive environment', the term is called in business) is the best nourishment for any growth. If you stop resisting and measure your strength against others, whether at work or outside it, these competitive events will not only be entertaining, but will also bring to the fore positive features and abilities that are suppressed during negative moods.

Horses are urged forward by spurring to the underbelly. People too, for that matter. To make someone feel that he is defeated, left behind and losing, triggers the same reaction. His effort then is to prove that this is not true. Eventually, the question of the bet or size of the enemy do not matter. It is important to realise that, as with external stimuli, we can motivate ourselves from the inside. We have the ability to return blows that did not actually happen and existed only in our imagination. This is called self-motivation. In the sensitive stage after a break-up, this time-tested strategy of successful people who do not need any opponents can boost our self-discipline.

DO NOT HESITATE TO USE THE SENTENCE:

"I am doing something nobody else has dared to do."

If you want to change your life, you must take a different path from people before you. All innovative projects at work are arranged like this. If somebody wants to move ahead, he must go places no one else has gone before. He has no idea what awaits him there. On the other hand, he knows that merely stepping into the unknown takes him further than someone who remained standing in one place, too frightened to move.

If you are not given the opportunity to participate in such projects at work, you could even try at home, for example, writing with a pencil held in your mouth, or writing backwards. Regardless of how unusual, or even impractical, the attempt is, it is important to realise that repeated practice actually leads to a skill that is unique throughout the world. You are doing something that nobody before you has ever done, and with every new attempt you are doing it better. If you look at yourself in the mirror, you will not see anything special. It is the same you all the time. And yet you are a person who is unique, who has no match. It is good to remind yourself that steps to new horizons are no more difficult than ordinary steps that are taken on a daily basis. On the contrary, with each new discovery you are acquiring experience. It is sometimes even amusing. This is fine. After all, there are never enough smiles.

DO NOT HESITATE TO USE THE SENTENCE:

"It is not perfect, but it is good."

We only have one chance to make a first impression in life. So each of us wants to make the first attempt look perfect. Sometimes perfection is the only thing we accept for ourselves. But then of course we torment ourselves all our lives because we cannot accept being imperfect. That we cannot be like it is in romantic movies. The workplace is a useful environment where one can get rid of such obsessions with perfection.

Because no man is perfect, no product or service invented by man can be perfect. And this is good. Anything can always be improved. Just look at TV advertisements and billboards on the highway. Products and services regarded as state-of-the-art a few years ago, are now considered outdated, and they are replaced by something more modern and advanced, something you can again not exist without. This applies in all industries, and they will keep improving those products and services which seem perfect today.

The cycle of endless improvement is a model that should teach us how to live after a break-up. It is irrelevant that life is not perfect. It never was such, and never will be.

What is important is that we keep on improving it.

DO NOT HESITATE TO USE THE SENTENCE:

"That was amazing work from you."

Let me set your mind at rest: nobody in the world is praised as much as he should be. This is the internal perception of every single man. We envy how much others are appreciated when it seems to us that they do not deserve so much praise. The reason, of course, is that our eyes are fixed on our own lives. That is why we think our problems are more serious than problems of others. And we are right, in a way. Not because our worries are really bigger or more important. But because they are bigger or more important for us.

To deal with problems (including a break-up) in a positive way, you need positive energy. Do you want a special dose of positive energy? Go to a colleague who achieved something good, and praise him. It does not matter when it was. Go back as far as necessary – you will always find something that someone else achieved. If you find the strength to tell someone, *"You managed that excellently!"* you can change that person's whole day.

It is not important what the actual achievement was, or even whether it was anything very significant. Just remind the colleague that people have not forgotten about him. And that they notice what he does for them. Praising others is a gift that is free, and yet priceless. Do you wonder how this benefits you? A good word can evoke a good feeling – just by saying it. We are not even talking about how the listener will start looking at you.

A person always stays close to those who do not consider him useless. He will be willing to do many things for you. Such as praise and support you when you need it most.

THIRD SOLITUDE THAT IS TOO DEEP: IN YOUR LEISURE
HOW TO RELEASE PAIN THAT RETURNS ON WEEKENDS AND HOLIDAYS

When you are lonely as a result of a break-up, the hardest time is not that spent with strangers, but the time spent alone: evenings, weekends, holidays.

You would like to think of something positive, but pain is stronger. It is always faster and drives you into a corner.

You feel this is a hopeless situation. You feel you simply cannot control your thoughts. Anxiety torments you so much that, paradoxically, you look forward to the new working day and to people whom you do not really like, but where you can hide in a crowd. Fridays become the worst days.

Just like Christmas, and Valentine's Day.

Life has reversed itself.

How to survive it? How to believe that everything will change one day?

Hollywood star Elizabeth Taylor once said wisely, *"Great happiness can be experienced only by someone who has experienced great tragedy."* Nothing is closer to the truth.

Regardless of how much you suffer in life, the future will compensate you with the ability to realise and enjoy the achievement of satisfaction.

The worst thing about pain after a break-up is internal. The wound is not external. It cannot be disinfected and bandaged. There is no cardiac surgery to correct this injured heart. Nobody else can heal you either. Only yourself.

It is similar to tension in the neck. You must first suffer the pain, then stretch the tense muscles, and relax them afterwards. It is like releasing the handbrake of your car.

Fulfilling the following laws should not be delayed. You will only be delaying help to yourself in relieving the tension in your neck. You can deal with pain in the heart, but it must not be allowed to last for too long. The pain must not spread to the other organs – you must not be prevented from going outside, communicating, eating, drinking, laughing and believing, just because of a paralysed heart.

Medication can help with every discomfort.

The medication that helps the heart is given in Laws 164 to 168.

INVEST IN YOURSELF, EVEN MORE IF NO ONE IS AROUND

Why should you care about yourself if there is no one to show your face to? Why should you exercise, lose weight or put cream on your skin if nobody will appreciate it? This is the kind of question asked by people who do not understand that their values, including their health, do not belong to others, but to themselves. Do not neglect your approach to a proper lifestyle only when you want to make a good impression on someone else. Learn to be sincere. Especially to yourself.

When you look around you, you will find that most people are trying to impress others, only a few are sincere to themselves. Do not let this dissuade you, try to belong to the select few. Describe your situation in precise words, specify what you need at that moment and what you can do to achieve it. People who have a hundred locks inside themselves are paradoxically those who most need windows wide open, to let in the fresh air to clear their thinking. People who like to switch off their thoughts in sadness are precisely those who need education and entertainment to clear them again. People who languish in depression paradoxically are those who are most in need of healthy meals, drinks and sufficient exercise − all of which helps them to recover energy and the joy of life.

Yes, all this is worth the effort.

But the effort will have a real meaning.

If you invest time, money or energy in somebody or something outside yourself, there is always a risk. But if you invest time, money or energy in yourself, you will never lose. Because an investment in yourself today is an investment in your future. The past, where you may have suffered a loss, will lose its power over the future. Begin to work on your future to eliminate any pain from it. Although the pain will always be part of your history, it will forever be contained in The Past.

INVEST IN FRIENDS

---

*L*ove meets Friendship and asks:

"Friendship, why are you in the world if I, Love, am here?"

Friendship replies:

"Because you cause pain while I heal it."

Remember this dialogue. It will help remind you that you need friends in any situation. They are people who do not usually solve a problem for you, but will support and accompany you until you solve the problem on your own. Because happiness does not come from outside. It comes from within.

Friends give us a hand so that we do not lose courage and balance when we are looking inward. We will find the solution to our problem with their assistance. And we will be proud of that (and of ourselves), and the greater the achievement, the prouder we will be.

LET ACTIVE VERBS INTO YOUR LIFE

Oh, how accustomed we are to adjectives. To everything that is sad, bad, painful, long-term. But you will set your heart and your mind in motion only with the help of verbs. They are ideal, because they personify movement. Learn to live according to verbs such as exercise, dance, travel. Of course, you will be tired at the end of the day. But your expression will change. It will reflect contentment, relief, self-esteem. These feelings arise after overcoming obstacles. Even if the obstacle is just a run around a nearby park.

Learn to distinguish between two types of rest. Being passively idle means inaction. An inactive body does not regenerate, but wastes away – under the force of negative verbs. Get up off the couch. Self-pity, accusations, excuses or procrastination will not improve your future. Only positive efforts lead to happiness. Yes, it means overcoming obstacles. Fortunately. Because obstacles cannot be tackled from a couch. You have to get up to overcome them. (But it pays – smiles, relief, self-esteem are already on the way.)

DO NOT BE AFRAID TO BE CONSIDERED A FOOL SOMETIMES

The most successful people are not those who achieve the most, but those who overcome the most. Do you want to be successful? Then realise that only madmen will take the route that nobody else would go. This is also the reason that madmen find things that nobody else does. So do not be scared of what appear to be foolish activities, adrenaline sports and things that can change you. Pursue new experiences, disregard the risk of falling, stumbling, getting hurt. After all — those who fall and stand up again are usually stronger than those who have never fallen.

Learn to live with folly and failures. You can be certain that you will be grateful for all the discomfort you have had to endure. Remember, the strongest people are not those who win every time, but those who do not give up despite failure. A failure which moves you ahead should be called Advancement. When you look at it in this way, it does not matter what life throws in your path. Regardless of how hard it is, you can overcome it if you get tougher yourself. So do not wish that life should be easier, wish that you could be stronger. Human strength is increased only when challenged by weights, burdens, obstacles. If you wish to achieve a lot in life, do not be afraid to go and meet failure halfway.

It is not victories, but failures that we overcome, that make us successful. Does this sound foolish enough? Then it's right.

TAKE CONTROL OVER YOUR THOUGHTS BEFORE THEY TAKE CONTROL OVER YOU

No problem can be solved by using the same thoughts that created the problem. No occasion or event can bring about a change, unless you change yourself and your attitude toward dealing with any situation. How do you change this? It is best to stop thinking negatively. To learn to laugh. You don't have to laugh because everything is good, but because you will start seeing the good side of everything. A smile does not necessarily have to express that you are happy. It often expresses something more important — that you are strong.

Weak people seek salvation in their surroundings. However, outside help is like a cold compress on a hot injury. Eventually, the cold pad gets warmer until it matches the room temperature. But there is no need to look outside, the cure is already there, on the inside. Where there is a problem, there is a solution too. As mentioned before, all that is needed is a change of attitude. Such as, just forgiving.

You do not forgive others because you are weak, but because you are strong enough to understand that others make mistakes. You forgive them not for their sake, but for your sake. Your forgiveness does not mean that you accept, understand or even approve the bad behaviour of another person. It only means that you acknowledge it and think no more of it.

What is crucial about forgiveness is that it is something that's done in the present. Finally you are doing something now. As if you turn a page after you've filled it with writing. What was, is no more — there is no need to rewrite what remained on the previous page, to reread what was unpleasant. Simply turn the page. That is enough. You are the one holding the pen, you are the one writing the new page.

THE FOURTH TOO DEEP SOLITUDE: ALONE AFTER THE DEATH OF SOMEONE CLOSE
HOW TO DEAL WITH ETERNAL LONELINESS

L*ife is a good, but ruthless, teacher.*

It teaches the most important lessons in the hardest way.

That is why you should not blame life so harshly. You should rather save your breath and words. Because you will need them when you thank life for its lessons.

What positive aspect can one find in the death of a beloved person? This is what I asked two months before my 22nd birthday, when my mother died literally in my arms. Without any warning, a sudden illness took her from me.

She was here one day, the next day she was gone – terrible.

That day influenced me more and more.

Even positively.

That was its message.

At that time, all I wanted was money, a career and achievements. Those were my crucial values. I trusted absolutely that they would make me happy. But none of these achievements could prolong my mother's life by a single minute. Suddenly I understood the real value of everything I had pursued until then.

On the devil's day, the day full of 6s and 9s (6.6.1996) I re-evaluated my life. I came to understand what is the most important. Not health – as we know, the people on the Titanic were healthy – but time. And the way you use it.

On that day, I stopped wasting time and postponing my dreams. I learned to see each new day as a gift, something special, and to live it to the fullest. I began to live as if I was going to die the next day. And to learn, as if I was to live forever.

Each time you come up against death you are forced to re-evaluate life, its meaning and its pathways. And to remind yourself that the direction matters more than the speed.

DEVOTE YOURSELF TO IMPORTANT PEOPLE WHILE THEY ARE AMONG US

It is strange that even when people leave us, they remain with us. Sometimes we are full of remorse at not having devoted ourselves to them while they were alive. Only when we lose someone, do we realise his value. It is the same with health. We hardly notice it while we have it.

Life likes gallows humour. And it is good that our greatest losses remain engraved in our memories. Only in this way will we stop ignoring opportunities that make us happy, stop putting them off, and also stop ignoring people for whom we cannot find time in the rush of our own importance. Life is a harsh school, which is not oriented to the past, but to the present. Its purpose is to make us aware of all the opportunities and people ahead of us, those we have not lost yet. The situation is something like a broken ankle – which never fully heals. It keeps paining again from time to time, reminding us to be more careful next time. Not to trample on important people in our life while they are still here.

Nobody can guarantee that they, or we, will be there tomorrow. And every day that we do not devote ourselves to them, we lose twenty-four hours that cannot be recovered, time that we will never be able to spend with them.

RETROSPECTIVE REGRET HURTS MORE THAN FEAR

Fairy tales teach us that we do not have to worry. But they should also teach us that if we do not take the step we are afraid of, one day we may experience a feeling worse than fear – regret. Over the opportunities we did not take advantage of.

Every man usually fears only until the moment he throws himself into the battle. Then all fear disappears, to make room for his strengths. So whenever you overcome fear, you will discover inside yourself the will to fight.

Everything bad that could happen in your imagination can hinder you. But do not forget that fear hurts less than the subsequent frustration from a lost chance. And, life is hard and does not bring the same opportunity twice. It teaches us not to hesitate. To take risks. Only in this way do we dare to grow.

So do not allow life to pass you by like a hand waving from a departing train. Behave in such a way that on the last day of your life you will be able to say: *"I can't believe I tried that!"* rather than *"I wish I'd tried that!"*

UNPLANNED ACTIONS ARE THE MOST OPEN

Nobody measures life by the blows that knock us down. Logically. If you counted them, you would be prepared for them. But life teaches us from childhood that unplanned actions are better. This is no mystery. The reason is that life is more resourceful than man. So it is often better to leave the director's baton to life.

Stop dreaming feverishly and planning convulsively how things should be. Let life flow on its own. Only in this way will you start appreciating it for itself. After all, as you well know, the best gifts are seldom wrapped as you imagined and wished they would be.

If you are open in your attitude, life will become simpler, free of needless bitterness and disappointment. Because suddenly you do not expect anything special from it. Every day can be surprising, adventurous, challenging. Learn to accept things as they are – whatever their nature. If you feel like complaining about things happening differently from what you wish, you should talk to yourself. Indeed, as is rightly said: If you want to make God laugh, tell Him your plans.

Whenever you are disappointed, it is only because you believed in an illusion that had nothing to do with reality. You only thought you were holding something in your hands that you never really had.

Live in the present, whatever it is. And change it by means of your own deeds and attitude so that it is exactly as you wish.

DO NOT RUN FROM SOMETHING

Whenever you try to run from something, you remain in the same place.

If I say, *"Do not think about eating a jam doughnut!"* most people will start licking their lips. All they think of now is the jam doughnut.

Your mind works by focusing on what you are thinking about. The context is not important. If you wish something to happen or not to happen, your mind will pay attention even to the things you wish to avoid. That is why persistent effort to move from a negative state forces our brain to deal primarily with this negative state. It is not a systemic mistake. If a brain is to find a solution, it must bounce away from the starting position. The problem is that if the mind does not find a constructive solution quickly, it remains at the negative starting point and cannot advance.

Even in the case where someone close to you dies, the solution is simple. Be positive. Do not run from what is troubling you, run towards what you want to experience. Retune your focus – from start to goal. Running from problems is a race that you cannot win. So run to the solution. Always run to a specific point, not from somewhere to a non-specific point. Run somewhere, not nowhere. Therefore, have a positive goal in any situation. Not a vague goal.

TROUBLES MAKE YOU STRONGER

What does not kill you, makes you stronger, a popular wisdom goes. And you know this is true from the gym. A muscle that you give sufficient exercise, strengthens. But what is sufficient exercise? Life brings many challenges to endure. All life's tests make us realise what we are capable of. If the tests are sufficient, they will exhaust you. Overwhelm you. Make you cry, rage and resist. Then you will know that you can manage more than you ever thought.

Many people suppose that they will acquire a new skill in the course of time. They will not gain anything; they already have everything within themselves. They merely have to stimulate, practise and strengthen the skills. Even the worst experience in life is a test in this respect. You do not have to worry that it will end badly. Because time will always help you. Even if you do nothing actively after the death of someone close to you, you will become reconciled with it in time. But it may take a long time. And it is a pity to waste time. You already know that time is the most precious thing in life.

DO YOU HAVE A PROBLEM WITH PERMANENT SCEPTICISM? HOW TO DISARM NEGATIVE THOUGHTS

*T*houghts beget deeds, deeds beget results.

In other words, the quality of your life depends directly on your thoughts.

If you believe that you are worthless, that you will never feel better or that there is no more beauty, it will become your reality.

Yes, this is how strong thoughts are. But this applies to positive ones too. So learn to disarm negative thoughts and make them positive instead.

A thought is a thought, you might say. This is not true. The difference between negative and positive thoughts is just as crucial as the difference between negative and positive life.

It seems like a paradox:

- People who are happy have experienced unhappiness in the past.

- People who are wise have made many mistakes in the past.

- People who love sincerely have hurt others in the past.

- People who have succeeded have failed many times in the past.

- Do not be surprised. We all learn.

Everyone experiences such paradoxes:

- The more you lose important people, the more you realise the value of those who remain.

- The more mistakes you make, the more you learn.

- The more new paths you are forced to seek, the more paths you will eventually find.

Human life is like Nature. Full of uphills and downhills. Light and darkness. High tides and low tides. All these natural phenomena build your realisation, gratitude and awareness of how much every experience costs. Failure teaches you humility, success teaches you to appreciate what you have achieved.

Thanks to this cycle, we can understand life and be useful to others. If someone survives a hard fall, he can advise others how they can cope with it too. If someone gets over a partner's betrayal, he can show others how to overcome such a situation too.

And if it seems to you that you cannot handle something in your life, remember it is just a feeling. You can cope with anything. We all can stand upright, improve and work on ourselves. It is often sufficient just to write a list of everything you think you cannot do. And then cross out the "not" every time. In this way, the list will change from a summary of what you cannot do into what you can do. A list of limitations turns into a list of challenges and long-term objectives. Goals you can aim at.

Changing negative assumptions into positive objectives is a universal way of overcoming any problem. The gap between inaction and action is often overcome by understanding that the way we live depends primarily on the way we perceive things.

THOUGHT BEFORE IT IS DISARMED:

Everybody can do it better than me

THOUGHT AFTER IT IS DISARMED:

Nobody can do it better than me, or like me

The only thing all people share is the planet. Otherwise, everyone goes his individual way from birth. Stop paying attention to what somebody else has or does. You

cannot live his life, follow his steps. Following another person's steps means to lose your own. Do not try to admire an original and imitate it, because it will only make you its copy at best, tormenting you your entire life that you are not living up to your model.

You do not resemble anyone, and nobody resembles you. The only limits you should overcome are your own. And the only person you can outgrow in life is yourself. Try to live today better than yesterday, every day, if possible. This is enough – this alone is immense.

THOUGHT BEFORE IT IS DISARMED:

What I go through is of no use

THOUGHT AFTER IT IS DISARMED:

What I go through is absolutely necessary

This applies in every phase of life, that the situation you are in is absolutely necessary for you to experience. Because if you cannot cope with something, you must learn how to do it. Behave like a juice extractor. Squeeze the good from the fruit (your situation), and throw away the rest. And avoid the bitter core entirely.

At every crossroad in life, you either choose the right path, or go to the end of a blind alley and have to turn back. Every step you take on any of the roads ahead is therefore a search for the right path. Failure gives you the opportunity to correct yourself. Have no doubt that you need to be in the place you are today, to be able to move where you want to be tomorrow.

Blind alleys are a precondition for all growth. All the bad feelings you have are informing you that you cannot continue in a particular direction. Forgive your body for not giving you clearer hints, e.g. by text messages to a mobile phone. Unfortunately, Apple Inc. has not invented iPhone Heart or iPhone Mind. The heart and the mind simply have no other way to let us know something than to communicate through our feelings. So listen to pain if you experience it.

Your senses speak through it.

THOUGHT BEFORE IT IS DISARMED:

I cannot get better

THOUGHT AFTER IT IS DISARMED:

I can get better

Everyone at any moment can get better. However, everything you have ever achieved, or will achieve, starts from what you have tried or will try. There is only one power that can prevent you from taking the next step forward. You are that power. This is how powerful you are. You can be your own salvation as well as damnation.

The smallest step in the right direction can turn out to be the most important in your life. No stairway that is worth its name can be climbed with a single jump. This is good. If you tried, the outcome might be painful – a fall from a height is painful. But progressive steps overcome any stairs. Regardless of the size, any dream can be reached by fulfilment of lesser objectives. So no day in life is useless, if you make some progress. Don't get angry at life because the progress is too slow. It has its exact purpose. Because whenever you stumble on the stairway of life you will know what to avoid on the next higher level – from where the fall would hurt you much more.

THOUGHT BEFORE IT IS DISARMED:

What was not possible yesterday will not be possible today either

THOUGHT AFTER IT IS DISARMED:

What was not possible yesterday can be possible today

Mistakes are the best teachers. What's more, the lessons are twofold. Firstly, man finds out what not to do, secondly, he is closer to understanding what he should do. On the basis of negative experience, a person develops a natural awareness of womanisers, drunkards, drug addicts, opportunists, bullies or gamblers. He was not born with this ability, but learned it from life. In a harsh way. He should thank life even more loudly for the lessons.

303

Break-ups are a particularly useful school. Usually they lead one to finding that life benefits from open doors with the inscription: *"If you want to enter, you can, the door is open. If you want to leave, you can, the door is open. But do not stand in the doorway blocking the passage."*

Do not waste intuition, time and energy by crying over spilt milk. Wipe the floor instead. Now you will beware of what turned out to be a failure, won't you?

THOUGHT BEFORE IT IS DISARMED:

My life will never be of such a quality

THOUGHT AFTER IT IS DISARMED:

The quality of my life is determined by the quality of my visions

It is up to every man to decide how he imagines his future and what he pays attention to in the present. If he focuses on regrets and disappointments, that is what his life will consist of. If on his development and success, then that is what his life will consist of. You can ignore your dreams, or live them. The choice is yours.

What you are capable of in life depends on how much you want it. If a particular dream means the world to you, you will follow it and not stop until you reach it. Success is no miracle if you are determined and persistent, but a natural reward for the effort to achieve what you longed for.

THOUGHT BEFORE IT IS DISARMED:

I am losing everything

THOUGHT AFTER IT IS DISARMED:

For everything I am losing, I get something back

Loss is profitable. It is a gain of experience. Loss and experience are directly proportionate to one another. The more painful a loss, the more valuable the experience. The most experienced people are those who suffered the most. They endured, because they learned to live with humility and see that, even if they had not reached

their desired destination, they had already gone a long way. There is always something you can be grateful for, can value or appreciate about yourself. Life never consists of a single chapter. One event leads to another. Life is full of changes, it loves alternation of chapters, and their moods. It forces us to cry, and to laugh. And to understand that a smile is possible even in the worst crisis. We smile especially because we can be strong and wise enough to accept things as they are, and we learn to write new chapters with the best will that we can at that moment.

THOUGHT BEFORE IT IS DISARMED:

The more scars I have, the more embarrassed I am

THOUGHT AFTER IT IS DISARMED:

The more scars I have, the stronger I am

People are ashamed of scars. Somebody said scars are ugly. While a scar is a beautiful declaration that the wound has healed and the injury is gone. It indicates that we managed to overcome pain, learned a useful lesson and grew stronger. Scars are strange tattoos produced by life. They mark people who deserve appreciation.

Scars do not disappear easily. And this is good. Respect those who have borne pain. They can be helpful to you. They know that the more life tempts you to give up everything, the more it can still give to you.

PREPARATION FOR A NEW RELATIONSHIP

The person who is not satisfied internally with himself is seldom satisfied in a relationship, because he brings the person he was dissatisfied with – himself – to the relationship. It is like a time bomb – sooner or later this person becomes the source of the problem, accusing the partner for not solving his problem. Be aware of this in good time when you are alone and strive to make yourself someone who will be a joy to live with. Even if you remain alone, it is in your best interest. Because you will live with yourself forever.

In the hospital where my mother's life was fading, I met an interesting girl. Every evening, she came to visit her grandfather, who hardly moved. The doctor told the girl that the old man did not have much time left. So the girl sat down close to him and quietly began to sing a melody to him. The man's temples shook and tears ran from his eyes.

I asked the girl what she was singing. "*The same tune he sang to me when I was a little girl. It helped me to fall asleep and not be afraid of the bogeyman and ghosts.*"

The girl sang for several minutes. I noticed the man's lips moving. As if he was trying to say something to his granddaughter. She lowered her head, listened intently and then kissed him on the forehead.

The man closed his eyes.

"*What did he say?*" I asked impatiently.

"*That when his mother sang him this song, she kissed him good night.*"

He fell asleep, calmly and happily, never to wake again. It is beautiful to have a loving person nearby in the last moments. And even more beautiful to be such a person for another.

THE FIRST OF THREE STEPS: HOW TO TIDY UP EFFICIENTLY WITHIN

Nobody in this world can work alone for a long time. An individual never has the same power as a tandem or a team. He never pulls himself together quickly enough after failures. Alone, he tends to get lazy, to give up in times of trouble. The solitary man also finds it harder to smile. We need other people.

Any part of the body weakens if it is not used, because there is no one to use it for. Sooner or later, you need to find a new partner. But to be able to find him, you must first seek. And not be a burden on him. Do not seek salvation in others, before you are absolutely at peace with yourself. It is impossible to find a close partner without renewed faith in people, just as it is impossible to mix a sweet drink if you only have bitter ingredients. What laws must you respect to be able to function fully in relationships again?

WHAT IS BEHIND YOU HAS NO CONNECTION TO WHAT IS BEFORE YOU

A ball of thread starts rolling downhill while you hold the end of the thread. The unrolled thread represents the past, because it is clear and visible, but it has stopped moving. Like the thread. It has stopped creating the past. While the rolling ball is the present. As long as you are afraid, you will keep repeating bad relations, unable to establish healthy ones. You must stop repeating the mistakes. Otherwise the situation will not improve. Therefore, remember these three rules:

1. What happened cannot be changed, but you can close the door behind it. Then what was created in the past will stay in the past.

2. What someone else has done to you has no connection with people who are yet to enter your life.

3. The person who hurt you need not be part of your life anymore. There is no need to concern yourself with this unpleasant person. He is lost in the past.

If you do not repeat old mistakes, there is no reason to torment yourself.

TAKE ONLY EXPERIENCE FROM PAST RELATIONS

If you can manage to look at your life with a detached view, you will find that actually nothing is tormenting you. You yourself torment yourself whenever you wish. Relations that did not work out give us useful experience for the future. Every lesson is helpful, even a bad one. Perhaps it was painful. But if someone is hurt, he will appreciate so much more a relationship in which he is not hurt. And anyone who has experienced betrayal will appreciate a partner who does not betray. Because of the lesson learned, he will value those properties in a new partner that he would have overlooked if he were less sensitive.

We stand in front of a clean sheet. Stop filling it with the past. Do not blame others. The greatest disappointment you can experience from this moment on is to disappoint yourself.

ENTER NEW RELATIONSHIPS SLOWLY

After a break-up, there is always the despair that you have finished reading a sad book and now do not have anything better at hand. That you actually have nothing at your disposal that you could open or read without being disappointed. But that disappointment is not in the book, it is in ourselves. Because we are bitter within and wonder why nothing tastes sweet. We behave like a polecat hiding in a hole – determined not to leave until the smell disappears.

I have already mentioned vampires. According to legends, people who were bitten by a vampire turn into vampires themselves. They hurt without knowing why. They feel a compulsion to make other people unhappy. Make sure you do not belong among them. Hasten slowly. Prudently. With a heart that has already shaken itself off and become regenerated. So that your relationships are not like in sport, which Mark Twain described as follows: *"Golf is a good walk spoiled."*

FAMILIARISE YOURSELF WITH PEOPLE WHO ARE SUCCESSFUL

Remember that every man represents the average of the five people with whom he spends the most time. Seek people who see life other than pessimistically, regardless of circumstances that come their way. Such people will be the best preparation for your impending meeting with that special someone. Why them? Because your immediate attitude will determine whether you want to frown or smile at the other person. A smile does not necessarily portray someone reacting to something amusing, but someone satisfied with himself.

The ideal positive models are people who are visibly more successful and happier than you are. They show the right path. You can gain the same well-being that they have achieved, but you must not turn away from them, or despise them. They will help you. People stronger than you can always lift you up, hold you, encourage you. Be in such company as often and as long as possible.

Work on your well-being. Life is too short to be petty, to spend it locked in your cell with everything that troubles you, wondering why it still continues.

Find new faces. Positive friends. One day, your future partner and the whole relationship will thank you for it. Because what you receive from them, you will bring to the relationship.

THANK PEOPLE FOR PROVIDING A USEFUL LESSON AND IN THIS WAY FULFILLING THEIR ENTIRE MISSION

When you find it easy to breathe a word of thanks to your former partners, you will know that you have fully digested a bad past and there is nothing rotten left inside you. Thanks for sincerity, a lesson, or even betrayal. Perhaps their intentions were bad, but that is their problem. If somebody clearly showed himself to be unacceptable for your future, he deservedly stays in the past.

Make sure you lock the dividing door properly. Wash your hands if they feel stained.

And focus only on the present from now on.

You have learned everything that you could from the past. You do not want to relive bad things. You can now undertake the second step.

SECOND OF THREE STEPS: RELATIONSHIPS YOU SHOULD NOT WANT AGAIN

Loneliness and solitude are different concepts.

Loneliness in a relationship is one of the worst sensations. You feel unwanted and alone, even in the company of someone. On the contrary, solitude, a temporary separation from people, is useful and you should make time for it now and then. Because solitude allows you to decide on your priorities, for example, never to accept a relationship again in which you feel lonely, even though by the side of a partner.

I understood loneliness at the age of 22 years. It was my first Christmas Eve. All alone, on the outside and inside. From the adjoining flats, I heard carols being sung, the lively tinkling of cutlery and laughter, while I faced a cold uneatable schnitzel from a supermarket and three empty chairs around the table.

Father had moved away, mother had died, my girlfriend had left.

On that evening, I cursed life – I was still stupid then, and did not know how important this experience was that I was going through; how much I needed to understand loneliness as well as solitude, to realise the value of having the right people around me. The right ones, I must emphasise.

That evening seemed endless and unbearable – which was good. It made it clear in my mind that I had to start working: firstly, on new relationships, secondly, on myself.

While solitude is a blessed state, when we are alone and we do not mind, because in solitude we return to our basic values and regenerate, in loneliness we are alone and suffer. The difference between these states is in the nature of the emptiness. Emptiness in loneliness does not mean there is something missing on the outside. There is something missing inside. As if someone has torn off a piece of your being, and it has not grown on again. You have to fill the empty space yourself. Yes, even if others take something in the break-up, you can, you must, replace it with part of your being.

The moment when loneliness hurts the most and we do not understand it, that is the most effective. This is when, piece by piece, we fill up the emptiness — the open wound within — by the potion which heals and burns at the same time. This potion is your understanding that you must not allow the pain to be repeated. In particular, you must not return to a bad relationship.

If you manage to free yourself from bad individuals, you will never be lonely at a table on Christmas Eve. Even if there is nobody else, the most important person of your life will be there. You.

And this is often more than enough.

Remember that every relationship is a living organism. Like a new-born child. It takes lots of effort and time before you bring it up as you want it, before it matures and begins to return the investment. Behave like a mountain climber, who is careful about who holds his securing rope. Make sure it is not anyone immature, childish, unreliable. He could pull you down.

DO NOT ALLOW A RELATIONSHIP TO BE LED ONLY BY ONE PERSON

When you paddle only on one side of a raft, the raft will spin around in the same place on the river. Relationships need tandem cooperation from both sides too. Only in this way will the raft float forward and not go around in circles.

You must realise that two people who join together in a relationship are different and must adjust their behaviour so that they do not continue as before, but complement each other. Think of it as magnets set in such a way that the opposite poles attract, not so that they repel. Such individuals still remain separate. They have considerable personal freedom, as well as responsibility. However, responsibility in a relationship increases. At the beginning, you are responsible for yourself, then for the couple, and eventually for your children.

No relationship can survive for long if it is tended only from one side. Imagine a tree groomed only from the right side, while the left side is entirely neglected, or even damaged by the breaking of its branches. The tree will not vanish partially, it will vanish entirely. Nor does trust between partners work in only one half. What would you think if a partner told you joyfully that he was faithful to you more than 90 percent of the time? No, trust is either 100 percent or nothing.

A unilaterally maintained relationship walks with a limp. It does not matter if the other leg is healthy. The whole body is limping. In the course of time, the overloaded healthy leg will also begin to languish.

Therefore, if you are in an unbalanced relationship, do not expect that you will remain in balance. If your relationship is weak, you will not remain strong.

NEVER AGAIN ALLOW A RELATIONSHIP THAT IS CREATED ONLY TO SATISFY ONE PARTNER

Idyllic TV shows feature Mr Big, who falls from above to give meaning to a heroine's shattered life. It is romantic to believe that someone like that will show up. However, this is not how it works in reality. Even if such a partner did arrive, the couple would never be happy.

Certainly, in desperate moments, it is tempting to find someone who would take care of you. You assume that the pressure you feel will ease off. But the contrary is true. The pressure will only intensify. If somebody is to lead you, he must first tie a collar around your neck and drag you by a leash. Such relationships do not last long. Or they are not genuine.

No partner can fill the emptiness you feel inside. Only you can do it. Unless you assume full responsibility for the emptiness inside you, you will not be happy in any relationship. Ignored scepticism is carried into the relationship like an infection. And the disillusionment only increases if you expect the partner to solve your problems.

Of course, it works both ways. A partner who does not feel complete must first accept himself the way he is. To reconcile himself with this and find possibilities for improvement. If somebody cannot get over the past and the present, he will also be unable to create an effective future. Everybody must build internal happiness, before he can share it with another person. If you do not feel any internal satisfaction, you have nothing positive to share with your partner and nothing you can use to make a positive contribution to the relationship.

Relationships where one member of the couple enters with debt will end badly. Indeed, they are like two batteries, one fully charged, the other completely discharged. After they are connected up, neither of them will be charged 100 percent. Each one will be half-empty. The first will lose its energy, the other will not feel sufficiently recharged.

NEVER AGAIN ALLOW A RELATIONSHIP THAT IGNORES THE NEEDS OF PARTNERS

To be constantly fulfilled, partners must feel comfortable and free in a relationship. Both must have sufficient choice, as well as subsequent responsibility for their decision. Then not the other, but the partner himself will be responsible for how he feels in the relationship. He must communicate in time, sufficiently and relevantly. Partners in non-functioning relationships practically do not communicate, and if they do, it is only to say that they hold the other one responsible for how they feel themselves.

In such relationships, where the needs of the other partner are not respected, it is impossible to plan anything without approval. Both partners feel captive. A compromise like this is a half-hearted solution for both. It satisfies neither of them. In bad relationships, a compromise is formed by the withdrawal of both. But such steps only increase the distance between partners. Both partners, and the relationship as a whole, are worse off.

In bad relationships, partners say: *"If you take care of me, I will take care of you."*

It sounds like barter.

On the contrary, in good relationships, the partners say: *"I will take care of myself because of you, and you will take care of yourself because of me."*

Where is the difference? It lies in responsibility.

In a good relationship, you cannot blame the partner if you do not feel good yourself.

If you understand that, you will also understand the difference between "*support*" and "*have to support*". Because it is all right to sacrifice yourself for others, if your sacrifices are made as a personal choice. But it must never be an enforced obligation.

NEVER AGAIN ALLOW A RELATIONSHIP BASED ON IDEALISTIC EXPECTATIONS

Idealism is an art form based on the search for an ideal, perfection, faultlessness. It is a direction which hardly belongs to human reality, because man is not perfect, and certainly not flawless.

Idealists seek an ideal partner in relationships. They cannot find him, because there is no such thing. In happy relationships, partners love and appreciate each other, not because they are perfect, but despite not being perfect.

Idealists believe they can repair someone who in their opinion is flawed, while people are in fact perfect in their imperfection. Because they are the way they should be. The problem with evaluating perfection therefore is not so much in the other partner as in ourselves. The less you expect from a partner, the happier you will be.

Why? Nobody will ever behave as you expect. Nobody else is you. He cannot give, understand and react like you. It is not his fault. Indeed, the deepest disappointments in a relationship are caused by idealistic expectations. If you remove your assumptions and prejudices about how the other should behave, you will reduce your own frustration.

A perfect relationship does not consist of perfect partners, but of partners who respect one another's imperfections.

NEVER AGAIN ALLOW A RELATIONSHIP WHERE THE PAST IS USED FOR ACCUSATIONS

The law does not allow a man to be tried twice for the same crime. So why is this allowed in a relationship? How can a partner be so cruel and cowardly as to push the other repeatedly, as if he still owed an apology for the past?

Business uses the concept of win-win situations. This refers to a mutually beneficial outcome. Never allow a relationship which, on the contrary, will culminate in a lose-lose situation. That is, one in which both partners eventually lose. If a partner who uses old mistakes by the other for repeated accusations thinks he has the relationship under control, he is mistaken. The contrary is true. He does not win but loses, twice actually.

The first loss results from not solving a current problem, but from reproaching the partner for some behaviour in the past. The second loss comes from going back to the old guilt to manipulate a person who has already served a sentence for it. It is the same as if you cut open an old wound and wonder why the new wound is not healing. But the situation actually gets worse, because now you have two wounds. And neither of them gets better, or even has a chance to heal, because you keep scratching at one wound while ignoring the other.

Partners therefore waste energy proving to the other that they have no guilt. In discussions they pose as less bad, restricting their relations with the other. But what happens is that they grow distant from each other, instead of trying to achieve closeness and harmony. They behave like hunters quarrelling about who shoots better, while forgetting where the target is.

Rather than listening to your partner's reproaches about where you were or what you did, it is better to stay alone. Because whenever you decide to be in a relationship with someone, you begin to live through his previous mistakes with him. If you do not accept a partner's past, you will not accept him either. And to accept someone in a relationship means, especially, not to misuse him.

NEVER AGAIN ALLOW A RELATIONSHIP BUILT ON A LIE

Trust is the foundation of any relationship. Without it, the relationship ceases to exist. Betrayed trust is an open wound that is difficult to heal. It makes you walk on tiptoes around the other, to handle him carefully, while the relationship in fact needs building. Once a link is damaged, it simply cannot hold the chain together.

Trust is a sacrament that partners should not gamble with. If you say to yourself seriously, "*I will not tell him, I don't want to lie to him,*" already this sentence is contradictory. And omission or concealment can also be a lie in a relationship.

A sincere enemy is always better than a false friend. Therefore in a relationship, pay less attention to what the other one says, and more to what he does. The worst partners are able to repeat a lie so often that you finally believe it. They take pains to make their lie your reality. But such people do not deserve your trust and relationship. Because the relationship is not true either then. It turns out to be a mere lie.

NEVER AGAIN ALLOW A RELATIONSHIP BASED ON EMOTIONAL BLACKMAILING

To blackmail emotionally means to use emotional punishment against the other, until he starts doing what the blackmailer demands. For example, when threatened, the blackmailed partner adjusts his behaviour against his will and his convictions. Sometimes he misleads himself into believing that it will be better to give in and the waters will calm down. No, they will not. Blackmailing is a methodology. It is never satisfied, never changes.

What is forced to change is you. But if you change according to somebody else's image, you stop being yourself. Even if you love the blackmailer in some perverse way, you must realise that being forced according to the other's wishes means that you are not good enough for him, and he does not see your real value.

Besides, you cannot be anyone else.

Only puppets on string can do this.

No man is a puppet. This is not his skill.

Because he has his own reasoning — for good reason.

If somebody wants a puppet, let him go and play with a dummy.

You can even recommend that to him, if you truly care for him.

Because such a manipulator will be happier with a dummy than with you.

NEVER AGAIN ALLOW A RELATIONSHIP TO BE LEFT ON THE BACK BURNER

When a chef has a pot that does not require immediate attention, he puts it on one of the hot plates that is further away. It is bad to have such *"chefs"* in a relationship. Run from partners for whom you are on a sidetrack and who refuse to talk about it.

You will feel that you are on the back burner if you find it difficult to say important things to your partner. There is already something wrong here. Nobody in a relationship should be handicapped because of his opinions or feelings. There should be no persuasion in a relationship, only discussion. Equal communication can remove any vagueness, doubts and wrong assumptions. These evil seeds are bred in the mind. Negative thoughts rot in the mind, until infection starts spreading from the person who is destroying his heart from within. In the form of hysterical scenes, threats, remorse.

That is why you must answer all questions in a relationship quickly. Deal immediately with things that are unpleasant and awkward. Treat a relationship like a body. To be healthy, the body must stretch, exercise, get proper nourishment. If a future partner ignores or trivialises things that trouble you, he is not the right partner. The right partner knows that the most valuable thing he can give the other partner is his time, attention and empathy. He does not put a boiling pot on the back burner.

THIRD OF THREE STEPS: ASSESSMENT OF SELECTED OBJECTS

What a partner should not be like

My friend looked everywhere for someone who would be the love of his life. Then he finally spotted her. In the Metro. Through a coach window. She was in the opposite train. They looked at each other, smiled, flirted without words. She then steamed up the window with her breath and wrote her telephone number on the misty glass.

He called her that very evening. She did not answer. He called again. She hung up. My friend dialled the number over and over and was getting very frustrated, when he received a text message:

"Only SMS, please. I am deaf."

Since then, I have been unable to reach my friend on the phone. He is on an intense course of sign language. To eliminate what might seem like an obstacle.

Hypothetically, every man can be given one chance. Or two. Or three. Almost everything in life can be renewed. The contents of a fridge that have been eaten. Muscles flaccid from non-use. Money you lost. It is even possible to renew self-confidence and love, if you lost any of it. But one commodity is irreversible: The time you lost with bad people can never be claimed back from life. Yes, it can be a valuable experience. But you can save yourself from repeating certain experiences.

If you squander time by yourself, you often do not realise it and do not mind. But if somebody else wastes your time and you sense it, it is annoying. Prevent this by

choosing an appropriate partner. How can appropriateness be recognised without a long period of testing? Watch the signals of those who are skilled.

Of course, they are only signals. You cannot be absolutely sure if the problem you suspect will really arise. To verify your suspicion, you would have to try living together. But getting out of a bad relationship is not as easy as getting into one. So be cautious, and at least talk carefully with the potential partner.

In advance. While you still have time.

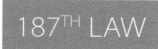

BEWARE OF A PARTNER
WHO IS HURRYING TOWARDS THE
GOOD TIMES

Listen carefully when he talks about his big plans.

Are his eyes bigger than his stomach?

Is he going to burden the relationship with debts?

Does he measure people by property, status, appearance?

Nothing of value in life comes by itself. Many people are so obsessed with happy endings that they forget about the journey to reach such endings. About the work required on this journey. Their views will by shown by their attitude to work, sport, or any effort that requires estimation of their own abilities. What happens to divers who sink quickly to the bottom of the ocean? What happens to climbers who climb quickly to the top of a mountain? A sensible partner realises that success is not about the point he reaches, but about the number and size of the obstacles he overcomes on the way to this point. It does not pay to hurry over obstacles. This will increase the probability of coming a cropper.

Responsible partners know that success consists of progress that you have to work on persistently, and if possible enjoy. This will give you motivation for further successes. Healthy success is not achieved quickly, and this is good. Only in this way can celebrations and joy continue for your whole life.

BEWARE OF A PARTNER WHO SEEKS SALVATION IN HIS SURROUNDINGS

Does he look forward eagerly to the announcement of the lottery winners?

To the next political elections?

To anything else where he cannot control the results, and yet believes he can be saved by them?

Whenever someone needs change and shifts the responsibility for it on to other people or circumstances, he clearly shows he has given up on arranging his own life, being responsible for his own actions. Such a partner solves even ordinary problems by waiting, postponing, passing the buck, chance.

If you have problems and do nothing about them, you cannot be surprised if the problems remain unresolved. Meanwhile you yourself hold the key to any change.

If you do not insert the key into the lock, it won't ever open.

BEWARE OF A PARTNER WHO EXPECTS THE RELATIONSHIP TO BE EASY

All long-term relationships seem idyllic from afar. But if you come closer, you will find that there is considerable work, self-sacrifice and effort behind every lasting success.

In each such relationship, the partners had to learn to deal with difficulties, to endure hard times, to use their combined strength to find the cause of the problem and, despite their different ways of thinking, agree on an effective solution.

No, no relationship is simple. Every one requires effort.

And double the effort if you are not alone. Because you have to work simultaneously on yourself and the relationship. You are supporting both yourself and your partner. While he does the same. Therefore you do not have to seek the energy in yourself every time you must exert it. Your partner can also provide it. Of course, this arrangement has to be fine-tuned, so that the partners strengthen and support each other. Then, in their own lives as well, they will manage more than they would have done alone. No, building a successful and lasting relationship is certainly not easy. But this is exactly why it is worth it.

BEWARE OF A PARTNER WHO ALLOWS TRUST TO BE OVERCOME BY FEAR

No relationship is possible if you refuse to give it a chance. To love means to enable someone to hurt you, and to trust him that he will not. You cannot function if you are worried that your partner might hurt you; you must trust him unconditionally. In a healthy, balanced relationship, you feel that the other person trusts you, and you must make it clear that you feel confident trusting him.

Real partners force fear out of the relationship by their combined strength, and especially by their deeds. If a potential partner is always wanting to see your mobile phone or is suspicious of you without reason, he is more of a time bomb than a human being. It does not matter when, but sooner or later he will blow up the entire relationship.

BEWARE OF A PARTNER WHO IS EXCESSIVELY SECRETIVE

You expect a reply, he does not write.

He is unpredictable, makes a fuss about everything, likes to arouse jealousy.

He thinks he is increasing his value, but he is actually destroying everything the relationship rests on – trust.

Each heart has 100 percent capacity: It can be filled with trust or mistrust. These components combine like oil and water. Where trust fades, mistrust increases. The heart filled with suspicion is poisoned.

You can perceive secretiveness as insincerity, which is closer to dishonesty than to truth. However, a relationship can move forward only with sincerity and openness. If one partner plays jealous childish games or hides his real feelings and concerns, he harms the relationship as much as someone who is really cheating or lying. An unreliable partner is like a stone in a gear mechanism. Hinders, disturbs and eventually destroys the gear.

Always try to give the best of yourself to the relationship.

Let the partner see clearly what you are worth.

Especially that you are worth his time. And he yours.

BEWARE OF A PARTNER WHO WALLOWS IN THE PAST

E goists talk mainly about themselves.

Those in love talk mainly about the other person.

And good-for-nothing people talk mainly about former relationships.

If you start a relationship with someone whose past relationships are not settled, you will probably become a ferryman. It is not a problem in itself to help somebody by ferrying him from the past to the future, but you must be aware of this in advance and understand that the relationship will only be temporary. Almost nobody admits this beforehand. Therefore, pay attention when a person you are interested in wallows too much in the past. The matter must be resolved. You must sort it out with one other. So that you do not find that you are accelerating in a relationship while your partner is braking.

BEWARE OF A PARTNER WHO DEMANDS RECIPROCATION FOR EVERYTHING

Do you want to pay together?" the waiter asks.

"No, separately," the person who plans to share all things *"good or bad"* with you reacts hastily.

But that is no partner. That is a tradesman. Check if his licence is valid for such trade. Love and business are two different worlds. In love, whenever you do something for the other, it is because you want to do it, you can do it, and it gives you pleasure – that is all the reward you wish. Love is like a dynamo – in exchange for effort, you receive energy. After all, you will be doing the best for the balance in a relationship if you give more than you take. While your partner does the same. The extra energy created will always come in useful. For the development of both the relationship and the individual members.

If you retune from the attitude of *"What can I GET?"* to the attitude of *"What can I GIVE?"*, you will be surprised how much you will eventually gain. The happiest people in a relationship are those who always wonder how to be useful to the other partner, while the unhappiest people ask *"What's in it for ME?"*

BEWARE OF A PARTNER WHO DOES NOT MAKE TIME FOR YOU

A relationship is like a garden. It must be maintained if it is to flourish. Focused attention is the most efficient nourishment. Such gardens grow quickly and profusely. To give attention to someone is like providing the necessary oxygen at a time when exhaustion makes it difficult even to fill the lungs.

People who are overcome by their own importance will be no comfort to you. They do not care, do not tend, do not give, but only take. However, this is not only about money. It can also be about kindness and concern. Therefore two people can care for each other, even though they are miles apart. And on the contrary, due to lack of concern, the couple can be alienated from one another, even if they are together.

When gardens are not cared for, they lose their vitality and become overgrown with weeds. Sooner or later, the garden will be invaded by pests. The gardener deserves this. He must understand that money, gifts or chemicals cannot save everything. And that a lack of interest harms more than even moderate care.

BEWARE OF A PARTNER WHO MAKES TIME FOR YOU ONLY WHEN IT PLEASES HIM

People enter into relationships to gain something they do not have alone. Especially support at times when they are uncertain about themselves. Alternately, they offer a helping hand. When someone asks for support, he is also available for the other, even if it may not be convenient or pleasant for him at the time – because this reveals most about his intentions and the resilience of a true relationship.

BEWARE OF A PARTNER WHO TALKS WHEN HE SHOULD LISTEN

It is important to stand in front of your partner and talk sincerely. It is even more important to open your heart and listen to a person who wants to be sincere. Focused attention is most clearly recognised in the ability to listen. This is a surprising paradox. Because listening does not require any energy – so why is it so hard to listen? The reason is that listening includes understanding, patience, self-control. Three components that confirm maturity, sincerity and interest in the other.

Most people who need to talk from their hearts just need an ear that will listen. A successful relationship is not about giving the right answers, but about asking the right questions. Partners do not primarily seek solutions; they can do that on their own. What they need especially is support. Therefore take note in good time whether the partner is willing and able to listen to you, and to understand you. Or, if he can accept what he does not understand.

The wisdom and maturity of a partner in a relationship are measured by his attentive silence while you are talking.

BEWARE OF A PARTNER WHO HINDERS OTHERS IN THE FULFILMENT OF THEIR DREAMS

It is an absolute precondition of love that, if somebody loves you, he should care for your happiness. While the key to your happiness lies in your visions and dreams. They direct, correct and motivate you. They are the light leading you through the dark tunnel of love. Dreams are what you are made of.

You can give people lots of second chances, even try to restrict or change yourself. But in the end you will find that you are not happy when you are with someone who does not allow you to be yourself, who wants to change you to fit his image, who reproaches you for your success, who robs you of your dreams.

A relationship must offer support, not injury. Healthy relationships are capable of finding a combined course of growth for both partners. Even if only one of them has a career, the other will feel fulfilment in the partner's success. Together they will share both pain and delight – as one. Therefore, pay careful attention to how much your potential partner supports you, whether he will support your growth.

Those who are the biggest obstacle to you in a relationship like to defend themselves by saying they are doing things for you with their best intentions, care for you and for your own good. With these words they indicate their selfishness, victimisation and efforts to control you. However to care for you does not mean taking you prisoner, but supporting, inspiring, being close by.

A relationship is not a combat. There is not a winner and a loser. There are either two winners or two losers. A relationship is a joint road followed by both partners.

BEWARE OF A PARTNER WHO SLANDERS HIS PREVIOUS PARTNERS

There is no reason for a partner to recall his past and bring negative things from it to the notice of a current partner. Why retrospectively insult people who were beneficial to you, whether it was a good or a bad experience? The current partner has nothing in common with the previous ones. And to bring old wrongs to a new relationship is like putting a rotten apple into a basket of healthy apples, and then being surprised when all the others become rotten too.

Of course, the flavour of previous relationships can be bitter, because they mostly had a bitter ending. They all ended with a break-up, otherwise they would still have been continuing. But all of them were a lesson and provided experience. Thanks to previous partners, you know better what to insist on, and what to avoid. Yes, the word of thanks is fitting. Because of thanks to mistakes in previous relationships, the new relationship can be more stable, wiser, better.

Be careful if somebody carries rotten apples and pushes them under your nose. A partnership is a bond that is formed by what you do now. Not by what happened in the past. Old rotten apples really have no place in a new life.

What a partner should be like

After death, a man looks at his life.

The guardian angel, standing by his side, points out: "Do you see the dual footprints? One set is yours, the other mine. I accompanied and protected you the whole time."

339

The man says angrily: "But where were you here, when I felt at my worst? I see just one set of footprints."

The guardian angel smiles: "That was when I carried you on my back, because you didn't have the strength to continue."

Partner. This is a word used in business as well as in personal life. Not by accident. Both types, business as well as life partners, share the same characteristics. This is how you can recognise them. Time will show the true value of a man. However, certain character-defining features can be recognised immediately.

CHOOSE A PARTNER WHO FACES PROBLEMS WITH YOU

Life is like a party.

You invite lots of people.

Some will leave early, others stay till morning.

Some laugh with you, some laugh at you, some do not laugh at all. None of them matters. Because the real friends cannot be recognised during the party, but only after it ends. This is when a few people stay to help you clean up. Usually they are not even those who were responsible for the mess.

Real friends, partners, will be among them.

You do not have a partner to tidy up instead of you. You can usually tidy up yourself in your life. But a partner is indispensable to stand by your side when you face problems. This does not only concern support. It also concerns his ability to sense that something is troubling you. To see the pain in your eyes, when the only thing that others see is your dissembling smile.

In tennis, such a person asks for time-out on your behalf. He suggests a time to rest when you need it. Not when you ask for it. His empathy is life-saving.

CHOOSE A PARTNER WHO CAN LISTEN

To listen does not mean to wait until you are able to talk again. To listen means to let the other talk, so that he knows that his opinion matters.

To listen does not mean to talk less, that is, to advise less. Less advising is always the best advice. People do not need much advising in life. What they need much more is that somebody should listen to them, understand them, give them personal feedback, if they wish to hear it, and especially that he should express his support at every step that they must take.

A partner does not have to offer the right answer. That is usually already within. You know what is good for you, although sometimes you cannot discover it. Or you are afraid, reluctant, ashamed to show it publicly. And if you cannot find the answer, you need to seek it, even at the risk of mishaps and mistakes.

Nothing about this is shameful, but rather enhances your experience. But you must feel that your partner is standing beside you. So that when you look back to the past with uncertainty, he will assure you that your choice was correct, even though it meant taking a longer path, or facing obstacles. Support means more than just sharing your beliefs about the past.

CHOOSE A PARTNER WHO ACCEPTS YOU AS YOU ARE

Everybody has different talents, viewpoints, makes decisions in different ways and at different speeds. It does not work if somebody advises you. Because you cannot change the way you are. Man is not a robot to be disassembled and then reassembled with new parts according to the ideas of someone else. We are simply the way we are. A partner can inspire you, offer suggestions, recommendations, but the final decision is up to you and you alone. You cannot think differently from the way you are made to think. If you were forced to, you would feel uneasy, controlled, awkward. Relations would suffer. If one or two pillars lose their supporting power, the bridge will collapse.

You will feel from the very beginning whether the partner will accept you with your apparent strengths and weaknesses, and whether he is wise enough to realise that these strengths and weaknesses are temporary. You can either develop the strengths fully, or eliminate the weaknesses. And if you feel you have a problem in accepting your partner the way he is and want to change him in some way, then you often need to ask yourself what you must change within yourself to see the partner differently.

Many years ago, I met an interesting girl who had a physical handicap. Her handicap was not visible at first sight. It was hidden beneath her clothes. When she bravely revealed it to me, I was amazed. She amazed me. In my eyes, she became an even stronger and more admirable person. Suddenly I perceived everything that she had had to overcome, everything that she had had to cope with. In my eyes, what she lacked was not a weakness. She had strength. She was not inadequate in any sense. On the contrary, I felt inadequate at that moment. She gave me the strength to stop complaining about minor problems and to start working on myself,

so as to equal her in activity, attitude and internal strength. She was my accelerator, not brake. Actually, I was the one hampering her.

It was as if I put her on a golden pedestal. I believe it was important for her, perhaps even epoch-making. If you feel that your potential partner does not accept you entirely as you are, perhaps you should reconsider whether entering into a relationship with him is the right thing for you. Because even partial non-acceptance hurts. And the right partnership must not hurt.

CHOOSE A PARTNER WHO BELIEVES IN YOU

The girl had a big, and seemingly unrealisable, dream. It was out of her reach, because she did not dare to pursue it due to physical problems. She wanted to become a deep-sea diver and photographer, but the doctors had warned her that she would have to do a lot of exercise in order to build up sufficient lung capacity to be able to return from the depths of the ocean with the heavy neoprene suit and the oxygen cylinders.

"Tell me that you think that this whole dream of mine is nonsense and I cannot make it. That I should stop thinking about it. Say it to me, please. I want to have this question solved for good," she insisted. I had to laugh, because in my view there was no question to be solved. This was her life's dream. An opportunity she could not let pass by. Whatever you can imagine and are willing to strive for, you can achieve.

"But do you realise that if I do make it, I would open a door to a spectacular world from which I might not want to return? Do you understand that I might wish to stay in those exotic destinations permanently?" Tears sparkled in her blue eyes and I had to embrace her. Yes, it would mean the end of our relationship. But no relationship is as important as personal dreams. Even if fulfilment of her dream was to mean our parting, I had to be the first to support her. Because I cared for her.

That was the moment that started a fundamental change of her life's direction. When she realised there was somebody who had no doubts about her ability. Who believed in her. People often mistake the word *"believe"* for *"trust"*. While in a relationship, it is important to believe IN the other. To support the partner in his courage to be himself, and motivate him to fulfil his life, to make his dreams come true. Mir-

acles happen if someone dares to make them happen. Miracles start with ordinary words and deeds that prove our belief in the other. In his success.

A partner does not have to do more. He does not lead the other by the hand. The other will achieve what he desires. If a partner believes in him, he can even achieve things that he has already given up hope about ever achieving.

The girl worked and improved her abilities, and today her fascinating photographs and films collect awards at festivals worldwide. I am proud of her. I lost a partner, but made a happy person.

I believe in you.

These four words cannot change the entire world.

Nevertheless, they can change the whole world of one person.

Because they can change the way the person begins to perceive himself as well as the world.

CHOOSE A PARTNER WHO CAN MAKE COMPROMISES

Official documents require the stipulation married. If you are not bound by a marriage contract, this must be indicated by unmarried. However, it is up to people themselves to grant one another whatever freedom they feel is appropriate in their partnership.

Partners must feel free, if they are to communicate freely about what worries them, what they dream about. In a free relationship, although confirmed by wedding rings, fresh air must circulate. Then people prosper in it.

In a relationship it is crucial to talk about your disagreements, before assumptions, fabrications and disastrous expectations turn into reality. Whenever you are jealous, something is devouring you, you feel indebted to the other. If that happens, you must talk about it.

Without communication, clarification and adjusting of values, no relationship will survive for very long. Partners must seek ways to understand each other and find solutions that are acceptable to both sides, without either of them having the feeling of being pushed into a corner.

Let me repeat: There is no winner and no loser in a relationship.

Only two winners, or two losers.

347

CHOOSE A PARTNER WHO KNOWS THE MAP

To know a map means to understand the reality of the present time, from the positive as well as the negative side. The right partner is able to understand the pressure of such times. He is prepared for ups and downs. He knows that nobody in the world is happy and successful all the time. He understands that troubled times, when the situation has to be brought up to date and made relevant, interfere with the relationship as well. More than ever before, people are forced to work on themselves, to develop. A partner should understand your desire to succeed, to do what you are convinced is right for you, even if it is a change into a new direction.

But a partner who always looks backward is living outside the advancing reality. He wants to hold time back. He wants to project on to other people properties and abilities that he does not have, and only wishes that the other has them. It is like pushing a boat from the water on to a dry bank, in the naive hope that the boat will grow wheels or sprout wings during the process.

Being contemporary also means to keep promises. Regardless of circumstances, to insist that a given word must be honoured. When a partner says that he will do something, he must do it, or at least do his best to fulfil this obligation. When a partner promises he will be somewhere at a certain time, he must make sure that he is there. Only in this way is it possible to trust his declarations of love, to know he really means it. Not just half-heartedly.

And especially, he should work on the map of relationships. He should be aware that a relationship cannot be built on lies. If he is unable to do something, despite his intentions, he must be able to admit it. Besides, if two people are to solve problems

together (and problems there certainly will be) and if they are to listen to each other, express their trust and find compromises, they must have time for each other.

From the moment of the first contact, you can sense if the prospective partner is capable of all this. You should never fight for a place in his life. And also you should never force him to make time for you. This is something he should do of his own accord.

CHOOSE A PARTNER WHO DOES NOT LEAVE

Unfortunately, there are people who stay close to you only as long as you offer what is beneficial to them, what they need at the moment. When this need passes, or they lose their desire, such people leave. If we refer back to the original comparison, such people are not those who help you tidy up after a party. On the contrary, such NON-partners are just wasting your time.

Take note of how your realisation affects the openness of communication from the very beginning. Do not minimise or overlook any minor uneasiness you have about the relationship now.

Speak up. Discuss. Demand explanations. Do not regret the time spent on this. Because time invested in communication in this phase can save incomparably more time in the future.

Tip for an optimal partner:

Why you should choose an optimist

An idealist lives in the world of ideals, but ideals (perfection) do not exist.

A realist lives in reality, but it might not be pleasant.

An optimist is a positively equipped realist.

He is not reconciled with the present, but believes that he will be able to create a better future. Winston Churchill, who also won the Nobel Prize for literature, for-

mulated it in these words: "A pessimist sees the difficulty in every opportunity; an optimist sees the opportunity in every difficulty."

Life's success, whether at work or in relationships, can be imagined as a road leading from wishes to realisation. The road can lead across slippery landscapes, via detours, through narrow passages, over unexpected obstacles.

Nevertheless, it takes you in the direction of the destination.

Moreover, you must believe it is leading in the right direction.

Our faith, which we can imagine as crash barriers on this road, is called optimism.

Man is not born a successful driver of this road, but becomes one. In the same way, man is not born a successful person and optimist. Optimism is not inherent. But optimism can be learned. As a fixed set of habits.

Why is an optimist the best partner for a relationship?

1st REASON: An optimist strives for the best result from all existing possibilities

An optimist is actually a positive realist. Regardless of circumstances, he believes that he can turn all usable possibilities into success. If he has a coin, he believes that he would get heads when tossing it, but, of course, the odds are 50 : 50.

An idealist, unlike an optimist, ignores risks and negatives. In our case, he does not even accept any other possibility than getting heads. He does not even perceive the coin has two sides.

A pessimist, paradoxically, is the reverse of the two mentioned types. He does not believe he will ever get heads. He is so convinced about it internally that he prefers not to toss the coin at all, as he considers it pointless.

A relationship with an optimist is characterised by faith in achieving the best result. This is very useful. He who believes, seeks. And he who seeks, finds. If, for example, an optimist and an idealist come to a lemon tree, the idealist picks the first fruit, convinced it will be as sweet as an orange. Idealists also turn into pessimists the

most often. The optimist in the same situation evaluates all the possibilities and turns reality into a positive outcome. If he wants to sweeten his life, he squeezes the ripe lemons into a glass, pours in water and adds sugar. And enjoys drinking the lemonade.

Yes, this is optimism. To believe in the best possible result — because you are able to influence it.

2ⁿᵈ REASON: An optimist respects himself for who he is

"Children, who of you think you can sing?"

Ask this question in a kindergarten.

All the children will raise their hands. Indeed, small children are natural-born optimists. They believe they can run, jump, sing and dance better than anybody else. And they are right. Nobody can run, jump and dance like they do. All children are therefore quite unique. And optimistic.

Ask the same question in the primary school.

You will see considerably fewer hands being raised. And the higher the grade, the fewer pupils will put their hands up.

In the high school, almost no one thinks he can sing. And it is advisable not to ask adults at all.

How is this possible? Why do people believe less in their skills as they get older? Shouldn't it be the other way round? After all, we practise, improve and gain new skills every day. As children, we were convinced we were perfect in everything, so we should be able to run, jump, sing and dance even better as the years go by. And perhaps we do. So why do we have no self-confidence?

Why are we so ashamed that we can or cannot do something?

It is simple. Because you have less and less self-respect. As you grow up — crushed by parents, teachers and employers — you hear so many judgements that you are not good enough. With each negative experience, and this applies in relationships

352

too, you tend to give up and crawl deeper into your shell. The older an employee, the more uncertain he is about his job. As if experience was dwindling, instead of growing. As if with increasing wisdom, human value was decreasing.

Unfortunately, this is the case for many people. By their willingness to conform, they lose themselves and their original value. They are convinced that they cannot influence their lives actively and are dependent on others. They are turning into pessimists.

An optimist also hears other people's opinions and judgements. He bears them in mind, but does not go along with them. He regards them as feedback, from which he can extract the good that he can use to his benefit. However, he takes the comments of others with a pinch of salt. He does not simply accept them mildly. His own navigation system guides him through life. It is called intuition.

Optimists mostly achieve their goals, not because they have more skills and knowledge than anyone else, but because they believe they can be better than they are at the moment. They count on each day bringing a new experience.

For a realist, his performance of today is the limit. He assures himself that what he has not achieved today, he will not achieve tomorrow either. And he is right, in a sense. Because if he believes this, then he will definitely not have more success the next day.

On the other hand, an optimist believes he can keep improving and go beyond his limit. That is why he tries to be as good as he can every moment, so that while acting in such a way he will become even better.

A pessimist does not look to the future, does not think about the future, but does not think about the present either. He looks back to the past, and, what is worse, does so with a negative outlook. He sees what he used to be like, and searches his conscience to discover how he could be so inexperienced. He does not believe in himself in the future either. He is more and more crushed, the deeper he goes into the past. An optimist laughs at this. He knows he was no better at the same age. And that all of us were inexperienced in the beginning.

3rd REASON: An optimist believes he is able to achieve higher goals

This paragraph is a blessing for a relationship.

Particularly for a partner who has run into trouble.

An optimist not only recognises the best possible result, but believes that this result can be achieved by anyone who is prepared to put in sufficient effort.

A pessimist in the same position will not admit the best possible result if he is down, and even rejects the idea that he might be able to achieve it.

Life is no persuader. It gives everyone what he asks for. And additionally, for the optimist, it provides the experience that the outlook for the future in any situation does not depend on his immediate abilities.

What you can or cannot do can always be complemented, improved, shaped. Your main worker, who builds your success, is inside your head. That is why the most successful person is usually the one who does not even consider the possibility of failure. Because if you think this, of course there is no way of succeeding, because you will not even have the self-confidence to try.

4th REASON: An optimist knows that life is a series of ups and downs

Although many pessimists would not like to admit this, an optimist does not live on another planet. His days are not only rosy.

The difference is that he does not mind going through bad stages, because he knows that they are part of life too. Nothing in Nature is more natural than change.

Just because something is not going well does not mean you have to believe that it will never get better. No, look into the future. After all, how many twists and turns have there been in your life? Indeed, life is like waves of the ocean.

An optimist does not ask the waves only to rise and never to fall back. On the contrary, he tries to get the best from both – the rises as well as the falls.

Change is the foundation of the optimist's satisfaction. Also because he does not look ahead or backwards, but at his feet right where he is.

5ᵗʰ REASON: An optimist does not separate the path and the destination

Success and happiness have one thing in common: They are not handed out randomly at birth. You have to strive to achieve them, both of them. How do you do that? The progress can happen in a mere second.

You only need to change your attitude.

To feel happy, it is enough to discover something in life that will make you happy, and pursue it. An optimist does not imagine success as a long path of suffering that will hopefully end at the finish line.

Because an optimist sees success in every step of progress on the way along this path. Those who feel successful and happy only after crossing the finish line do not experience any satisfaction along the way. That is why so many people steer clear of the path to success and happiness. They think it looks too long and difficult. They do not realise that the source of happiness and success is actually found along the whole path. Every day. Every single moment in which we surpass ourselves.

An optimist is often already happy, because he sets goals that please and motivate him. He always has something to strive for, something to grow for. He loves the path he is following more than the finish line, which he does not actually need to reach. For the optimist, success and happiness are therefore like light radiating from his own person and attitude, rather than circumstances that enter his life. An optimist does not mind that there will always be things he will never own. Even if he was the richest man in the world, he knows there will always be something more to get.

An optimist therefore is someone with the healthiest energy. Because at every moment he can tell himself that no matter what he desires, he already has enough of everything. Nevertheless, this does not prevent him from believing that he can achieve even more.

6ᵗʰ REASON: An optimist talks positively

It is characteristic of an optimist that he will try to lead a positive life, regardless of events and circumstances that cross his path and that he is unable to influence. His mood is not determined by what is happening around him, but by how he interprets it. And especially by the way he talks and thinks about life.

When a young pessimist gets a good mark at school, he thinks: "*Hmm, I was lucky. It will be worse next time.*"

When a young optimist gets a bad mark, he thinks: "*Hmm, I deserved it. It must be better next time.*" And when he gets a good mark, he thinks: "*I believed it. I worked on myself and it paid off.*"

What is the main difference between these two types?

A pessimist finds difficulties outside himself, he sees them as insurmountable and permanent.

An optimist finds difficulties especially within himself, sees them as surmountable and temporary.

An optimist is especially able to deal with his anxieties. His faith is like the sun, which can brighten the sky after heavy rain, until a spectacular rainbow appears.

Yes, an optimist's attitude to life is just like that.

7th REASON: An optimist avoids negative people

For a healthy, untainted atmosphere in a relationship, it is particularly important for an optimist that it is not contaminated by envious and bad-tempered people. Either he avoids them completely, or ensures he spends as little time with them as possible. He knows that a group can grind an individual down. Indeed, the attitudes and thinking of people whom you meet the most can become the accepted standard, whether you wish it or not.

If an optimist seeks out somebody new, it is someone who thinks the same way he does, someone who knows that optimism starts from nothing, because he can build self-confidence by gradual successes. That is why optimists are in the habit of setting higher goals than they can achieve at that moment. For this, you need sufficiently inspiring models and supportive people who lead you to self-improvement and growth, and who will remain close to you even in the case of temporary non-success – to keep providing courage and enthusiasm whenever there is a risk that, due to a single failure, you might lose heart and decide that your enthusiasm has completely faded.

No, as long as you are alive, you have your attitude in your hands.

Optimists believe this. It is not bad to be in a relationship with them, is it?

PART 3 | NEW PARTNER

HOW TO (CO-)WORK ON THE RELATIONSHIP

None of us can promise to be with the other till the end of his life. But you can promise that you will be with him till the end of your life. A promise, like any word, is just an assumption. Only deeds give it meaning. So, on what foundations can a long-term relationship be built? What can destroy it, even at the very beginning?

BALANCING ON THE EDGE OF THE PAST

You can be prepared for a new relationship. Both the partner and you. But then déjà vu comes. A moment which we experienced with someone before. And you immediately recall the series of negative events that followed the same moment and ended with a break-up.

These alarm signs are useful – whenever you approach the edge of a familiar abyss, they warn you to be more cautious this time and keep on in a healthy direction.

We live under the restraint of prejudices. These stem from the past and say very little about the present. They ignore how you have changed and what you have learned in the meantime. The old pain simply reawakens. However, it does not belong to your present anymore. It ached in the past. Thanks to the pain, you remember that you must not repeat the same mistake that accompanied it. Yes, thanks to past pain, you grow wiser.

In warm weather, I take a blanket, call my dog and take a few treats for both of us and head for Petřín, a hill with an observation tower rising above Prague, and we have a picnic on the grass, where many couples are relaxing too. I like to watch them and enjoy seeing the clear difference between couples who have a long history together and live without mutual barriers, and those whose relationship is just beginning and where there still seems to be an invisible glass between the two. They are together, but hesitate to touch each other. Once there was a slightly tense student, trying to break just such a glass separating him from a slightly older, rather casual lady companion.

He wanted to make a perfect first impression. He wore a white shirt, a bow tie, he made the effort to be very attentive, gallant and romantic. He sat the woman on the lawn, poured her tea from a thermos bottle, he had even prepared the words to win her heart in advance. They were written on a sheet of paper which he pulled out when he eventually plucked up the courage.

"*Love is like a rainbow. Colourful, it can conjure up a smile,*" he read and looked at the listener. She did not react. He looked perplexed. "*Well, it is also like an ocean, deep and beautiful.*" The woman looked around. "*Or like the sun, it shines and warms.*" She yawned, looked bored. His chin was trembling. But he wanted to read everything he had so painstakingly written down. "*And love can also be like rain, because it cools down and refreshes.*"

Nothing. An embarrassed silence. It was obvious that his selection of poetry did not appeal to her. It must have been a terrible feeling for him.

Using the last remains of self-confidence, he threw out the last prepared line: "*Will you allow me to show you the love described here?*" The hand holding the paper shook nervously. She mercilessly shook her head.

The destruction was complete. At that moment his mask fell. Crushed, he bent his head and – for the first time, he was himself.

At that moment she exclaimed: "*This is what I want. I do not long for love from poems. Always show me only YOUR love.*"

HOW TO AVOID HEADING INTO AN OLD DEAD END IN A NEW RELATIONSHIP

A hint of a partner's insincerity.

An old wound carelessly touched.

A partner's doubts about you.

Ouch, how are you supposed to convince yourself and your aching gloomy memories at that moment? How are you supposed to believe that the new partner will be better? Would it not be more secure to turn from the blank sheet of paper, today's potential partner, back to the old well-read book, to the former partner who perhaps disappointed you, but from whom at least you know what unkindness to expect? What if you are wasting your time by blind faith and even the new partner does not realise your value until he is left to stay alone?

Such theorisation is an anchor. The object that lies at the bottom of the sea and keeps the boat in one place. To lift the anchor means things like deleting old contacts from your mobile phone. Burning the photographs of someone who hurt you in the past. Dissolving your gnawing memories.

To lift the anchor also means to bet on one direction. You may wonder: What if the waves toss me against a cliff after I weigh anchor? Is not it safer to remain at anchor, even if the water is calm?

These thoughts return, whenever you stop adhering to the following laws for a very new relationship:

363

A FEELING OF HUMILIATION IS ALWAYS A SIGNAL TO CONSIDER A CHANGE

It could be just an isolated case: the partner's emotional outburst, frazzled nerves, simply an exception. But it could also be the first warning of an approaching storm. You do not know. But you do not need to experience a crashing storm. That is why it is important to realise that this is exactly the time to talk to your partner and remind him of your principles and values. In particular that:

The meaning of life is to live. Not to survive.

To live, really live, means to act in such a way that you feel happy. You tend towards relationships in order to be happier than when you are alone. Unhappy feelings in a relationship are a clear signal that something must change. What you are living in clearly is not fulfilling your need.

A partner must be able to control himself. He cannot claim that it is beyond his power. All the instruments of self-control are contained in the body. Happiness is your inner feeling. If you are not happy, the problem is within. Not in other people or events. It is especially in your attitude. Instead of looking outwards to find somebody to blame, look inwards.

Cast light on: 1) what you feel, 2) what you think about it, 3) how you will react to both.

The background of a partner's outburst can be manifold. If there were unexpected, troublesome changes in his life (job), remind him that we are never powerless. Even when we feel powerless, it is just a feeling. We have immense power. Our life is our responsibility. You cannot always change what is happening outside you, especially

364

the way someone else behaves. After all, everyone is a sovereign person. You cannot control what he will do. His life is his responsibility. But you can always have an influence on what you allow in your life. Whenever a nervous partner changes his view of life, his life will change on its own. And the way to positive deeds will open for him. If he remains negative, he will only destroy.

UNLEASH YOUR PRESENCE

These three words sound strange and ambiguous, so let me explain. A barely noticeable event can trigger negative feelings in a relationship. A thought flashes through the mind that all partners are bad and the same. The feeling that the new partner's behaviour is strikingly similar to that of your former partner suddenly grips you like a pair of pliers. Why is this happening?

Expectations are usually the cause. Mistaken assumptions usually hurt the most. Fabricated images in a relationship about what the partner is supposed to do/not do, how you should/should not behave. The greater the expectations, the greater the level of disappointment.

Whenever your expectations are disappointed, you feel unhappy, although it is not always a partner's mistake, but most often a mistake on the part of your expectations. Try to expect nothing for a moment, only watch to see what comes your way.

Disappointment will disappear.

Curiosity will increase.

You will begin to look around the corner of the street of life, and learn to prepare for anything.

Start to live in the present moment.

More for yourself than for others.

More by your perception than by outside judgements.

Start to see today as a gift, which you cannot use tomorrow, because each day lasts only a limited time.

And instead of constantly being on the watch for time that has not come yet, you should live in the time that is here now. Then you will discover that it already contains all the miracles you long for in the depths of your soul.

You must have eyes only for today.

YOUR SUFFERING IN A NEW RELATIONSHIP CAUSES NEEDLESS RESISTANCE TO WHAT IS HAPPENING; DO NOT COUNTERACT IT AT ANY COST

Every partner is different. If you feel like comparing the current one with a previous one, you can always find positive as well as negative differences. The fundamental problem is that such comparison does not bring anything positive to the new relationship. It says nothing distinctive about the partner.

Man is no construction set that can be assembled from pieces that suit us the best. You cannot change the partner, it is meaningless to regret what he does not have while the previous one had it.

Nobody is so perfect as to be perceived as perfect by everybody. You can see your partner as being 90 percent perfect. If you want to see him negatively, you will notice the missing 10 percent. And if you are especially obstinate, you will start seeking someone who has that 10 percent. In the end, you will be willing to exchange the 10 percent you missed for the 90 percent you actually liked.

Rather try to stop resisting what you have. To focus on the present means to unfocus both the past and present. With this step, you start noticing more what is happening, not what happened or what might happen. It will help you to find satisfaction with what is and what you have, rather than regret what is not and what you do not have. You will be more satisfied, not because you did not have something previously that you realise you have now. Only you ignored it. You could not look

at the present positively. Moreover, whenever you can realise what is or what you have, you are able to work further and make positive changes.

To be able to define the terminology correctly:

What is, always means that which is to be.

People mistakenly believe that what is to be must only be an ideal. While in fact what is to be is what you urgently need at a given moment to learn and thus improve your life. That is why life sometimes also needs to include negative experiences in what is to be. Only this guarantees that you do not step into the same muddy puddle in the future. Negative events push you further than positive ones.

When you accept that what is = what is to be, you will understand that all the rest of your thoughts is just you disputing with your own faith. Therefore, suffering enters your life only when you defy what is. Do not forget that, although you cannot influence everything happening to you, you can influence the way you react to it.

Your reaction is your strength. You have strength only in the present.

COMPLAINING ONLY WORSENS EVERYTHING, RATHER SEEK SOLUTIONS

In a relationship, just as important as knowing what to do, is to make up your mind what not to do. For example in moments when you can no longer stand your partner disturbing your privacy and entering areas that used to be only yours; when he switches television programmes; when he wants to spend time differently to what you were used to; when he enforces his priorities and demands compromises from you. This is when you consider leaving, to be alone again.

People unable to cope with change, who feel overpowered, would like to conserve time. But this cannot be done. They tend to complain. Aloud and to everybody who is nearby and can hear. Which does not help anyone, and themselves even less. In life, you never get where you want to be by merely complaining about where you are now.

Complaining solves nothing. It is a pointless activity. It does not work as an efficient long-term tactic or strategy. Because each step in life prepares you for the next step. To stand in one place and complain about the previous step serves no purpose and is unnecessary. Indeed, the next step can already correct the previous one. You are wasting all your time and energy howling at the moon like a wolf.

If you take only 10 percent of the time and energy spent complaining and use that for solving the problem, you will be surprised how quickly life will start functioning again. All of us have more power and influence over our destiny than we realise. Whenever you stop complaining and marking yourself as a helpless victim, you will reveal that you are stronger than you thought. However, only when you use this power in practice.

EVEN A SHORT STEP IS PROGRESS

A relationship is the most fragile at the beginning. Both partners have their hands close to the emergency brake to stop the train before it gets far from the platform. At the beginning, they also feel how different they are, they are not so attuned to each other by shared habits and time spent in compromise. In the first serious quarrel they may fall back to the old scepticism, feel sorry for themselves, stop moving. They are not as compliant yet, easily fall silent or boycott communication. Suddenly simply nothing, silence.

How to survive this dangerous vacuum?

How to overcome this early crisis if the other does not want to talk?

How to survive a vitally important beginning, when young outgrowths must take root and become stronger stems, when they need nourishment, which in a relationship is the feeling that you miss each other, but which is hard to express without communication?

A little thing helps in that temporary solitude. One small step forward each day. You will start feeling better and stronger. This is what you should do today. One step. Even a small one. Everybody prefers something. To write your feelings off. Enjoy the company of friends. Devote yourself to hobbies, family, work. Small steps make the greatest difference. Because they are simple and everybody can take them, even somebody who feels crushed in a relationship. The gem of this small step is the discovery that the next step will seem reasonable too. And so will the following. Until you find after some time that you have surfaced from the inner suffering. That you are prepared to accept reality, whatever it is.

Not the steps, but what is happening inside your head, is the hardest. Because all of us are inclined to magnify ourselves. It seems to us that our life is illuminated by rows of lights, that we are playing the main role, and the world will collapse if we

fail. This is just a feeling. Not a fact. Just look around. There are millions of people with problems. Often bigger than yours. And it seems to you that their problems are easy to solve. Not because they are simple. But because you can keep a detached view, as other people's problems do not clog the centre of the cosmos. We lack such a detached view when facing our own problems. They seem to overwhelm us.

Whenever you stop being egotistical and realise the wider context of the problems, it helps to do away with self-pity. You will find out that you do not have to feel pity for yourself, because your problems are not the centre of the world. The remedy for your pain is already in the question: What do people around me need? To think about others is the best strategy. Not only will you stop magnifying your own problems, but you will also be useful and your life will become meaningful. Just by helping somebody else, you will stop feeling futile and useless. And you will realise that all people have an opportunity to change. Even if the change is to take place only in your heart. In the perspective through which you look at your surroundings. In decisions that will immediately transform life.

Never underestimate your power, whether in terms of helping others or yourself. And do not undervalue any day that is left. For example, by repeating old mistakes, and therefore also arriving at the same results.

NEGLECTED COMMUNICATION

Partners believe they understand each other, although they never get such first-hand experience. Parents always have the best instructions for life for their children, without actually caring about their own needs and personal views. People usually quickly finish communicating so that they can catch up with the sports broadcasts, TV shows, work that has priority. The simple belief that we know the other best, unfortunately leads to complex ends. While we adjust to something existing only in our imagination, we often do not see what exists in reality.

My French friend Melchior met a girl who became blind during an injury. Her handicap was still recent and she had nothing but scorn for the world, hatred, anger, animosity for other people. She gradually lost all her old friends, not because of her blindness, but because of her new attitude to life. Only Melchior did not allow himself to be repelled. This irritated her. She wanted to hurt herself, to degrade herself.

"Don't you see that I am blind? Poor man, you have eyes and yet do not see anything? Look," she put his fingers on her empty eye sockets.

"The two of us can never be happy together, you are healthy, I am a cripple. It would not work for us, understand that finally!" the girl shouted. Rather embarrassingly, she was not aware of one significant factor.

Melchior listened to her self-torment, shrugged and replied: *"Fine, I respect that. I just wanted to do my best that you should feel happy. Take care and try to open the eyes that are more important – eyes in your heart."*

Melchior is blind too. But she did not know.

QUESTIONS THAT MUST NOT BE MISSING IN A NEW RELATIONSHIP

People mistake *"communication"* and communication.

The first communication is shallow. Because the participant has the impression that he will be praised just for taking part in it. The following is an example:

"Hi, what was new today?"

"Nothing. And you?"

"Also nothing." And silence.

People often complain that they do not get the right answers, but they do not know how to ask the right questions. They ask without interest, and thus start a conversation which leads nowhere. Their relationship therefore stays the same.

Communication is the key to a relationship. Communication can deepen and open it, if the other person is not uninterested. When you ask the right questions, you will hear answers directly from the heart. You will learn to ask because you really care about what the other person feels and what he needs to tell you. Not only will you learn more, but you will really get to know him. If you do not seek meaning and depth in a relationship, then you are not able to ask questions that are meaningful and deep.

Questions that show how much you care for the other are a key to his heart. You can build a successful relationship just by asking questions. So do not start with questions floating in the air without substance. Start on the ground. Your questions will build retaining walls that will protect the partner whenever he might feel depressed, useless and overlooked in the relationship. It does not matter whether it was just because of his wrong impressions. You already know that feelings lead to thoughts, thoughts to actions and actions to results. So what laws can you use to protect the partner?

ASK THE PARTNER AS OFTEN AS POSSIBLE:

"What made you feel good today?"

Why do people enter into relationships if they feel happy alone? Because a functioning relationship works better with energy. Shared joy is double joy in such a relationship, and a shared worry is half a worry. But it is necessary to start sharing both joys and worries.

Regardless of how you feel, it is already strengthening if you know you have a partner who is interested in the reasons for your temper. A partner is one of the few people whom you can be sure wishes you success. Because it involves him too, intimately. The more positive energy you emit, the more positive he will feel too. Because we are like connected vessels. That is why it is pivotal to stand by a partner and to share your happiness and worries with him.

And why ask in a positive way? Why not ask what made the partner feel bad today? Positive questions lead to positive answers. Positive answers can only use positive terms, formulated on the basis of positive thoughts and feelings. A mere question can change a person's mood. All days in life are not good. But there is something good in every day. This is the task of the troubled partner, if it is a problem for him to look at an ordinary day in a detached way. Even if the day brings nothing good, you must remind the partner that life is change and the days to come will certainly bring something good. With a little help.

Remember that happiness in a relationship depends on the quality of the thoughts put in it by the partners. On how positive they are and on their perspective. One day you will see that you can laugh about things that made you sad in the past.

ASK THE PARTNER AS OFTEN AS POSSIBLE:

"What makes you feel lonely and unimportant?"

Sometimes we feel we are facing all the demons of the world. However, in a relationship there are two of you to face the demons. And even if the two of you do not defeat them, it will always produce something positive. Fighting a common enemy gives a relationship cohesion.

People in pairs do not give up as quickly as when they are alone. You have a better chance if there is somebody who will mobilise you and cover your back. There is a shoulder to lean on, and hands to embrace and support you.

So listen to a partner when he is frustrated, stay with him when he needs to think things over, offer him a shoulder when he wants to rest a heavy head, and a handkerchief when he feels like weeping. Be nearby under all circumstances. Why, do you ask? Because this is what a partner does.

ASK THE PARTNER AS OFTEN AS POSSIBLE:

"What should I do to make you feel loved and appreciated?"

Bad partners dislike it when the other is disappointed or annoyed. As if he is not allowed to be human. These bad partners even ridicule, insult, degrade the other partner. Yes, they make him feel worse. Which does not help the relationship, and neither of the partners.

What if you present *"the best speech of your life"*, in which you are brimful of stupid anger and which you will regret later, to yourself in the mirror first? What if the partner's miserable feelings are caused by your inability to express enough love and interest? What if the mistake is on your side?

Everybody has a right to weak moments – because it is human. In a relationship, it does not matter how sure you are that the other will support you, there is always good reason to spend some more time on strengthening the basis of support. To love and be loved in return are the strongest emotional experiences, and they should be expressed as often as possible, because they generate amazing energy. For both partners.

Do not feel embarrassed if you are revealing your heart. Tell the other partner openly what he means to you, what you appreciate in him and what you admire in him. Most relationships disintegrate because of words that are left unsaid. Do not wait for tomorrow – only in the present can you express how grateful you are for the other.

ASK THE PARTNER AS OFTEN AS POSSIBLE:

"What are you afraid of in our relationship?"

A negative question creates a negative reply. In this case, it has a purpose – to drive a partner's worries away. Regardless of what reply you get, do not judge it, but respect it. Just answering the question already reveals courage. Having the courage to answer sincerely shows human vulnerability and fragility. The answer you will hear can be something you find embarrassing and foolish, perhaps you will even feel offended. But forget about your ego. What is important is that you received an answer. Analyse it together. I repeat: without ego.

Learn to be grateful when your partner points out any problem he feels. Do not get angry, do not be insulting. Thank him, because his words, perhaps negative, warn you that the problem is on a short fuse.

This question is like an X-ray machine. Like under roentgen rays, it localises the source of the problem. It must not stop with the localisation though. It must be like being at the doctor's, you must endure the discomfort of the problem being examined, the pain of the wound being disinfected and cleaned. A bad partner would ignore and belittle the wound, letting it suppurate. The same as a coward who cannot admit any possible failing on his behalf, or an incompetent person who is unable to correct problems and deficiencies constructively, even if they are pointed out to him. It is not easy to live with someone like that.

To love means especially being aware of the feelings of the other, and being willing to find the strength and self-confidence to accept even unpleasant answers from the partner. This question triggers an essential healing process, which shows the

depth of your feelings for the partner. Bringing the whole discussion around the partner's reply to a close by a friendly smile, an embrace and relief on both sides promises a long-lasting positive relationship.

ASK THE PARTNER AS OFTEN AS POSSIBLE:

"How much do you love yourself today?"

Sad people often complain that others dislike them. But do they like themselves? You should not automatically expect more love and respect from anybody else than from yourself. If you do not feel and cherish love and respect for yourself, you will feel weak and useless, and nobody will be able to talk you out of it. The feeling does not come from anyone else but yourself. So if a partner wants to feel happy both in the relationship and a job, he must start with himself.

Creating a contented relationship is always harder than creating a contented self, because both partners must be happy. If each partner is satisfied with himself, he has a strange synergic strength that gives energy to the other too. Loving oneself is the key to happiness. Because happiness works on the principle of light and dark. The less dark there is inside, the more light there is. And vice versa. There is good reason for the saying that if everybody took care of himself, all the people in the world would be taken care of.

So, in your own interest, try to support the other, so that he never needs to beg for love, respect and attention. If he begs you for it, it means that he does not have enough self-love, does not respect himself sufficiently, does not pay attention to himself. If he had sufficient self-love, he would be able to bestow love not only on himself, but on you as well. A partner who dislikes himself is a threat to the whole relationship. Because partners in a relationship are like mountain climbers. They secure each other. If one does not like himself sufficiently and takes risks, he endangers the other at the same time. Yes, it is nice to be kind to others. But in the first instance, be kind to yourself. Teach the partner to give priority to kindness towards himself. For the sake of both of you.

ASK THE PARTNER AS OFTEN AS POSSIBLE:

"What haven't we discussed yet?"

It seems as if this question is empty of meaning. Many partners do not even ask it. Yet it contains everything.

It is not asked in the hurried, that is, obligatory conversation. Because such a question is the opposite of shallowness and lack of interest. It shows that you care about the partner so much that how he feels is important to you even when you are not together. If he had an important meeting at work, ask how it went, but also, for example: *"How did you feel during the meeting? What did the other party say? What was your reply to that?"* (a whole series of questions can develop). You can talk to your children in this way too, for example, about their first date.

This question indicates interest. The main thing to show is that you care about the other. Do not be worried about what you may hear. Questions are crucial in a relationship.

THE PARTNER LOSES STRENGTH

When a man wants to measure his significance, he does not need a tape measure. He just needs to think what he can do for people who at that moment cannot do anything for him. The first such person for whom you can exert your greatest effort is your partner, at a time when he feels crushed by life. Either you can abandon him, because lifting him up would take too much of your energy, or you can grit your teeth and be with him in the situation. You could think that by supporting him you are losing time and will have to pay for it. While in fact you are making an immense investment in the relationship.

It is when your partner's lungs weaken that your breath is needed the most. See the other as if he was part of you. Your Siamese twin. When (together) you pull through the difficulty, you will discover that your approach was no illusion. Because you really are inseparable. Beautifully close in an embrace, thanks to the resolved problem.

I noticed one young couple in the park.

He, Mr Uneasy, went all around the houses.

She, Mrs Impatient, was encouraging him.

When he hesitated and would have liked to take her hand, she grabbed his.

When he was ashamed to embrace her, she directed his arm.

When he was shy about whether the time was right for a kiss, she accidentally brought her lips closer to his.

But still the relationship was on uncertain ground, and the hesitant boy was aware of it. He needed to make his feelings clear.

He swallowed, and then took the plunge for the decisive move:

He: *"Do you think I'm handsome?"*

She: *"No."*

He sheepishly: *"Do you want me as your boyfriend?"*

She: *"No."*

The boy turned pale and trembled. He wrenched himself from the girl and broken-heartedly walked away.

"Wait!" she called after him.

He turned, as if for the final blow, tears in his eyes. She ran to him, squeezed him in her embrace and said:

"I do not think you are handsome. I know you are GORGEOUS.

I do not want you as my boyfriend. I NEED to be your girlfriend.

And if you leave, I can't live without you."

THE MOST IMPORTANT KINDS
OF SUPPORT IN A NEW RELATIONSHIP
COST NOTHING AND YET ARE
PRICELESS

It is beautiful to be a great small man.

So small that you can be overlooked in a crowd.

But whose greatness can be perceived by the heart.

This is what a partner with capital P is. The person who stays, even when the whole world has left. Who supports and pushes the other ahead, even if the whole world forces him back by its negativity.

A Partner usually transforms ordinary moments into extraordinary ones, and unhappy times into happy times, just by being there, by standing beside you. To encourage someone, it is often necessary to take his hand, so that he knows he is not facing his problems alone – regardless of how big the problems are. Not to be alone is the most important human need, even seen in children.

PROD THE PARTNER IF HE NEEDS IT

Unfulfilled dreams bring lots of sadness.

Disappointed expectations.

Lost hopes.

But it hurts even more if you don't allow yourself to pursue what you really want. As French writer François de la Rochefoucauld said: *"Whatever others have done to us we can deal with somehow or other. The worst is what we have done to ourselves."* Man is never considered ridiculous because of the qualities he has, but because of those he pretends to have. Especially if he pretends to himself.

Therefore, a real partner inspires you to become the person you always wanted to be, but did not find enough courage to try to be. Perhaps you did not have the right support or motivation to step over your hesitation, to overcome your fear.

Those who help you do not need hands to push you ahead. They use kindness, encouragement and praise to prod you. Then your half-hearted steps and incomplete determination turn into deeds done with confidence and a full heart.

SPEAK THE TRUTH AT ALL TIMES, ESPECIALLY IF THE PARTNER IS SERIOUSLY AT RISK

False people walk silently past you when you make fatal mistakes and are not aware of them yourself.

False people betray you without your awareness, even if you trust them fully.

False people keep silent, even when you are unwittingly hurting yourself.

No, you are not stupid. But they have enough distance and do not see the details (like you do), but see the whole in a broader context.

They could warn you, but will not do so. They are happy if you waste time – the most precious commodity you have in life.

Of course, being friendly and smiling at everyone brings you lots of acquaintances. But you do not need to build up a specific number of friends. What you rather need is a few friends who are genuine. Who will tell you the truth, even though it may not be pleasant for them to say, and certainly not for you to hear.

People are afraid of telling the truth. Whenever you require it from friends, you will suddenly find you don't have many friends. This is not a problem. At least the real ones will stay. The others will rather say something that is not true just to get out of the situation. They prefer to kill you in the long term, rather than heal you with a single blow.

Sincerity is the only way to face up to all the risks the other is struggling with, and show him a better way. Of course, you must respect his view and his decisions, because it is his life. If he insists on his way, stand by him. And do not reproach him

when his plans fail and your warnings prove to be justified. Do not be a know-all. Keep supporting him and provide warnings about possible new dangers.

You have to learn to recognise the point up to which it is still useful to make your own mistakes and learn your own lessons, but after which failure can have devastating consequences. Imagine a tightrope walker, for instance. You will not help him if you simply approve of his idea of walking blindfolded on a rope stretched above the city. This might be the limit beyond which he will not be able to learn from a possible mistake.

SUPPORT THE PARTNER UNCONDITIONALLY

L ove does not accept conditions.

It is either unconditional, or it is not love.

Remove from your thoughts the phrase, "*I will not support you if...*" or "*I will support you because...*"

People in love always pay in advance. Without thinking twice. Because support in the right relationship is beneficial for both. Even when only one partner gives, both are recipients.

One gets support, the other gets the feeling that he is being useful.

PUT IN AN EXTRA EFFORT TO UNDERSTAND THE OTHER

People are completely different from one another, it is not easy to know what the other thinks. Sometimes you have to describe your whole life to the other, so that he has at least some idea of what you are experiencing at any given moment. It is always easier to ignore than to help. Because help and support require an active approach, with extra energy put in. To help or support means using your energy to destroy the negatives that surround your partner.

Feelings are particularly difficult to describe to a partner. They are insubstantial, have a colour, no physical existence. Besides, the colour can change all the time. Also, a partner who finds himself in trouble can be reluctant to talk about it, thinking that his sad tale of woes will be a burden for you. Everything loses its meaning for him, he does not even see why he should confess what *"cannot be solved anyway"*.

There is all the more reason to stand by this person. You do not have to force the words from him. Just support him with your presence, by a simple embrace. Do not enforce any of your own solutions or ideas on a partner who feels he has hit rock bottom. You do not have to act on his behalf or manipulate him in the belief that you would solve the same situation better. No, you would not. You cannot even imagine what your partner is going through.

Put the maximum effort into just being there with him. Although it might not seem much, it is often more valuable that all the riches in the world.

STAND BY THE PARTNER AT ALL TIMES, BUT DOUBLY SO IN DIFFICULT TIMES

W e feel an affiliation with those who smile at us.

We avoid those who frown at us.

But you must not ignore a partner who falls into a negative state. The mere question, *"What happened?"* can have a healing effect on the other.

No relationship will survive long without sincere interest. Because every relationship like that is dead. I emphasise the word sincere. Why?

Although you always provide support, do not see it as paying your partner and doing it for what you can get out of it for yourself. That would be as small-minded as counting the pennies to see how much each partner contributed to a shared budget. The main currency in a relationship is not money, but support. That is also why the words I must do not exist in a relationship, but only I want. The more so, when a sincere interest makes you uncomfortable, because that means you do not like sharing something unpleasant with the other.

A relationship can be entered by strong individuals. Because you can give to others only what you can give to yourself. Therefore, treat a partner in such way that he thinks about himself. Help him to like himself better. Indeed, this is how you began to work on yourself. And you made it. Your partner can make it too. If you, the source of his inspiration, do not leave him.

A RELATIONSHIP CAN BE CRUSHED BY MODERN TIMES

Times have changed. Everything is electronic now.

A sentence written on paper could not be changed before. Now you can erase any word with a click of a button, or you can amend a public promise on social network.

We are starting to communicate with people only through a monitor, without ever feeling their breath, hearing their real voices, or holding their hands. That is enough for us. Our feelings are limited to emoticons, even serious issues can be treated lightly. With modernisation, robots and automation, we should theoretically have more time for each other. In the past, you spent a whole day to travel 100 kilometres, now it takes an hour by car. In no other time in history were people so close and yet so isolated from one another. We are so unsettled. The computer dustbin is bottomless. You can throw away any document you do not like, and start writing it from scratch again.

The same approach is emerging in relationships. Why solve problems and work on improving the relationship if it is easy to throw a person into the dustbin and open a new file?

The man at the florist's shop standing in front of me ordered: "*31 flowers please. Give me 30 of these red roses...*"

And the last flower?" the florist asked.

"*Add an artificial one,*" the man surprised her.

The customer is always right. So the florist prepared the strange bunch without comment. The man paid and left.

I saw him in the street a few minutes later. He handed the bunch to an overjoyed lady, who impatiently tore off the wrapping paper. She was horrified when she saw the plastic flower among the living ones. I went closer to hear the man's explanation:

"I wish you all the best. I will love you until the last flower in this bunch withers."

HOW TO BUILD A TIMELESS RELATIONSHIP FROM SCRATCH

Why do so many partners stop building when problems arise?

Why do they break up the relationship, claiming that it was not possible to continue with that partner any longer, rather than trying to find a way to make it work?

Why has compromise become a forbidden word and why do people prefer to start another relationship, rather than solving their disagreements?

Why have trivialities – which some people consider tiresome, but are actually very simple to deal with – disappeared from love?

Why do people forget how amazing love is when we talk about it, and even more amazing when we show it?

How can you survive these impersonal times in which someone who tries to build a long-term relationship is seen as abnormal?

How can you get rid of the modern technology that interferes with your life and dehumanises something that is elusive and immaterial – such as merely being together?

Observing the following laws can bring some ordinary personal feelings back into the cold technological times:

SET ASIDE A TIME JUST FOR BEING TOGETHER, AWAY FROM MODERN TECHNOLOGY AND CURRENT WORK

In the past, a couple could enjoy time spent alone together. Today, people are not alone anymore. They are constantly online. Available to anyone who contacts them. Slaves of online relationships that penetrate into their privacy.

It is the rare individual who is capable of something as unthinkable as putting off the smartphone, turning off the laptop, and talking face to face, not via Facebook. He knows that the partner's expression is different from a photograph, that a conversation is real compared with texting or Skype. In brief, he is a real living being, not communication shortcuts and emoticons. His hands can be touched physically, and you can feel his heartbeat, soul, energy. He knows that kissing warm lips is more satisfying than staring at a cold monitor.

Of course, with all the iPhones, iPads and other iThings we are more in, cool, trendy. However, no mobile application can replace live laughter, dancing in a passionate embrace, a romantic walk under the stars. I understand that everything human is starting to belong to the past. Things that were once normal are now becoming rare and unusual. We would rather spend time with Angry Birds than with close friends.

But give it a chance. Even if you feel you're so busy that you can't stop, make some time for your partner. Not because someone suggests you should do so, but because it is worth it. None of your so-called friends from the virtual world will do as much for you as a real living partner. And do you know why? Because a living partner is part of reality. Virtual friends are only the result of your impulses.

BE WITH YOUR PARTNER

W hat law is this?

Does this sentence seem to be missing something? Does it seem incomplete? But that's it. It may make you think again.

Of course it is natural to be with your partner. Fine. But what about really BEING with him when you are with him?

The strongest human emotions include delight on the one hand, when you are with someone who is important to you, and anxiety on the other hand, when that person is not with you. These are two opposing feelings, but they lead to the same behaviour.

In both examples you show the partner how much he means to you. It is best to do it when you are with him. Therefore, when you are with him, really be with him. Devote sincere and focused attention to him. Give him the most precious thing in your life – your time. Without looking at a watch, or thinking of your next meeting, or about tomorrow's business. To give your own time to your partner is the most valuable gesture you can make.

People you care about are too valuable to be ignored. You do not have to buy them expensive gifts. These are only material objects. You do not have to make excuses and say you have no money and have nothing to give your partner. All of us can save something that does not cost even a penny – time spent together. Do you know why this is the most precious? Because it does not break, wear out, get lost. And it will remain in the memory for a lifetime.

PAY COMPLIMENTS

There is no reason to criticise the other if he fails.

There is no reason to abandon the other if his path is difficult.

There is no reason to ridicule the other if success remains beyond his reach.

There is no reason to humiliate the other only because you were right.

It does not matter if the partner is worthy of admiration at any particular moment or not, appreciate him. Although his weaknesses may rise to the surface of his character at a particular moment, remind him of his strengths. Do not try to be the judge who condemns what someone did wrong, or the coach who shouts out what must be improved. Try to be the third option – support. Support has the most difficult and yet the most important purpose. To stand by the other, just when it is the most important, when he is not doing well.

There is no ideal relationship which emerges and lasts while ages and ages pass by. There are only challenging relationships on which the partners work continuously and, by a combined effort, advance toward an ideal. Such a relationship is not formed by people who are perfect. But by people who are equally imperfect and who are suited to each other. People who sometimes find themselves at rock bottom and who get stronger and more resistant just by overcoming the greatest difficulties.

Although the partners are attracted initially by external appearances, sooner or later their senses will begin to see under the surface, beneath the outer husk. The soul, the heart, the energy, thinking. They will begin to perceive the essence of the person, not only the shell.

This is when they really fall in love.

Physical beauty changes with age, sometimes fades. But internal beauty can grow eternally. Just close your eyes and look with your heart. Give your support, regardless of what you see.

More precisely, support what you feel.

DO NOT MAKE AN AVALANCHE FROM SNOWFLAKES

Whatever the vice and wickedness, man is so ingenious that he always finds enough reason to regard evil as an advantage. That includes telling lies.

An insincere partner claims that he cares about the other, so he does not tell her unpleasant things. In fact, he cares so little about the partner that he is insincere to her. No, insincerity is not a manifestation of perceptiveness and consideration, but the inability to cope with the truth and its consequences.

It can start as a folly. Like an innocent flirtation. But that leads to the first lie. A lie is like an avalanche. It starts with a single snowflake. The pile of snowflakes keeps getting bigger and bigger because of other lies piling up. Its volume increases, because you do not only lie to others, but also to yourself. You lie to your conscience, start losing sleep, remorse grows and grows. You know that you would not want to live with a liar yourself.

Yet, you must.

Because you are living with – yourself!

We often lie only to protect our fragile egos. That is the only thing at stake. We are so cowardly that we cannot bear the consequences of deeds we are responsible for.

Let's look at it from the other side. Let's stop finding excuses. Let's accept personal responsibility for what did not work out. If you think that your confession will hurt the person you care for, admit these mistakes all the more readily and face the deserved consequences. Confess the truth, not because of the other person, but because of yourself. Accept the hard school of life. You deserve to see an intimate

partner with a broken heart and in tears. If you have any conscience, this tragic image must be engraved in your memory for your whole life. And you will learn.

Apology is the best glue for a long-term relationship. After all, all of us make mistakes. Perhaps the apology will not be enough compensation for what you have done to the other, but it will be good for both of you. You will help the other to find a better partner, and at the same time you will help yourself to start creating a better Self. To behave so that you are not ashamed of the truth.

If you erred, well, it happened. With an apology and a correction, you have done your duty. Now the ball is in your partner's court. *Can he forgive you? Will he be able to support you in a difficult moment? Can he find the good in the bad? Can he conquer his ego and, together with you, find an acceptable way forward for both of you? Or is he unable to be a partner with a capital P?*

To support a fallible partner is his responsibility.

WHAT YOU COOK AT HOME, YOU MUST EAT AT HOME

T his is an almost ironclad rule for this day and age. The more you think about it, the more you realise this. It goes like this: Never publish anything negative about a partner or a relationship on the social networks. This would be similar to shouting it aloud from the rooftops for the whole world to hear.

Weak people like to make fun of others in their posts online. They forget that the main message is not in the content of their contributions, but in the name of the author. The person who writes the text primarily publishes information about himself. In this case, lack of judgement, low values, his small-mindedness and anger, instead of taking a detached view. No letter tells as much about the recipient as about the sender.

Therefore, do not wash your dirty linen in public. Do not think that you will win people to your side by doing this. A relationship is a special scale with two arms and only one bowl. The bowl belongs to both partners. If someone burdens a partner, he burdens the relationship too. Not to mention that the majority of relationships are incomprehensible to other people. They wonder how the two individuals can stay together, what they see in each other. Often the reason is that outsiders see only the superficial side, a mere shell. They are unable to put themselves in the shoes of the other, to see into his soul. To understand the interior of another person, you have to use your heart. However, only a close partner is capable of this. For all others, this person will remain opaque, like a fruit, which it is impossible to see into.

So do not allow anyone from among your acquaintances – and even less so anyone on the social networks whom you don't even know at all – to advise you about your relationship, or to interfere in it or decide for you. If you have made a mess at home, do the cleaning up with the help of your partner. Until you've done that, do not invite

anyone else to your home. He would only trample the crumbs into the carpet due to his clumsiness.

Two people are enough to reach a compromise solution in any situation. If they are mature enough to seek it.

KEEP YOUR PROMISES OR, EVEN BETTER, SURPASS THEM

Success in life rests on two activities:

1. decisions,

2. actions carried out in response to these decisions.

People often have difficulty achieving success because they are unwilling to commit themselves to some action. And even more difficult is keeping the promise. A long-term relationship works on the same principle. But it is more difficult than the commitment itself.

In a relationship, you are confronted every day with promises made to yourself, as well as to your partner. However, you cannot postpone, manipulate or wriggle your way out of promises made to a partner. That is why so many young people prefer to stay single. They can deceive themselves more easily, and it will not taint their reputation or ego, because nobody will ever know that they have deluded themselves.

A good partner in a relationship stays committed to his promises. He keeps the overall objective in mind. He will always remain faithful. He knows words alone are not enough. He must act too. Actions speak louder than words. Promises made to a partner must be kept, but not only that. They should be surpassed. If you are a step ahead of your partner's expectations, you give him more than he expects – at no loss to yourself. On the contrary, you will gain something. You gain someone who knows he can trust you.

The effect of relationships in which both partners give more than they take continues for a long time after the relationship has ended. Why? Because you have given your partner something that lasts many years into the future.

402

BE LOYAL TO YOUR PARTNER

This is not about loyalty in love, but about the ability to stay together not only in good times, but also in bad. Stand by your partner in the dark, not because you want to stand in the dark, but because you do not want your partner to stand alone in the dark. Whatever happens, be on his side, and do not be afraid of the dark or the shadows. After all, shadows indicate the source of light. Learn to find their meaning and causes.

Being loyal to your partner is not a choice. It is a priority. Because such loyalty can mean absolutely everything for your partner.

MALE EGO

*M*en do not have an easy time in relationships.

Even if a woman achieves nothing else but bringing a new life into the world and bringing up a child, she is useful to mankind for this reason. If a man does not participate in the bringing up of children, he can degrade himself to the position of a mere inseminator who is useful to mankind for only a few minutes in his life. A man simply needs more than that. He needs some success. That is why so many men try to advance to the top positions in companies as well as in politics. Men want to command the world, and yet cannot reconcile themselves with the fact that the world they control is not exactly thriving. Besides, in terms of productivity, men are not as efficient as women, who are able to manage the household, their children, the husband and do their own work all at the same time. So the male ego suffers. However, be aware that ego is an important element that saves men, and women should understand this if they want to have a happy relationship.

The male ego can be unpredictable in a relationship. It can disrupt everything. A man controlled by his ego can stop having his wife's interests at heart if she is more successful than him. He can become unfaithful to boost his self-confidence, to "dominate" the woman, so as to show her that she does not have control over everything, and, if nothing else, at least she is dependent on him emotionally. The male ego is an insidious parasite. Because it gnaws from the inside. However, a clever woman can take advantage of the male ego.

A certain couple visited the café regularly. He believed they were more than friends. She thought they were friends at best. He was becoming increasingly desperate to try to express his ardent feelings toward her. She obviously did not share them, and with every date, during which she only wanted to chat, she found increasingly fewer reasons to come the next time.

One day, when he was again awkwardly trying to express his love to her, she jumped up, knocking over her cup of coffee, and shouted out for everyone to hear: *"For God's sake, stop those sweet words. You are just a friend to me. Can't you understand? I do not want to see you anymore."*

She slammed the café door as she left.

She did not shatter the glass, but she did shatter the male ego. To pieces.

In the following weeks, he was just a shadow of the man who had gone to the café. Although he had been very talkative before, he now hardly said a word. He was no longer a man. More like a robot, moving around mechanically with no human spark.

Then one day, when the man was sitting staring into his coffee, the door burst open and the woman entered. She went straight to the surprised man, sat down beside him and said: *"I miss your words. I realise how much I need them. I will never hurt you again. Will you give me one more chance?"*

The man brightened up. His ego reawakened. No doubt, this was the moment it had been waiting for all the time.

The man straightened up, laughed bitterly and cried out: *"Only a madman would give a second chance to a person who has hurt him once already."*

Then he took the hand of the woman, now with tears in her eyes, and added: *"But I am mad about you."*

WHERE A WOMAN CAN BE BETTER, AND THE MAN MUST ACCEPT IT

God arranged things wisely. He gave man a model – woman. A model, which man will however not admit as such. Contrary to men, women undergo a managerial speed course. It is called maternity. No man is so well trained by life in personnel management, planning, time management, crisis communication, motivation strategies, improvisation and efficiency. Women begin with a helpless creature which, from the first moment, can do nothing but cry and mess, and from that they are able to build an independently functioning unit that can walk, talk and bear responsibility. Although children are often brought up harshly, they have a strong emotional bond and loyalty to mothers, which no employee is likely to feel for a human employer. Indeed, it is no accident that during divorce proceedings, judges entrust most children to the care of their mothers, although men may have a higher salary as well as a more stable background.

Men used to humiliate women by their force. But it was of no use in the end. Nothing good came from it. Today, men are backing away from their physical supremacy. They have stopped making fun of women and laughing at them, because they realised that reality is different from their jokes. The male ego in a relationship must reconcile itself with the fact that the woman is often more successful.

If a man stops being a slave to his ego, the success of the woman would strengthen the whole relationship. However, the man often feels inadequate because of the woman's success, that he is a failure. And later he perceives the woman as a rival who must be belittled, dishonoured, destroyed.

Women need not understand this, it is enough just to accept it. This is a systemic mistake in the male software. Well, nobody is perfect. Ego does have its meaning. Men need praise. Assurances that they are not useless. And women still need men

who want to change the world, just so as to be appreciated by the woman. But they can be a support for one other. Because man has what woman does not have. And woman has what man envies in her.

The only way a man can obtain the things by which a woman exceeds him is to persuade her to cooperate. Make a partner from the rival in the relationship. Learn to respect women for their strong points and get inspiration from them. Because they really can be inspiring.

RESPECT WOMEN FOR WEARING MASKS AND YET REMAINING THEMSELVES

Women paint on new faces every morning. As if they wanted to deceive men, it seems. But then you come to a corporate meeting where there are only men. They do not wear make-up, yet they deceive. They pretend to be better than they are. They cheat, lie, promise, but do not keep their word. So who does the most deceiving?

Women apply make-up to themselves. Openly. And naturally. For that matter, in Nature, females also highlight their attractive features to get the attention of males. And they do it successfully, because the males will arrive.

But why do men deceive? Why do they claim superiority over one another? Are they ashamed of their real faces, do they feel inadequate? Do they put on masks to cover reality?

Women also put on masks, but remain the same under them. Men try to fulfil an ideal by hiding behind psychological masks – some kind of private idea of what they should be like at work, what they should achieve. The problem is that, by all the deception, they tend to forget who they really are and what advantages they have.

If women apply inferior make-up masks, they can damage their skin. If men apply inferior psychological masks, they damage their character. That is why men should find inspiration in the way that women treat their less than perfect external features without damaging their internal qualities.

RESPECT WOMEN FOR NOT EXPECTING TO HAVE PERFECT FEATURES, BUT TREATING THEIR IMPERFECTIONS TO BECOME PERFECT

Men like to watch action movies and dream of manly perfection. Women go into the maternity hospital in an imperfect condition and bring a product into the world. Regardless of the appearance of this product, which the woman cannot influence, the woman considers her child to be sufficiently good.

For her, the child is the most beautiful in the world.

But sufficient is not the final word for the woman. Sufficient means initial. The woman works with the basic product, the infant, for at least 18 years. She teaches the child patiently and does not give up. During the period of time that the woman brings up the child, some men do not achieve any usable product, do not complete a single project.

A woman can do this. Because, contrary to a man, she is able to work with imperfection. Although she did not choose the child and has to accept him as he is, she considers the child sufficiently good to bring up someone better from it. During this period, the man might see in his own wife somebody who is not worth being faithful to. Even in shorter periods than 18 years. Mothers are devoted to building up their children. However, which man expends so much devotion to building a relationship, or to some other project?

Women have a deeply rooted conviction that the perfection of a product does not arise from its properties, but from theirs. Men can learn from this. The first big

challenge in life is to discover who we really are. And the second challenge is to be satisfied with what you find. Women are aware that they will not change a child's nature, but they are determined to work on eliminating the deficiencies and improving the strong points. For women it is essential to remain committed to the goal. They can sometimes behave as if they are wearing blinkers, walking on like draught horses and not listening to other people's opinions about their (bad) upbringing.

No woman is born a mother.

She becomes a mother who learns how to deal with a child.

A man should work the same way on each incomplete product. And he should start with himself.

RESPECT WOMEN FOR THEIR SELFLESSNESS

To devote 18 years to a single project. Often along with other work. Women manage this while bringing up (several) children. They have admirable patience, endurance and character. Being a mother is a commitment from which it is impossible to deviate, to be released. Woman undertake this long-term project regardless of the stage of their own lives at which these 18 years begin. Why do women have such a drive, but men not?

Women see further than just the horizon of their own lives. They wish to leave something meaningful behind. More than only property. Women, unlike men, can build something during their lives that cannot be converted into money, and yet whose significance exceeds all the properties and careers of men. The reward for women is that children remember until their last day the time, the energy and the love their mothers gave to them. They burn their names not in trade registers, but in hearts. They are wiser. Perhaps they understand stocks and shares less fully, but they understand real values better.

Men should realise that the things they do only for themselves will perish with them. But the things they do for others will outlast them.

RESPECT WOMEN FOR NOT AVOIDING CHANGE AND GROWTH

A man often hesitates. He is reluctant to make a change because he does not know what lies ahead. He is afraid of loss, a bruised ego, bankruptcy.

What if these were the feelings held by a woman who is about to give birth? Why does she go on, despite all doubts about pain and uncertainty? The woman at that moment risks much more than a man. She has no guarantee that the birth will proceed without problems, or that the partner who was with her in the moment of pleasure will remain by her side in less enjoyable times.

Of course, women are not stupid. They know the divorce statistics, they know how women end up in divorce courts. But they take the risk anyway. Because they know that it is the only option for them.

A family means growth for them. Their own fulfilment. A higher value, because three are greater than two. And even if the man leaves the woman with the child, two will be greater than one. Actually, the worst risk a woman undergoes in maternity is an unsuitable partner. Women are able to venture into a long-term project, which maternity is, and endure long-term hardships, in the case of an unmarried mother. For a child, they are willing to renounce a career for the rest of their lives. Although men like to describe women as gold-diggers and materialists, the contrary is true. Mothers can limit their pleasures, such as fashionable clothes and cosmetics. They are willing, as sole wage-earners, to live in a single-room flat, but they never give up building their project, their child.

Mothers are the most capable entrepreneurs. Because they think about what they do and where it leads. They know that if they want to understand their past, they only have to look at the present – the conditions they created for themselves. And

if they want to understand the future, they only need to look at what they are doing now. Women understand better than men that those who keep repeating the steps of the past do not grow. That is why women are not afraid of change.

RESPECT WOMEN FOR NOT GIVING UP WHEN THINGS ARE AT THEIR WORST

Men cancelled compulsory military service for themselves. When things get tough, men think they should be avoided. After all, even in war they allow themselves the privilege of raising a white flag and surrendering. Man always has an escape route handy. From any situation.

Women cannot cancel their service to themselves. They have not created a professional army of women who will bear children on their behalf. All women are prepared to continue going to maternity hospitals. And they do not give up at birth because the situation is not developing as planned, or is unpleasant or not really enjoyable.

Also, when women bring up children, they are aware that there are no permanent failures, only temporary ones. A mother does not bring her child back to the hospital if he is naughty. No, she works with what she has, to improve the product, regardless how difficult the situation. And she keeps doing it. Every day, every minute, every single second. There is no holiday from the job of being a mother.

For men, mothers are a better model than Rambo is. Mothers prove that what seems impossible at a given moment can be coped with anyway. Mothers can always take at least a small step ahead, even at the most difficult time. And they will do so all the more readily if things are not going well. Because they do not want to remain in such a situation.

RESPECT WOMEN FOR NOT ATTEMPTING MICROMANAGEMENT

Many men can handle their careers, and yet they fail, drown in microproblems that are irrelevant in the long term. A man is able to keep to only one direction, sometimes even the wrong direction.

Women manage to cook on several plates at once. And to care for their children and husband at the same time. They manage both the household and work. They do not have more limbs or time than men. They set their priorities differently. Because they are managers, not micromanagers.

Micromanagement is the desperate effort to control and solve every detail. A micromanager believes that if he grapples with every single detail, he will solve the whole. The contrary is true. The more he occupies himself with details, the less he is able to see the whole. He devotes care to one tree, and then does not see a problem affecting the whole forest.

On the other hand, women often manage things in a complex way and so that the result is sufficient. They do not need the result to be perfect. That is why a woman's result is not always what men would regard as correct, but at least women make progress. A family managed by a woman always functions well enough. Because women have learned what many men have not – not to waste time, but to be efficient and productive. There are positive results achieved by women. Everything is washed, cooked, cleaned.

Nature also helps women. Because women weep more. Eyes that are washed quickly are able to see possibilities that were not apparent because of blindness. This also leads to productivity. Women simply do not like to waste time. That is why they are also not guilty of micromanagement, when they have bad partners.

RESPECT WOMEN FOR NOT WAITING ENDLESSLY

Women are so strong that they leave things that have no future, and so wise that they wait for what they deserve. But they do not wait endlessly. They have their limits. Women understand that it is one thing to dream, and another to act. Women do not have the feeling that life owes them something, which they will get one day. No, women do not want to wake up and discover that the time for what they wanted so much has passed. Such as to start a family.

Women are driven by nature and understand the value of time better than men do. Maybe it would be the most reasonable to have a baby in retirement, when they have more spare time for bringing it up. However, women are able to ignore words like sometime, another day and later. Women hate these words. At the end of life, they want to have a list of accomplished goals. Not a list of excuses why they did not achieve the goals.

Women know what it means to assume responsibility for their own life, as well as for other lives. Men should learn from them that if they want to achieve something, they must stop dreaming about it and take steps toward achieving it. Women do not wait for someone to do things in their place. They know that nobody will do anything on their behalf. This does not refer only to giving birth. Women understand that *"sometime"* means right NOW, that the *"someone"* is ME and that the *"something"* is what must be done NOW by ME.

FEMALE ASSUMPTIONS

Female assumptions stem from female intuition. Women take the advice of their inner voice seriously. Because it is seldom wrong. Men can laugh at them because they do not have any evidence for their convictions, no facts, but women do not need such things. Because of maternity, they are anchored to Nature more than men. Women therefore perceive what men do not understand. They have good foresight and, especially, do not forget.

The female code is similar to the animal code. Animals carry within themselves the hereditary information that man can harm them. Even cubs that have never encountered man have a genetic code that teaches them entire legends about what happened to their ancestors in the past.

Therefore, men should not underestimate female assumptions, regardless of how irrational they may seem. They are based on what happened. Men can heal innate female distrustfulness in only one reliable way. By correct behaviour, which will leave the woman in no doubt that she has at her side not an average but an extraordinary man.

I was having a meal at a street café. Then I noticed a couple arriving in a big, luxury car.

The man went to the other door, offered his arm to the woman and held an umbrella over her. He led her to the table, helped her out of her coat and pulled up a chair for her. When she rose to go to the bathroom, he stood up until she had left the table. When she returned, he stood up again and held the chair for her. Later the waiter brought in a big bunch of flowers and a bottle of champagne. The man knelt down and kissed her hand, as if they were just going to get married. Yet, they were celebrating their fiftieth wedding anniversary. Both of them were over seventy.

I met the man in the bathroom. I complimented him on his perfect gentlemanly behaviour and asked him for a piece of advice so that I could also have such a beautiful and deep relationship. He smiled and told me something I will never forget:

"Young man, there was once a time when everything important flashed through my mind in a single second. That was when I stopped looking for the ideal woman and decided to be the ideal man."

BE LIKE A SHERPA, AN IDEAL PARTNER, IN A NEW RELATIONSHIP

A Sherpa is a mountain guide. He leads his client to the top of the mountain and lets him have all the glory. Sir Edmund Hillary is known as the first man to climb to the highest peak in the world, Mount Everest. However, the New Zealand mountain climber was not there alone. The whole time he had a devoted Nepali by his side, Sherpa Tenzing Norgay.

The right man should behave like a Sherpa.

Like a second Self for his woman.

To be the solid shoulder to lean on, the stronger arm to lift and hold her when she does not have enough strength to support herself.

Men are usually stronger than women. They can choose how they will use their strength. They can hurt a woman, or can give her the support and protection she needs.

A Sherpa never deliberately leads his client to places where he would be in danger and then leaves him there to die. He does not need any written contract. This behaviour is natural for him, part of his code of honour and dignity. Although the client may have worries or negative feelings, the Sherpa's attitude will reassure him.

A woman's trust is not automatic. It must be won, worked for, deserved. The man can do it, if he is a real Sherpa. Then the woman's worries will be reduced or eliminated. Because the woman will understand that she is in the right, reliable hands.

FOLLOW THE MAN WHO IS A WISE GUIDE, NOT AN IRRESPONSIBLE ONE

A Sherpa knows that he cannot influence the weather and natural occurrences. He knows that these events can lead him into dangerous situations through no fault of his own. He knows it is no use trying to fight Nature.

It is necessary to adapt to events and to use them to your advantage. Do not complain about high waves where it is impossible to swim. Rather take a surfboard and learn to move on the high waves faster than by swimming. Exploit the situation to your advantage.

Life usually destroys those plans that deserve to be destroyed, although at the beginning we do not understand this. For everything that life takes from us, it provides something else. Yes, we can lose an important thing or person, but we will always receive some "notification" – an experience or message which we would not understand otherwise. We do not have to understand everything right away in life, often it is enough just to accept it. If we do so, we go along with the flow of events.

Avalanches often block off a Sherpa's plans, make him pause, re-evaluate the planned route and appreciate what he has achieved already. A Sherpa will always remind us to be grateful in cases where we tend to forget and then complain. With a positive Sherpa, you will more easily outlast a snow storm hidden in a sheltered spot, and thanks to this you will even feel recharged with more energy and determination to continue afterwards.

The right Sherpa will not reproach you if you do not go as far as he wished, and if you do not have the strength to continue immediately.

He will not seek negative answers but, on the contrary, will always search for a positive approach. In short, he will always continue with the flow.

FOLLOW THE MAN WHO TRIES TO KEEP YOU ON YOUR PATH

Regardless of whether you are doing well or not, there will always be somebody who will want to hinder you, divert you from your path, knock you to the ground. Because nobody wants to be unsuccessful alone. A Sherpa will remind you at that moment that you do not need anyone's approval to make your dream come true. Nobody else needs to understand your personal desires and the way you wish to acquire experience – not even a Sherpa, only yourself. Although your Sherpa does not understand your path, that does not mean he cannot respect you for the courage with which you venture into unknown places, that he will not support you in what you want to achieve because you believe in it.

A Sherpa is no judge or jury, he is primarily a protector. He makes sure you remain on your path. It does not matter if the path is short, or is a dead-end leading nowhere. If you are convinced that you need to go on this path everything is fine. There is nothing more important in life than your own path. The path symbolises your wishes, your aim, your happiness. Everything is in your dreams and your heart. And a Sherpa knows there is no other time to do it, only this short life.

You do not have to prove anything on your path. You do not have to compete with anyone. You prove everything to one person only – yourself.

Although your planning is fraught with worry and uncertainty, life is wise and rewards you right from the beginning. Every step along the way in which you overcome obstacles and problems will make you happier. Not only are you getting closer to your goal, but you are in fact already living your dream.

The right Sherpa knows that if you tried to follow another person's path just to please him, you would give your happiness to him. And be dependent on him afterwards.

To find a partner who will keep you on your path means having somebody who will move you in the direction of your dream.

FOLLOW THE MAN WHO BELIEVES IN WHAT YOU FEEL AND IN THE DREAMS YOU HAVE

Austrian mountain climber Reinhold Messner was the first man to climb all 14 eight-thousanders in the world. He got to the highest one, Mount Everest, as the first climber ever without supplemental oxygen. Then he crossed Antarctica without the help of dogs and technology. Let me stress that these were all first-time-ever feats. It means that he tackled all these ventures knowing that nobody had ever achieved them before. He had enough opportunity to doubt whether he was up to the task, or whether it was even humanly possible. What led him on? He did not know whether it was possible or not.

His drive was strong belief.

Strong belief is not something that can be proved. It is just a feeling in your heart. However, believing has a fundamental influence on human fate. It directs our thoughts, and consequently our deeds. If someone seeks a better way, because he is convinced that there is one, he will find it. And if someone does not seek a better way, because he is not convinced there is one, he will not find it. The biggest barrier in the path of the fulfilment of our wishes is therefore inside us. We can achieve anything we attempt. But first we must believe that we are capable of achieving it.

If you listen to all the negative thoughts surrounding you, you will quickly lose belief in yourself. Especially if people who have not achieved anything similar themselves discourage you. They might not even mean you harm. After all, they are right from their point of view – it is impossible for them to do it.

However, their discouragement says more about them than about you. More about what they themselves have not achieved than about what you are able to achieve. Therefore, do not allow your dreams to be taken from you. Have a bodyguard by your side who believes in what you feel and is willing to support you through thick and thin. Like a Sherpa.

American boxer Muhammad Ali said it correctly: *"Impossible is just a big word thrown around by small men who find it easier to live in the world they've been given than to explore the power they have to change it. Impossible is not a fact. It's an opinion. Impossible is not a declaration. It's a dare. Impossible is potential. Impossible is temporary. Impossible is nothing."*

FOLLOW THE MAN WHO PRE-CHEWS THE HARD BITS

It is natural that to achieve a goal you've never achieved, you must take a path you've never taken before. You do not know the path, therefore you might stumble or encounter an obstacle you don't know how to cope with. You might feel doubts. Give way to remorse. To regret. What's worse, you can't stop yourself. Such moments test a relationship.

A bad partner would dance on your grave. If he did not want you to grow, he will be pleased that *"he was right"*. He would know this was a precedent that he could always point to later: *"Don't do it. You know how it ended last time. Do you want to get hurt again?"*

A Sherpa knows nothing can inhibit you like the past. People have difficulty reconciling themselves with the past, because they cannot change it. They forget that all the mistakes they made in the past are the source of their current wisdom and the spring of experience. You would never learn without making mistakes.

A Sherpa must remind you of this. To communicate with you whenever you are uncertain. And if some worries are indigestible for you, he must pre-chew them in communication with you. Only in this way can you digest and build your future.

FOLLOW THE MAN WHO DOES NOT ALLOW YOU TO ROT AWAY

No Sherpa will let a mountain climber freeze in a snowdrift. He will not let him lie or stand for long in such a place. He will set him going. He will get him to safety. When you feel like stopping, a Sherpa will remind you that change is life. And that to get positive results, you must make positive changes.

Every decision is a risk. However, in the snowstorm of life it is more dangerous to remain in one spot than trying to get away from the storm. Whenever you do not want to repeat yesterday, change today. Everything you are afraid of will disappear when you start doing something about it. Therefore, a Sherpa will make sure that your dreams are bigger than your worries, and that your deeds speak louder than your words.

If you strive for success, you can fail. But those who do not strive will certainly fail. If you decide to succeed, there will always be some opportunity. Opportunities are like buses. There will always be another one. But you have to meet it halfway.

A Sherpa is well aware that you could stumble with every new step. That is why he stands by you and emphasises that there is nothing more important than trying one more step.

Without him, you might not stand up again.

But he will not stand by and watch if you do not try to stand up.

FOLLOW THE MAN WHO SEES SOMETHING POSITIVE IN EVERYTHING

There is no heads without tails. And vice versa.

There is experience hidden in losing, or danger hidden in winning. The defeated can be determined, just as the winners could be humble. If they have this attitude to life, they swim on the wave of growth. A Sherpa can guide you in this stream. He brings you down to earth when your self-confidence flies dangerously high, and supports you if you stop believing in yourself. Whether you are doing well or badly, a Sherpa will lead you into remaining productive.

Of course, the moments when you fail to achieve your goals have their reverse side. The reverse side is the fact that the relationship is strengthened at such times. It reveals the real cohesion of the relationship and gives a reason to embrace and kiss. Without successes, love can grow. As we see, love can grow in any situation. As long as the partners recognise the good in everything.

FOLLOW THE MAN WHO IGNITES YOUR SELF

Satisfaction in a relationship depends upon the satisfaction of all its members. However, only somebody who fulfils his values can be contented. Such a person is not ashamed of his own deeds or words, he can say what he thinks, and do what he says. A contented man simply goes his way. He stops being a false car from a used-car dealer with a turned back odometer, repainted rusty bodywork and an unreliable engine with a restamped production number. Such false cars will not go far — and neither will those using petrol diluted with water.

To be contented, man needs quality fuel — to be honest not only to others, but especially to himself. Only in this way can he fulfil his values and derive positive energy from his satisfaction. A Sherpa does not need to explain anything to his client. He knows that your own path in life is the most important. It requires courage to continue against everything, but it is always worth it. This is the life's mission for a Sherpa: To help himself by helping others.

CLASH IN THE UPBRINGING OF CHILDREN

Two different people bring somebody into the world who is different from both of them. So, there are possibilities for new differences of opinion in a relationship. And new clashes will come if children are misled away from being themselves and become dependent on others.

Many parents think they will make life easier if they remake their children according to their own image. However, this assumption is wrong. Dissimilarities will not be reduced, but on the contrary there will be more of them. Because the child will have to create a fourth person, who is neither mother nor father nor the child himself. He will be a copy of someone else.

Therefore, the Laws of Love must apply to children too.

Be the best possible example to them.

Perhaps children are not perfect at obeying their parents.

But they are perfect in the way they imitate their further lives.

In the Law Faculty, I had a classmate whose appearance was not very prepossessing. Shabby clothes, worn-out boots, he never bought textbooks but only borrowed them from other classmates.

Sometimes he did not even have enough money for lunch.

But he never complained, smiled a lot and was positive.

I could not resist asking how this was possible. He replied: *"I come from a region with high unemployment. Yes, I am probably the poorest student here, and I strug-*

gle to afford basic food. But whenever my parents call me just to tell me how much they love me and think of me, I feel like the richest man in the world. And do you know why? Because at such moments I have no doubt that I have everything I need in life."

HOW TO BE THE BEST EXAMPLE TO CHILDREN

All parents want their children to be smart and happy. But what do they really do to achieve this?

To make the question clearer: What do parents do to make sure that their children are smarter and happier in life?

Because children are like flypaper. What they hear, sticks to them. Like a tape recorder, they repeat everything, even what we do not want them to. So think twice about the example you are setting your children.

We, parents, should really do something to make sure our children are smart and happy.

What about starting with ourselves?

DO WHAT YOU SAY

Every parent is the main example for his child. Unfortunately, also in the negative sense. Therefore, remember that it never matters what bad things are happening to us, because we can always make them even worse. Children hear what you say. And they see what you do.

Do you complain about bad times and say that even worse is to come? And do you say this in front of the children whom you brought into these times? What about creating a better time just by your attitude? The only limitations to tomorrow's successes are those buts we say today. It is not fate that brings change to people. The most successful people in life are those who do their best to reverse a bad situation. Children learn by watching us when we curse, postpone, resign ourselves to unpleasant circumstances; when we listen to negative people who tell us to do nothing, or do something that we regret later; when we regard what we have lost as more important rather than what we managed to save; when we see what we have not achieved as more significant than what we have achieved; when we try to manipulate others to make them feel guilty about our failures.

We must set the example for our children to learn that in life it is never possible to work with what we do not have. No builder can build walls with bricks he does not have. Therefore, he must not count the bricks he does not have, but count the bricks that he does have. So always start by looking at what you have. This is where your focus must be. It is pointless criticising what we have. On the contrary, we must value what we have. To focus on what we have is a positive act.

But in doing so, beware of this:

Most parents think they are a good example to their children by telling them what to do. However, children learn more from the way adults really live their lives. The difference between talking and doing can be huge.

Do not tell your children how they should live. Rather keep your words to yourself. We teach children how to live by our everyday conduct. Let's live the way we urge our children to live, let them watch and imitate us. Do not try to preach water and drink wine. Let's practise what we preach. Or forget about preaching. Because it will be meaningless anyway.

Parents are the first models for children.

Children try to become what their parents are.

Therefore, let's be as we want our children to be.

Let's change into what we wish for our children.

Let's do what we expect from our children.

Let's demonstrate what we want them to admire.

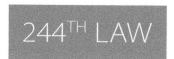

FIGHT UNTIL YOU SUCCEED

The defeated stop if they fail.

Winners stop only after they have succeeded.

Therefore, let's deepen the winning mentality of our children. It will be beneficial for them.

A winning mentality means especially thinking in the present. Imagine a boat on the open sea. Among threatening waves, in a wild storm, battered by lightning. The captain goes below the deck and happily reads in the log entries from the previous month: *"It is beautifully still. Sunny weather. An idyllic day."*

The captain dives into the past and nobody is handling the boat, it is out of control. The sea plays with it as with a puppet. Is this the fault of the boat? Of the weather? Or of the captain?

Yet, so little was needed. He merely had to attend to the boat in the present.

Children can be cruel (to each other), because they are vulnerable. They have difficulty enduring other people's judgements and overcoming their own sorrows. They have to learn to fight. But they have to act, like the captain, in the present.

In order to act in the present, you must focus on the present. Forget all the previous reasons for weeping, and the causes of the pain. What was, must be accepted as an unchangeable fact. Until you have dealt with what was, or even as long as you still think about revenge, you are focusing on the past.

Let's teach children to understand the development of events. To understand that they do not have to worry about things they cannot change. And, on the other hand, to take things they can influence and use them to their advantage.

Mistakes do not matter. What is important is to hold the boat on course. Even more so when the weather gets worse.

Never forget during upbringing that life is like a novel. What matters most is not the first chapter, but the last. Also, children write their own novels. Whenever they dislike a chapter they have written in cooperation with life, they do not have to waste time and energy by tearing it up and rewriting it. They just need to turn the page — and they will see a new blank page. The first new word will be written by the next thing they do.

BELIEVE IN YOUR CHILDREN

The thing is not only to believe your children. It is more important to believe in them.

To believe in somebody's ability is the greatest compliment you can pay that person. And that does not exclude children. Whenever you see that the child is fighting for success, admire that regardless of the result. And regardless of whether he succeeds or fails, be prepared to help or advise, if the child desires it.

I emphasise the word prepared in the previous sentence. Do not impose yourself at any price. Children must work through their own mistakes too.

Ordinary and simple faith in your child can fill him with self-confidence and conviction that he can cope with even the most difficult things. Let's realise that children are young, and any obstacle that seems minor to us can seem huge to them. Because they have not overcome it yet. We already have.

Whenever parents or teachers make it clear to the child that they consider him competent enough to cope with his own tasks, his learning results will improve significantly. Belief is the strongest driving force. It enables the child to be the best he can be at every opportunity.

Let's not stop children if they get close to our limits. Allow them to continue and try to achieve even more than we could imagine.

The possible success will be especially their achievement.

But partially ours too.

Simply by allowing them to be better than you, their model, you are being good parents.

436

If we believe in our children, the children will believe in themselves. Then in the future they will themselves become the person they can turn to with confidence when something troubles them.

They will not need us anymore.

This is what human evolution is about.

PRAISE CHILDREN FOR EFFORT, NOT FOR TALENT

Stand by children, but never take from them the responsibility for the result. Do not give them the false impression that somebody will always arrange good results for them. On the contrary, praise them for every effort, so that they realise they must take full responsibility for their actions and that they create their own destiny.

Personal effort is what children can easily control. If they get into the habit and put more effort into the activity, their results will improve. This will teach them the value of perseverance, and they will understand that constant effort is the way to improve themselves. It is essential for children to realise that they can control their own success.

Most parents make the mistake of praising their children for their talent. But talent is something they are born with, not something that is in the child's power to control. Focusing on talent is not the way to react to failure. Talent is just a precondition. It is applied only through work. Effort is what develops talent. A child who is led to believe that he succeeded thanks to his talent could come to feel that talent is natural, that he will never lose it and that it will always come to his rescue.

But merely relying on talent will inhibit growth. Talent is a natural advantage, yes, but it has to be worked on if there is to be improvement – and this is only possible by training, studying and diligence.

That is, by growth based on constantly increasing effort.

PRAISE CHILDREN ONLY WHEN IT IS DESERVED

Praise can be defined as a pause on the path to success. As an opportunity for a small celebration.

A small one, because praising must never last long. Too much praising can turn into a permanent pause. Lifelong satisfaction. An overpraised child tends to stop working to improve himself, because he feels he is already *"good enough"*. He is led to believe this from our exaggerated praising, a distraction on the way to success.

The overpraised child also becomes confused. You praised him for something, but you do not do again, because you want him to keep growing. If he learns the alphabet (and is deservedly praised), it does not mean that this is sufficient for the rest of his life.

Praise is the sibling of faith, because we want the child to learn to develop this quality by himself. That is, we want him to learn how to apply self-praise adequately and constructively, so that he has this skill in the future when there is nobody else to praise him like we did when he was young. Children who do not learn how to praise themselves will feel disoriented, incompetent, inferior as adults. Disappointed, they begin to change jobs because an employer is not a parent and does not care about the growth of a specific individual. For an employer, any employee is replaceable.

Therefore, be cautious and economical with praise. Children must also experience failure. Let them know what defeat feels like, if it is justified. Let the child think about the defeat, examine its causes, that is, explore the sources of learning. Although it hurts to see your child defeated, give him some time to benefit from the experience. And then support and motivate him again, so that he does not remain

despondent and negative. Help the child to feel the greatest intoxication there is — the sweetness of victory that comes after previous defeat.

Why is such victory so sweet? Because we know how much we worked after the previous defeat and how we benefited. Therefore, let us support our children in experiencing both. Successes, but also failures.

ALLOW CHILDREN TO CREATE THEIR OWN HEALTHY RELATIONSHIPS

Parents like to appoint themselves to the role of ruling over every aspect of their children's lives. They know everything *"better"* than their children, even what friends they should have. Just imagine if someone had been made our guardians for everything, even deciding who our lifetime partners should be.

It is definitely a good thing to influence the attitude of children to life by exposing them to the right company. They will not be able to make a negative choice in a circle of positive friends. It is also known that the easiest way to improve a child's school results is to let him sit next to a smart and supportive classmate. Because children are easily influenced. They pick up each other's good and bad habits. But this is nothing new to you. You already know that you are the average of the five closest persons with whom you spend the most time.

Despite everything, respect the child's opinions and tastes too. Healthy relationships are not only those that we consider healthy, but also those that our children consider to be healthy. If you feel any uncertainties or problems in this regard, discuss it with your child. Teach him to understand that it always depends less on where he is, and more on who is by his side. What's more, that thanks to the people by your side, you can change the place where you are.

Also in relationships, children need to get bruised sometimes. Do not turn away from them at times when this happens. Stand by them and be the first they can turn to, when their first love or friendship fails, as you warned them. Do not forget that the value of a relationship is not measured by the size of personal truth, but by the extent of support.

CULTIVATE GRATEFULNESS
IN CHILDREN

P arents in advanced countries establish diaries of gratefulness for their children. Children can enter in them all the good for a given day. At schools, when children have to make a speech in front of their classmates, they talk more and more about recent accomplishments that they are proud of.

Being grateful for what life has brought or what we have achieved ourselves is a little thing that makes a big difference. Because it allows us to think positively. To be aware that there are always reasons for happiness, optimism and determination. It is not because there would be a big change in life. It is just that we begin to notice beauty more. And if our children are to do so, we, the parents, must do so first.

REDUCE STRESS, PARTICULARLY AT HOME

People who have achieved their desired happiness and success in life are like armies that have defeated the enemy. If you ask these *"soldiers"* who have achieved the most on the *"battlefield"*, they will confess that what helped them more than the weapons chosen along the way was their preparation, the background they had. They had somebody to rely on, and they could be confident that there was someone who empathised with them.

Children are not subordinate to parents. They are partners, equally unique and distinctive. They have individual personalities, their own values, and every day they acquire new specific experiences. They must be respected just for their dissimilarity, for being who they are.

A relationship with children is like any other relationship; it works on two basic principles: The participants in this relationship 1) appreciate the ways in which they are the same, and 2) respect the ways in which they are different. Therefore it is senseless to emphasise, victimise and punish children for their difference. Try to exemplify, by your experience, the path to a healthy and safe life for them. But it is up to them to find their own happiness on this path.

Inspire them to try to change the things they don't like. And if they can't be changed, at least to change the way they think about them. This is always possible. Teach them that if somebody hurts them deliberately and it is hard to change the other person or prevent it, they should accept it as a fact that is simply happening, and to adjust themselves to it accordingly.

Do not try to arrange life for your children. After all, we ourselves do not know where our steps will lead. Teach children to have the courage to listen to their intuition.

443

Explain to them that this inner voice does not follow reason. Reason always recommends the safest and easiest way. While intuition does not seek the most comfortable or the easiest way. It searches for a life path. It leads us to obstacles that we have to overcome; that will make us rise early because we are eager to overcome them; that will provoke, motivate and entertain us; that will give meaning to life and will make us happy.

Reason is wise, because in the end it always acknowledges that intuition was right. Because it has nothing to add. After all, how can a path on which you feel happy be unreasonable?

Therefore, do not shout at children if they have different ideas about life. Do not even shout at your partner. Rather try to talk about the issue calmly. Communicate.

It is no accident that public roads are a means of communication.

They are a means of getting from somewhere to somewhere else.

The way to a better relationship. Long-lasting. Happy. Productive.

A relationship in which all the links have their own unique value and positive meaning.

A relationship in which these links feel better together than separate.

A relationship in which these 250 Laws of Love work.

444

PETR CASANOVA

P etr Casanova (∗1974) is the founder of the FirstClass.cz online concept, the FC magazine, and the First Class Academy educational system of personal development. He is married to Jana. He has two sons, Jakub and Daniel.

Each of us is unique. We differ in genes, education, desires, chosen paths and acquired experience. Also in our moods which change from moment to moment. How can two different people agree on a common direction that suits them both without strife? How can they overcome the discrepancies caused by their natural differences? When compromising, how can both sides in a partnership win and not lose? This book explains 250 laws of a happy relationship, in which the couple is more than just the sum of two persons, and in which partners can also achieve more in their working lives than alone.

Lightning Source UK Ltd.
Milton Keynes UK
UKHW031844170820
368391UK00009B/112